IMAGES
of America

OLD SACRAMENTO AND DOWNTOWN

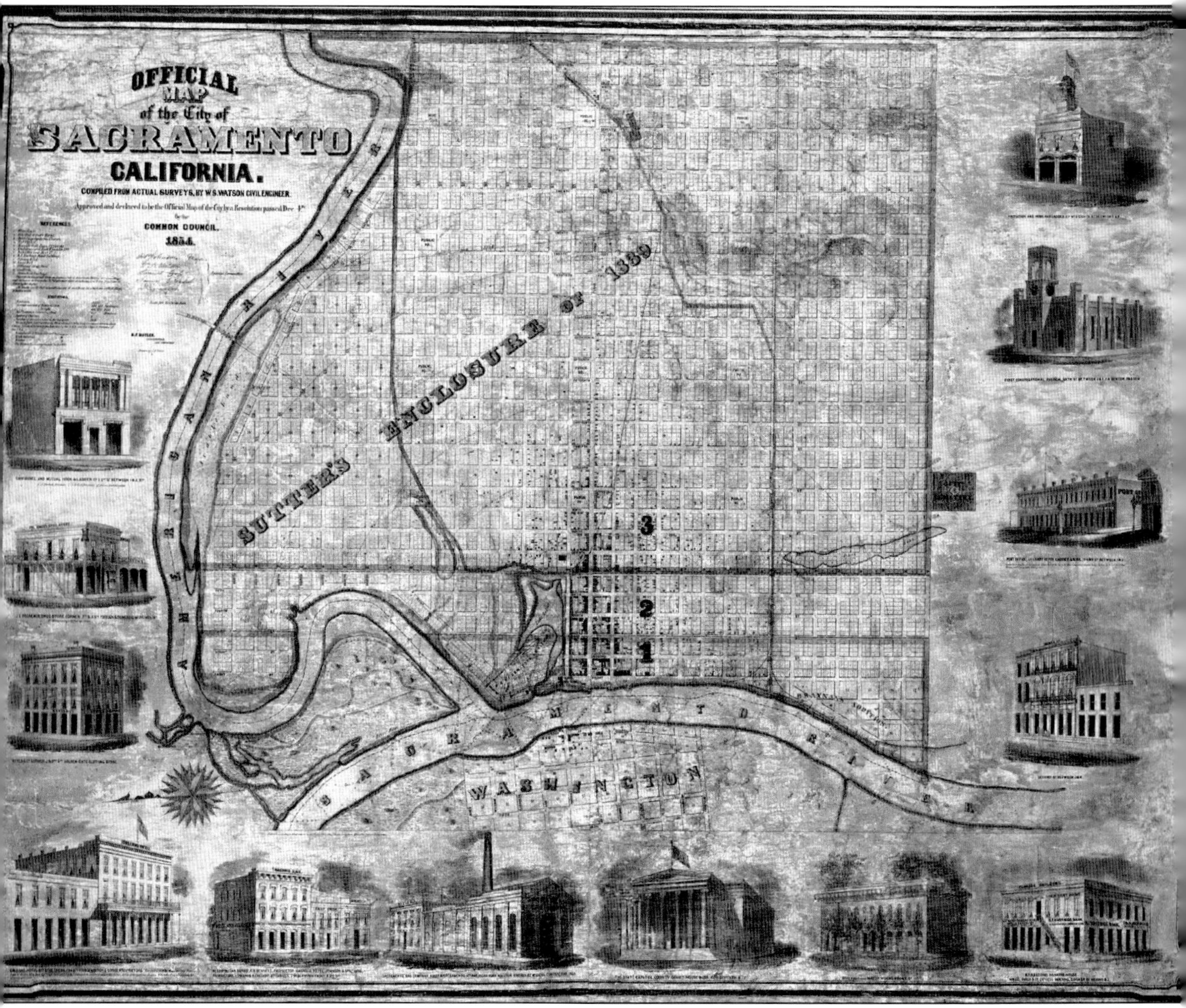

Of the few early maps of Sacramento, this is one of only three known original lithographs. J. H. Pierce drew it in 1854 from the surveys of W. S. Watson, a civil engineer. The map shows the locations of most buildings in Sacramento, while the legend indicates the types of material used for construction—brick or wood. Important parts of this map are the illustrations of the more impressive and significant structures in the city. Other noteworthy features are the statistics it provides for Sacramento: a city of 3,256 acres and a population of 15,000; an average number of 244,400 travelers in a year; 8 churches; a distance to San Francisco of 115 miles by steamship, equaling a trip of about 8 hours; and a note of its fire companies with an enrollment of 400 members. This last item was likely included as a result of the devastating fires suffered by numerous other 19th-century California cities, including Sacramento's own 1852 fire that destroyed a majority of the city's buildings. (Courtesy City of Sacramento Collection.)

ON THE COVER: A streetcar turns from Seventh Street onto M Street, around 1921, on its way to the City Wharf. The M Street line ran a circular route from the docks on Front Street to the Western Pacific Depot at Nineteenth and K Streets. Streetcars, in one form or another, operated in Sacramento from 1861 to 1946. (Courtesy Don Rivett Collection.)

IMAGES
of America

OLD SACRAMENTO AND DOWNTOWN

Sacramento Archives and Museum Collection Center
and the Historic Old Sacramento Foundation

ARCADIA
PUBLISHING

ISBN 978-0-7385-3123-6

Published by Arcadia Publishing
Charleston, South Carolina

Printed in the United States of America

Library of Congress Catalog Card Number: 2005939052

For all general information contact Arcadia Publishing at:
Telephone 843-853-2070
Fax 843-853-0044
E-mail sales@arcadiapublishing.com
For customer service and orders:
Toll-Free 1-888-313-2665

Visit us on the Internet at www.arcadiapublishing.com

To James E. Henley, Sacramento's preeminent historian, we dedicate this book. Without his prescience to collect and document Sacramento's history, there would be no Sacramento Archives and Museum Collection Center.

CONTENTS

ACKNOWLEDGMENTS

This book would not be possible if not for a large number of people who assisted us, whether they were aware of it or not. First we would like to thank the good people at Arcadia Publishing, particularly our editor, Hannah Clayborn. We would especially like to thank the Sacramento History Foundation, who sponsored this project. Our thanks also go to Steve Huffman, executive director of the Historic Old Sacramento Foundation, for his support of our efforts. And finally, we would like to thank Jim Henley, our patient manager, who has probably forgotten more about the history of Sacramento than the rest of us will ever know.

Volunteers have always been a vital part of Sacramento Archives and Museum Collection Center's (SAMCC) archival operation, and over the years we have had quite a few people assist us with projects. Specifically we would like to thank volunteers Kevin Morse, Bill Gaylord, and Greg Tracy, without whose help this would have been a nearly impossible project. And to all of our other volunteers, thank you! We could not do what we do without you.

We have drawn on our extensive photographic collections at SAMCC in preparation for this book. We would especially like to thank the photographers who are the ultimate source of the over five million images in our collection: Joseph Benetti, the Frederick-Burkett Studios, Eugene Hepting, David Joslyn, the McCurry Company, Ernest Myers, the Pope Studios, Ralph Shaw, the many *Sacramento Bee* photographers, and all the others too numerous to mention.

We also send our appreciation to the families of these photographers, who were often the actual donors of the images. Our thanks to the collectors: the California State Library, Frank Christy, Jim Henley, Eugene Hepting, Mead Kibbey, Ted Leonard, Bob McCabe, Eleanor McClatchy, Ernest Myers, Don Rivett, and the Sacramento Public Library. Your appreciation of history makes all this possible.

INTRODUCTION

Sacramento is known as the "Gateway to the Goldfields," "River City," and "Camellia City." By any name, when gold was discovered, Sacramento became the center of California. It was only logical that it would also become the capital, the true center of the state. Sacramento has come a long way from its humble beginning as John Sutter's personal fiefdom. During the more than 150 years of its existence, Sacramento has accomplished much. It has overcome fire several times and floods (up to this point) with at least one fairly ingenious concept, and then a more practical solution. Most importantly, Sacramento has survived the vagaries of governing one of the largest bureaucracies in the world and its ever-increasing need for office space.

This should not be considered a definitive history of Sacramento. It is more of an attempt to tell the story of some of the key events, places, people, and trends that have defined the city, and more importantly, defined it as a great place to live and work.

John A. Sutter Jr. and Sam Brannan founded Sacramento in 1849 with land given to the city that was originally granted to Sutter's father, Capt. John Augustus Sutter. A team led by Capt. William H. Warner, a civil engineer of the U.S. Topographical Engineers, did the city's original survey. The team included Lt. William T. Sherman and Lt. Edward O. C. Ord, both of whom later gained fame as generals in the Civil War.

This book's time frame spans roughly 150 years, beginning with the actual founding of the city in 1849. It necessitated leaving out stories of the Native Americans who populated the area prior to the city's founding, and of John Sutter's settlement of the area. While it is understood that these two stories are important and compelling, space and time considerations made telling them impossible. And as this is a mostly photographic history, the dearth of images from that period also affected the decision. Additionally, the book's geographic scope is defined by the city's original 1849 grid, albeit cut in half, bounded by what is now Broadway, north to the American River, and from the Sacramento River east to Fifteenth Street. The Governor's Mansion is included in this book, even though it is a bit outside the boundary. This was done because of the building's historic significance and its connection to state government. All images used come from SAMCC's collections.

The book starts with a large chapter on Old Sacramento, as this area is the true beginning point of the city. A large portion of Sacramento's history is centered in this small area. While much of that history is lost forever, fortunately a good deal has been preserved through the efforts of the historic community and city leaders. The next three chapters cover more "official" aspects of Sacramento, such as government, public safety, and transportation. The following three chapters look at the day-to-day life of its residents—the culturally diverse neighborhoods, the business sector, and what Sacramentans did for fun. The last chapter documents the large-scale redevelopment projects of the West End that so drastically altered the city.

The old saying, "a picture is worth a thousand words," rings true for this book. The criteria used for choosing the photographs boiled down to those that illustrated the dynamic life in Sacramento as it changed over time. More than just pictures of static buildings, street scenes, or portraits, the selected images depict action and move the story along. It was also important to choose images that had not been used in the many previous publications about Sacramento's history. However, some photographs were so superior, or others captured a scene so perfectly, no real alternatives were suitable or available. Generally, the chapters were organized chronologically, but, as many of the chapters cover several topics, it was not always possible to follow a strict date order.

SAMCC grew out of the early Landmarks Commission. This organization was responsible for the core collections that developed into what the archives have become. The commission evolved into the Sacramento Museum and History Commission responsible for developing a museum for Sacramento. As a result, collections began to grow, with the largest expansion between 1977 and 1983. During that time, the Sacramento Museum and History Commission became an official division of Sacramento city government, creating the official archives.

The Historic Old Sacramento Foundation's (HOSF) mission is to conduct interpretive historical programs in order to improve Old Sacramento's value as a historic and cultural asset. HOSF conducts regular walking tours of the district with the help of a dedicated corps of volunteers. They advocate for a major gold-rush museum and attraction, increasing the number of historic events, and improving the marketing of Old Sacramento as a destination and a place to learn history.

One

Old Sacramento

Preservation for Use

By Amy Whitlatch

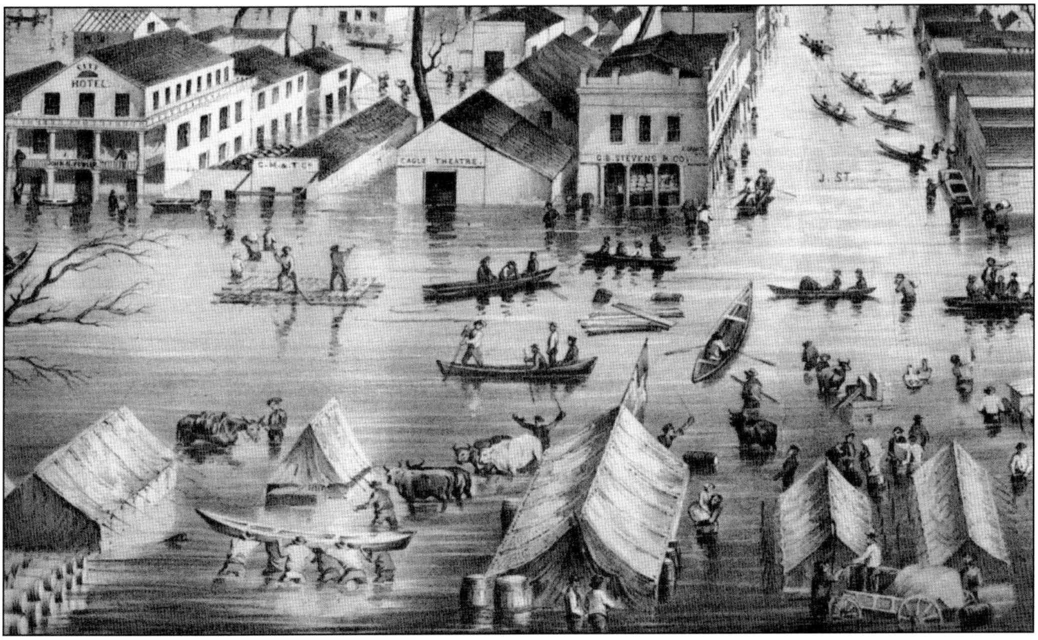

Old Sacramento is the foundation for many ideas and values, and the site of the merger of those who came by land and sea to live the story of the gold rush, where California moved from an ox-cart economy to the richest state in the nation. Over the levee of the Sacramento River flowed a quarter of a million immigrants along with floods, fires, and devastating disease. A stagecoach empire would stretch out over the western half of the continent. The Pony Express would give up its precious mail to a riverboat for the final journey to San Francisco, and on the levee with the turning of a shovel full of earth, a transcontinental railroad would span the continent and insure the social and economic ties that would bind the future of the nation to the future of California. The Old Sacramento Historic District is a national historic landmark because of these events and many more. In this lithograph, the early city and its citizens struggle for survival in the rising water of the "Great Inundation" of January 1850. (Courtesy Eleanor McClatchy Collection.)

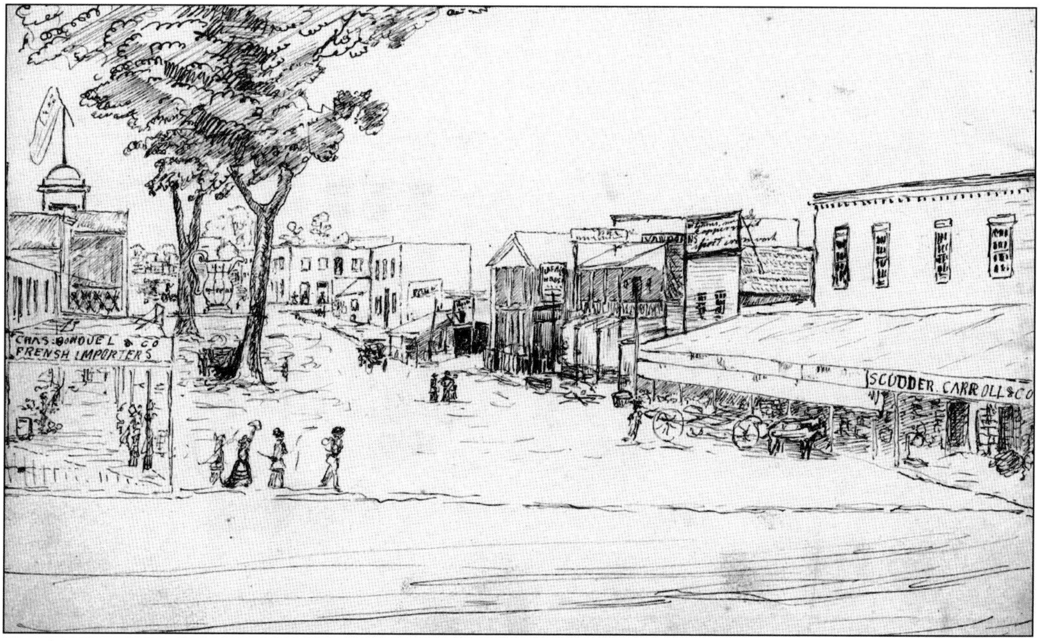

Established in 1849, the city formed along the waterfront and up J Street toward Sutter's Fort. Emil Lehman sketched many street scenes prior to the fire of November 1852 that turned most of the town to ashes. Several artists drew the activities along the waterfront, but Lehman's drawings are the most important in depicting development east of Front Street prior to the conflagration on November 2 and 3, 1852. (Courtesy Eleanor McClatchy Collection.)

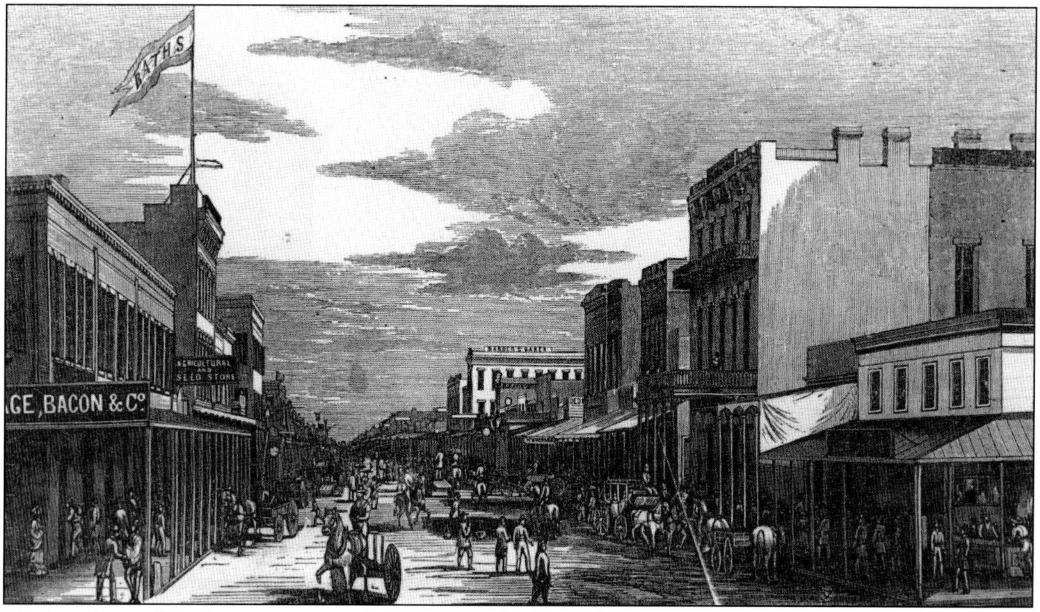

With indomitable determination, the city published an illustrated history in 1855 despite two fires, a cholera epidemic that killed hundreds, and several floods. This illustration of J Street shows the resiliency of the city and its residents. The Vernon-Brannan Building, the nearest three-story structure on the right side of the street, still stands today. The building on the left side of the street with the "Baths" flag has been reconstructed. (Courtesy California State Library Collection.)

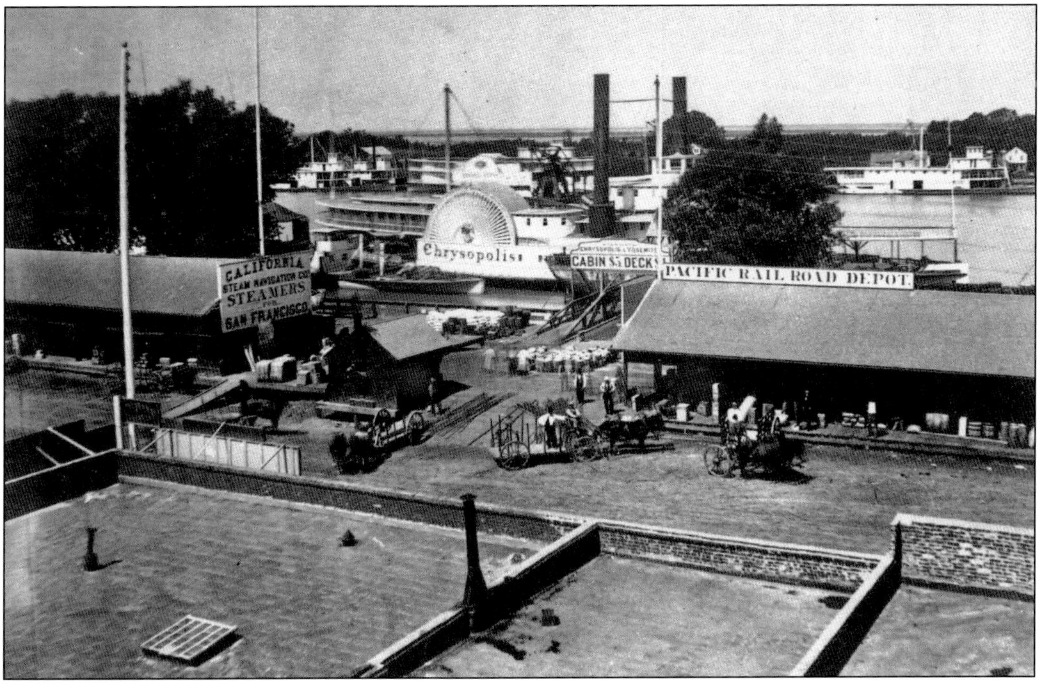

The Sacramento River was the most important transportation corridor in the state, tying Sacramento to San Francisco. Riverboats like the *Chrysopolis* plied the river before there were any paved roads or a railroad. The records of the Sacramento harbormaster show 363 sailing ships and 238 riverboats calling on Sacramento in 1852. Competition between vessels was keen and would often lead to racing. Occasionally a boat's boilers would overheat and explode, causing horrendous injuries and deaths. (Courtesy Alfred A. Hart Collection.)

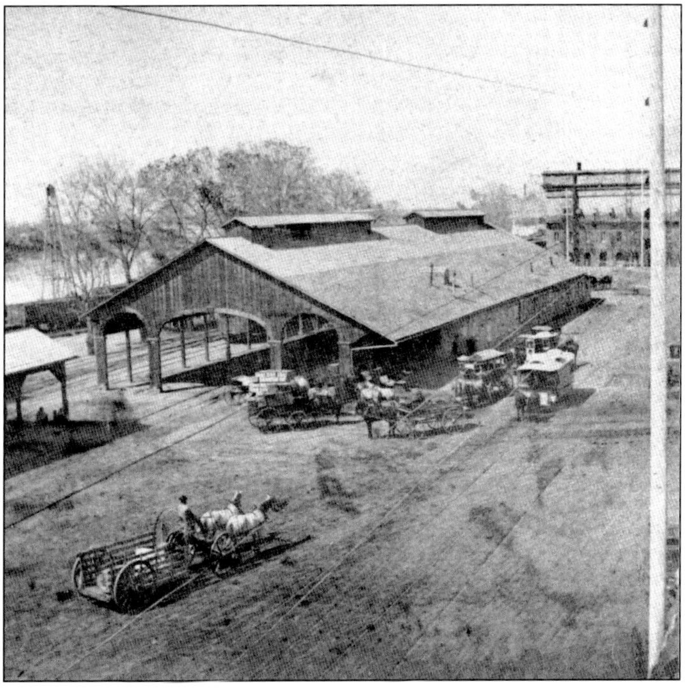

The first Central Pacific passenger station was a crude slant-roofed shack that would be converted into a tool shed. In 1867, the Central Pacific built this arcade station that interfaced with horse-drawn wagons, trolleys, and omnibuses. Local hotels would send baggage boys to the station to compete for the business of new arrivals. Clearly, the station contributed to the general prosperity of the region. (Courtesy City of Sacramento Collection.)

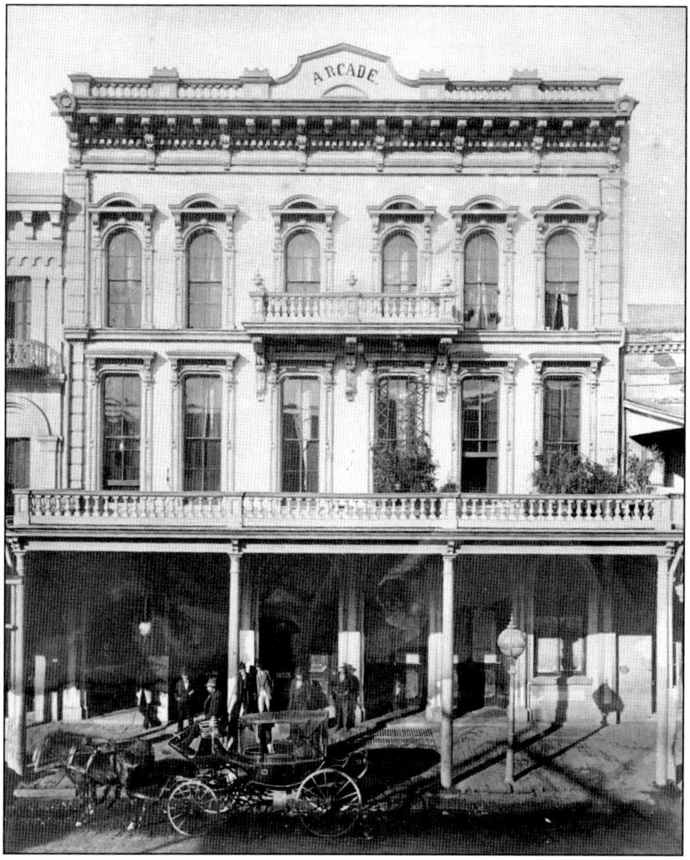

Most of the hotels along Second Street competed for visitors arriving by train. From 1869 through 1872, the arrival of new immigrants to the state rivaled the numbers that came for the California gold rush between 1849 and 1852. Each hotel tried to secure a share of newcomers with their own inducements. In this photograph stands the Arcade Hotel, which probably adopted the Arcade Station's name as its own. The building standing today is a reconstruction. (Courtesy City of Sacramento Collection.)

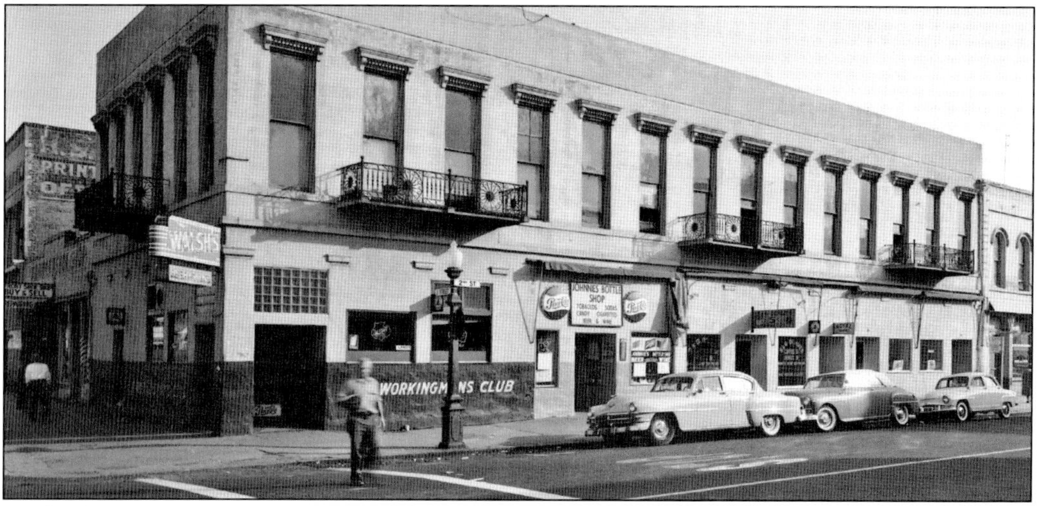

In the first 50 years following the completion of the transcontinental railroad, the businesses located in Old Sacramento usually prospered and then relocated out of the area. Cheap hotels and bars, along with labor agencies, occupied the old buildings. The area continued to deteriorate into the region's biggest slum. By the late 1940s, the area was declared a problem in need of a solution. In the 1950s, redevelopment was advanced as the answer. (Courtesy City of Sacramento Collection.)

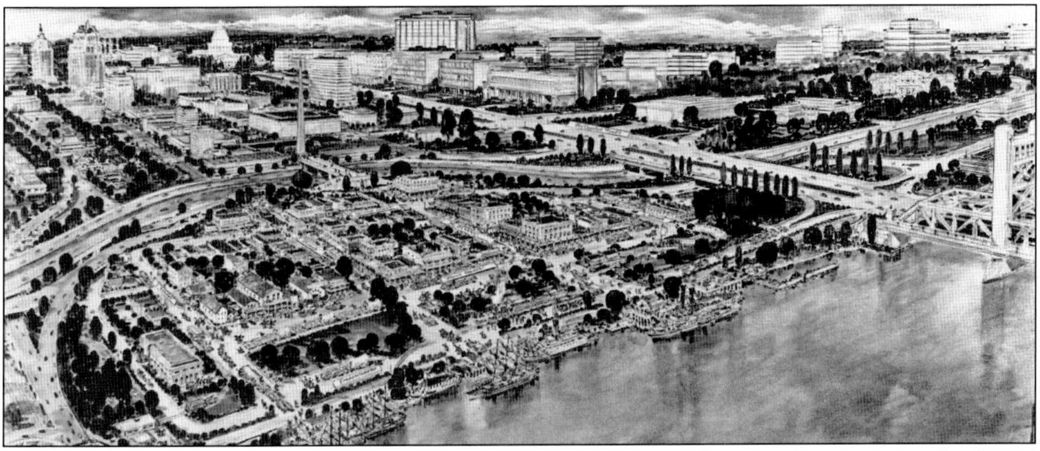

Once Old Sacramento officially became a redevelopment project, planning documents and political decisions would define the boundaries of the area. Interstate 5 would be pushed east away from the river to permit the preservation of buildings along Second Street. The California State Parks declared one third, or seven acres, as a historic park. This rendering helped local officials to understand the vision and potential of the historic district. (Courtesy Frank Christy Collection.)

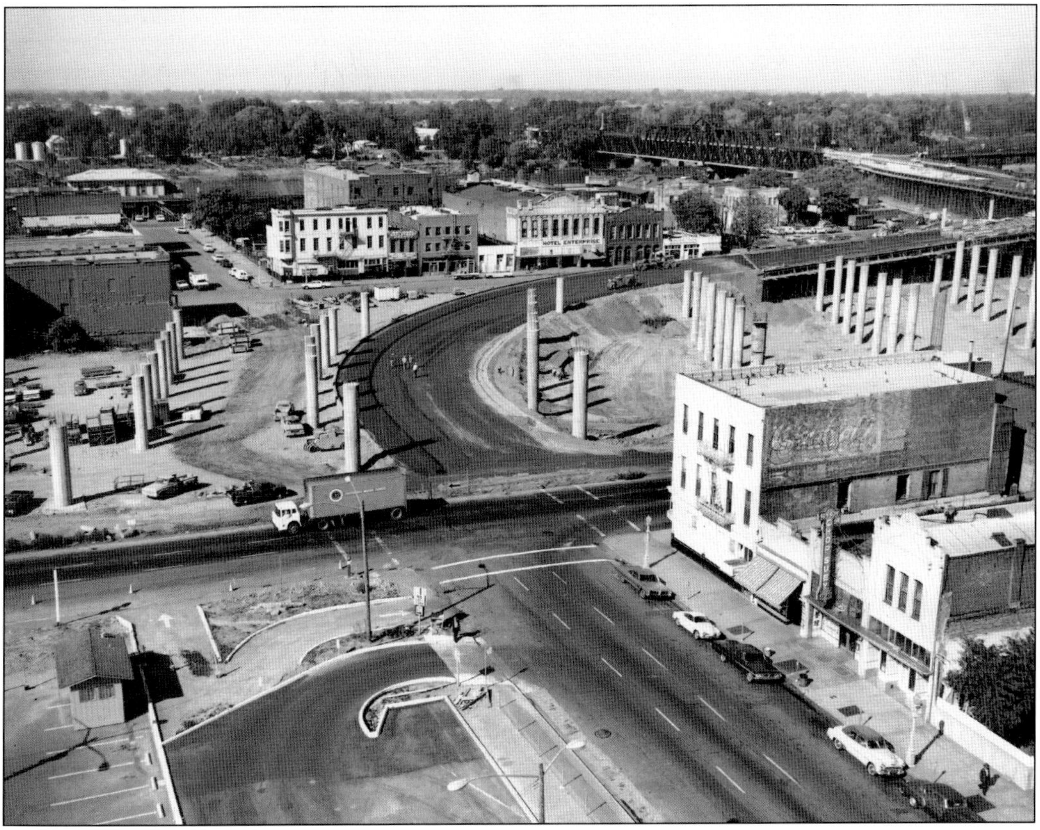

The construction of the Interstate 5 freeway left a great scar across Sacramento from north to south. It would, as a physical and psychological barrier, delay the development of Old Sacramento for many years. From this photograph of Third and J Streets, looking west in October 1967, it is easy to visualize the destruction of the area for the freeway. (Courtesy Frank Christy Collection.)

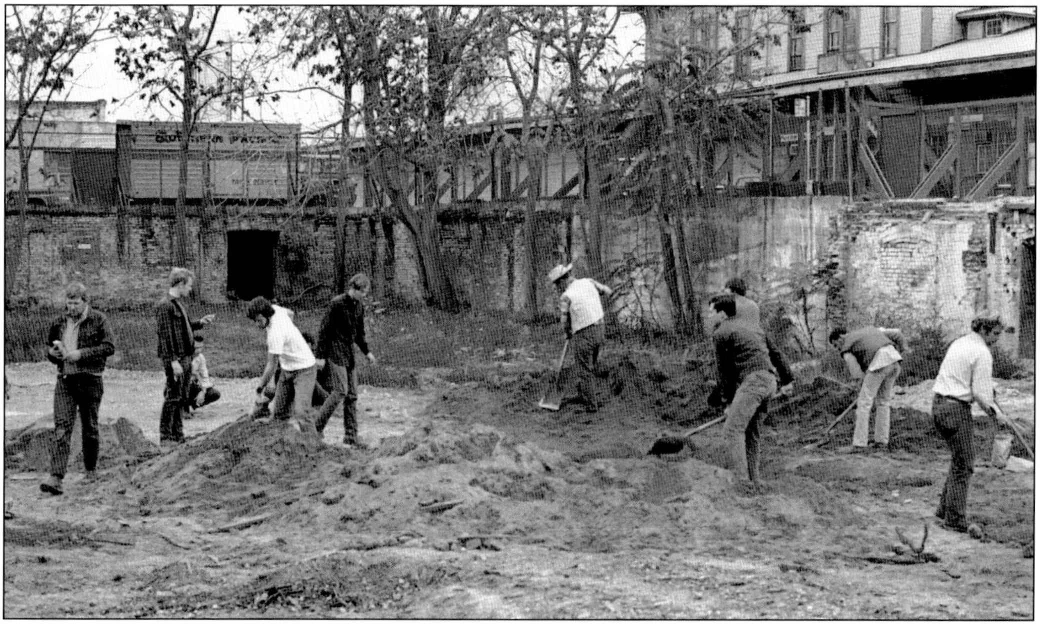

Delays in construction of the freeway provided an opportunity for extensive urban archaeology within the freeway's footprint and Old Sacramento. In this November 1970 photograph, students from California State University, Sacramento, under the direction of Dennis Smart, excavate along Front Street at the site of the City Hotel. Artifacts found provided information about the people and businesses dating back to the gold rush. (Courtesy City of Sacramento Collection.)

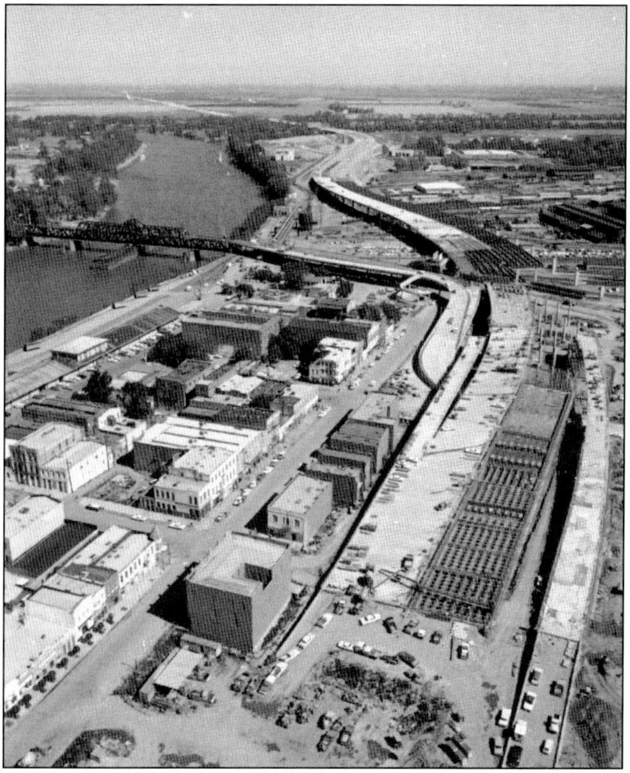

Until the freeway was completed, little progress could be advanced in the historic area. This May 7, 1968, aerial photograph is from L Street looking north. The realignment of the freeway to preserve the historic district is very apparent as is Old Sacramento's isolation during the construction of the freeway. By 1969, the Redevelopment Agency funded the restoration of a building to encourage the project's development because of the district's isolation. (Courtesy *Sacramento Bee* Collection.)

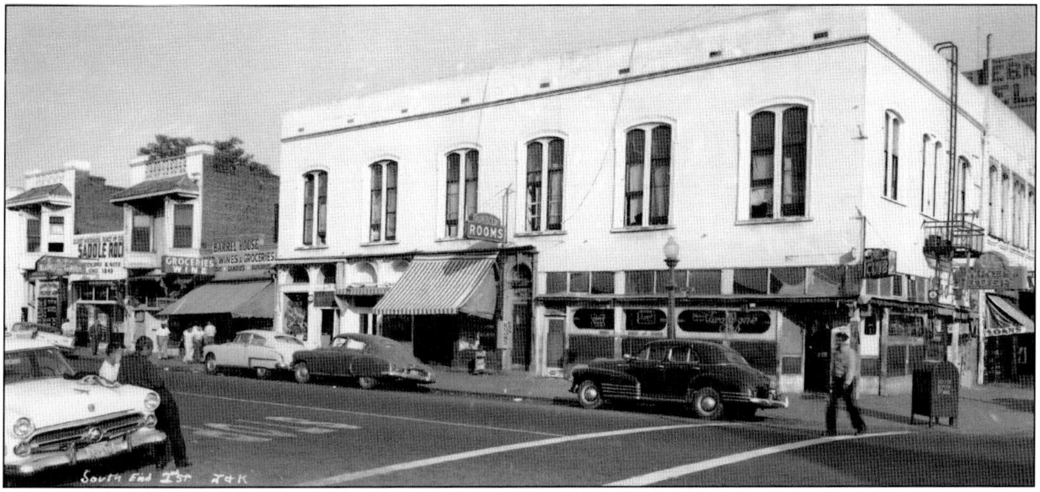

The structure selected for the demonstration project was the Morse Building at Second and K Streets, named after one of its early owners, John F. Morse, who was a doctor and editor of the *Sacramento Union*. Morse is also credited with authoring the first published history of Sacramento in 1853. This photograph of the building was taken in the late 1950s for the Redevelopment Agency prior to its restoration. (Courtesy City of Sacramento Collection.)

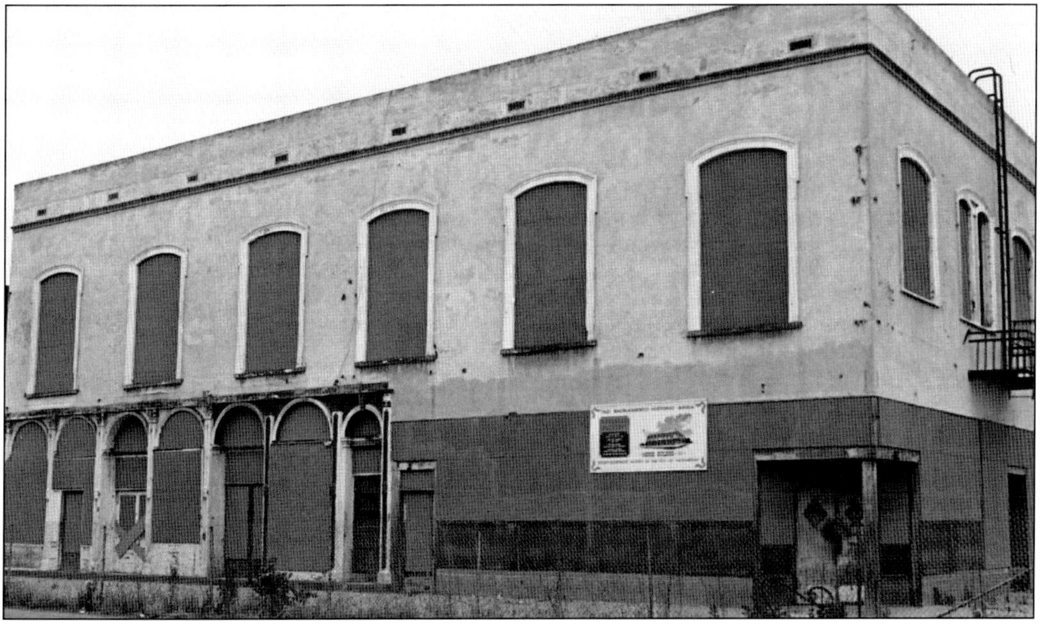

In 1969, when the Redevelopment Agency began restoration on the Morse Building, it had deteriorated significantly. This photograph was taken on December 24, 1968, just before restoration was to start. The agency took the opportunity to explore several structural solutions in stabilizing the building. Many proved impractical and were not utilized in later restorations. (Courtesy *Sacramento Bee* Collection.)

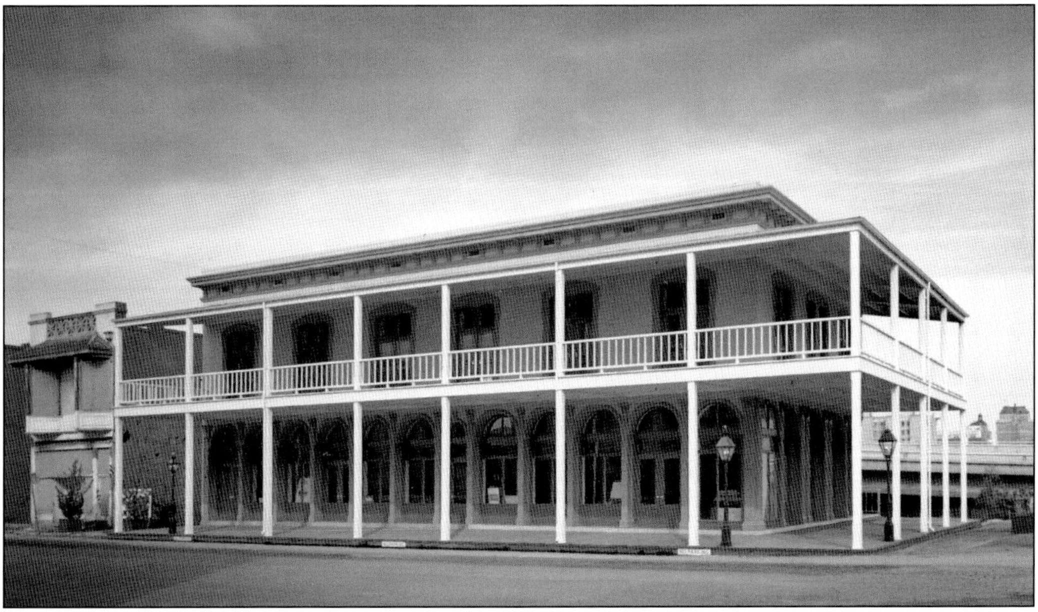

The Morse Building, when completed in 1969, was opened with an exhibit of artwork commissioned by the Southern Pacific Railroad in commemoration of the 100th anniversary of the completion of the Transcontinental Railroad. The center of the exhibit was a model of a proposal for a California State Railroad Museum, which a few years later would become a reality. (Courtesy Ted Leonard Collection.)

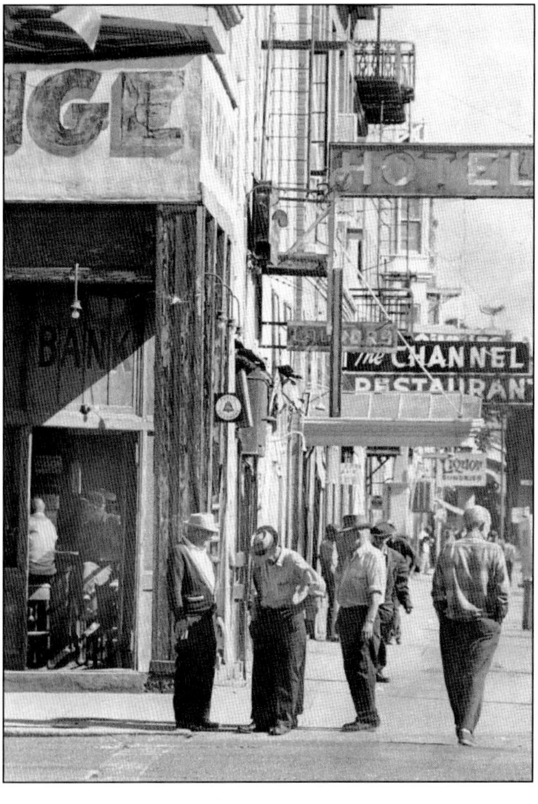

Even as the Morse Building restoration project was about to begin, across Second Street the derelict district was very active. This street of cheap hotels, restaurants, bars, liquor stores, and missions was memorialized by local filmmaker Richard Simpson as the *Marshes of Two Street*. This photograph was taken on September 15, 1968, looking north along Second Street from K Street. (Courtesy *Sacramento Bee* Collection.)

Before redevelopment, Sacramento Buick automobile dealer Newton Cope, who dabbled in collecting California memorabilia such as advertising, paintings, and architectural remnants, envisioned a quality restaurant located in the most historic part of the city even though it was a slum. In the mid-1950s, he purchased a firehouse on Second Street that was being used as a warehouse for used restaurant supplies. (Courtesy Frank Christy Collection.)

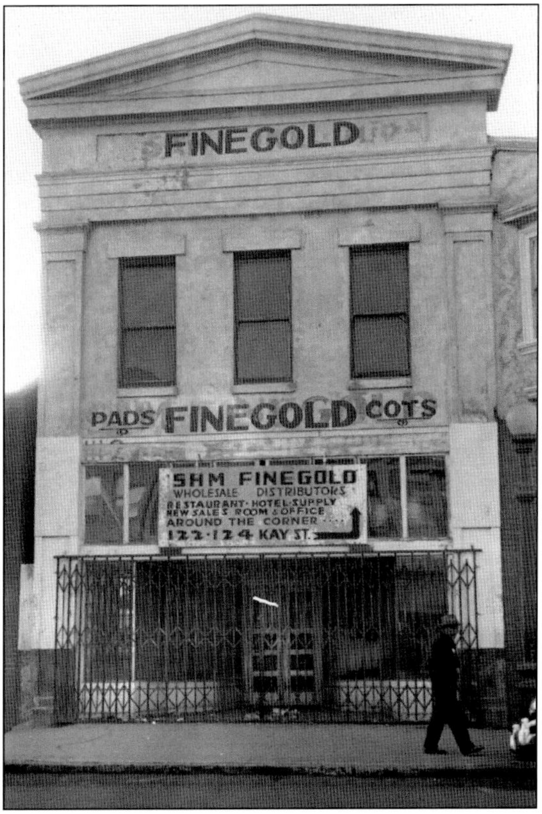

Cope's restaurant, called simply the Firehouse, was located in the Sacramento Engine Company No. 3 building and became one of the most successful upscale restaurants in the community. For many, the trip to this island of affluence in the city's worst slum was their closest personal contact with the conditions of the West End. In a sense, the Firehouse planted with the public the potential for a historic district. (Courtesy Bill and Shirley Gaylord Collection.)

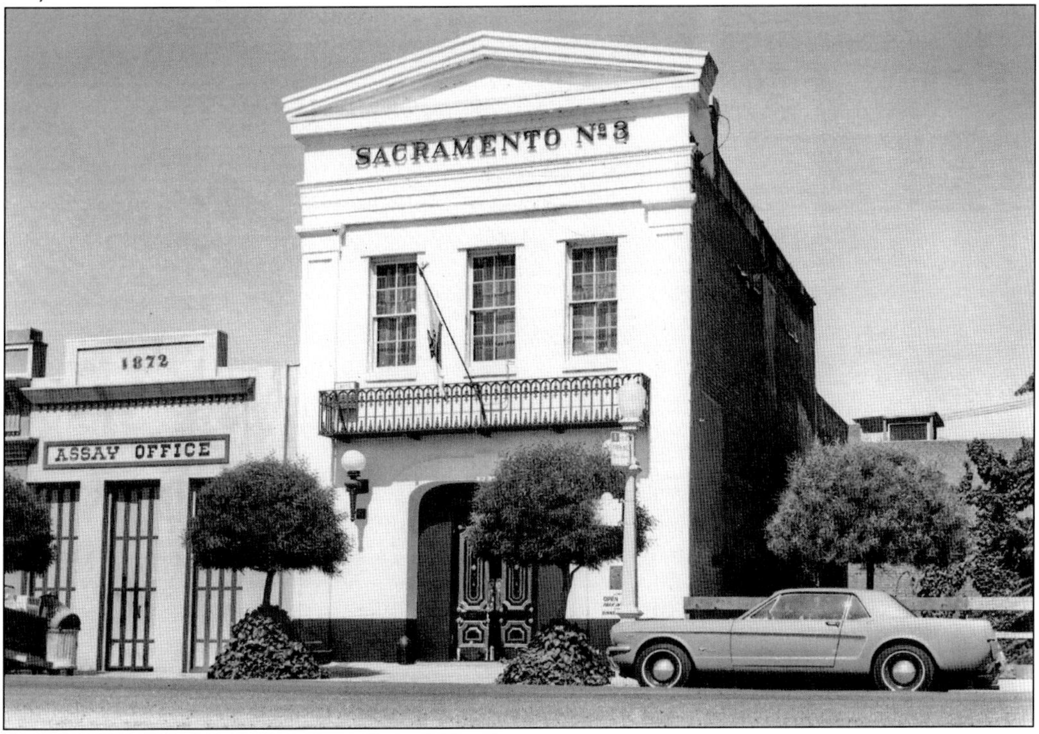

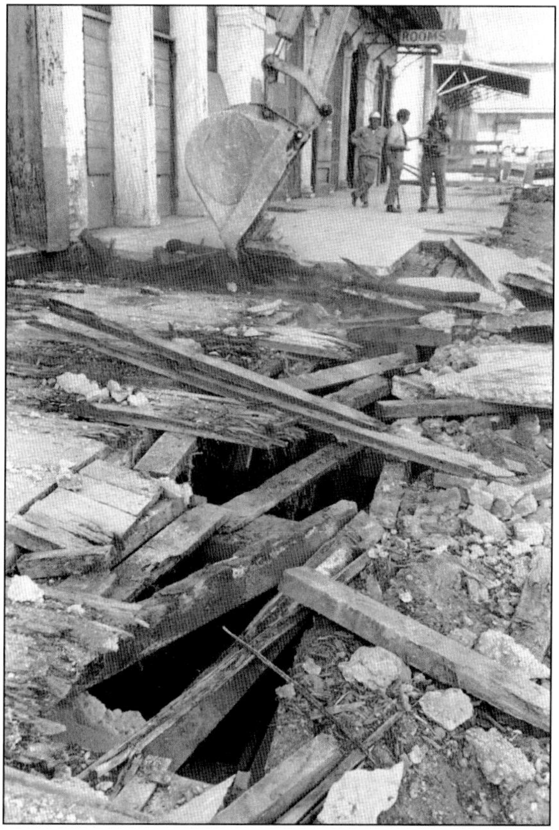

After completion of the Morse Building, the Redevelopment Agency decided to aggressively develop the public infrastructure necessary to stimulate private development. They placed modern utilities in the streets and rebuilt streets and sidewalks. In this October 1971 photograph on J Street near the B. F. Hastings Building, the concrete sidewalk is being removed for a new wood one. It was a surprise to find older wood sidewalks beneath the concrete. (Courtesy *Sacramento Bee* Collection.)

As restoration and reconstruction of buildings began in the historic district, some tradesmen, such as mill workers, were well versed in the crafts and techniques of their predecessors. Others had to relearn and gain proficiency through practice to recreate past techniques. In this photograph, a cornice is being constructed in 1974 for the Howard House Building being restored on K Street. This cornice can be seen installed in the next photograph. (Courtesy *Sacramento Bee* Collection.)

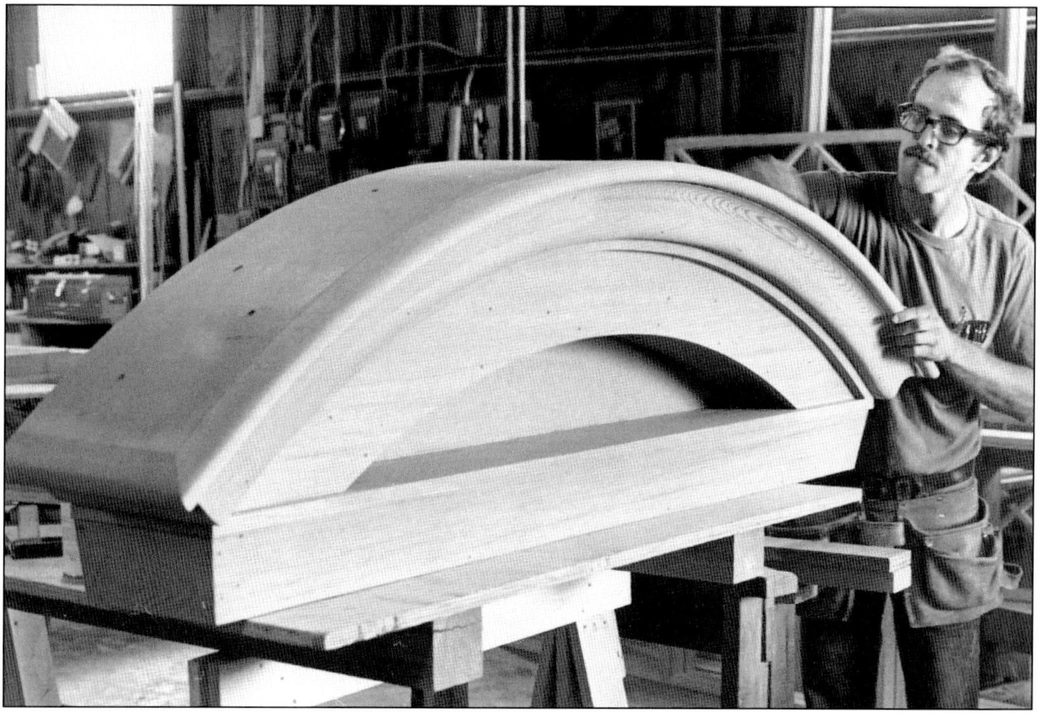

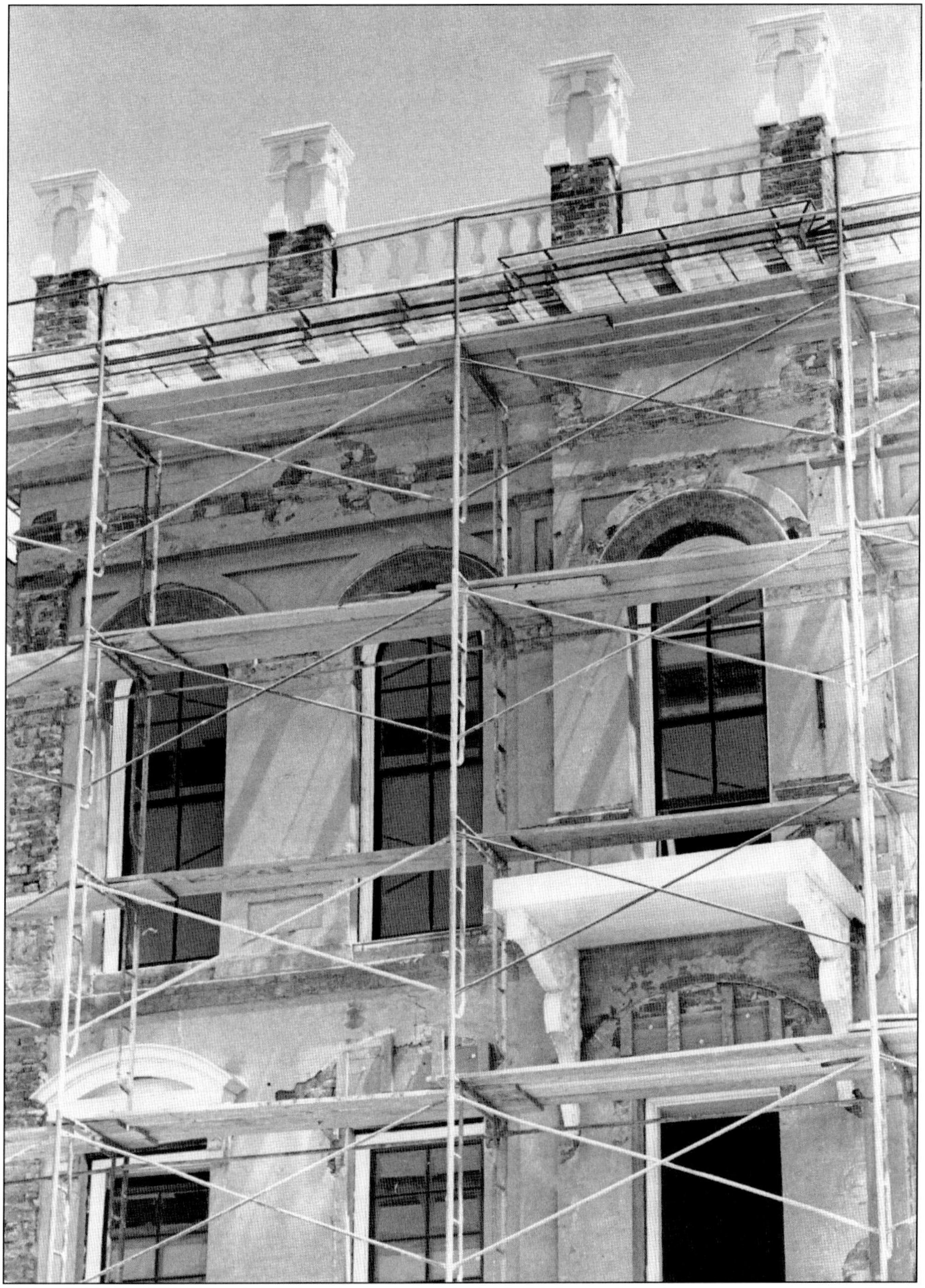

The Howard House and Lady Adams Buildings were purchased and restored by the non-profit Sacramento Trust for Historic Preservation. In this photograph, much of the exterior wood millwork had been installed. The bigger challenge of the exterior plaster work was about to begin. Complex moldings had to be completed in place in wet plaster, a skill almost lost by the modern plasterer's trade. (Courtesy *Sacramento Bee* Collection.)

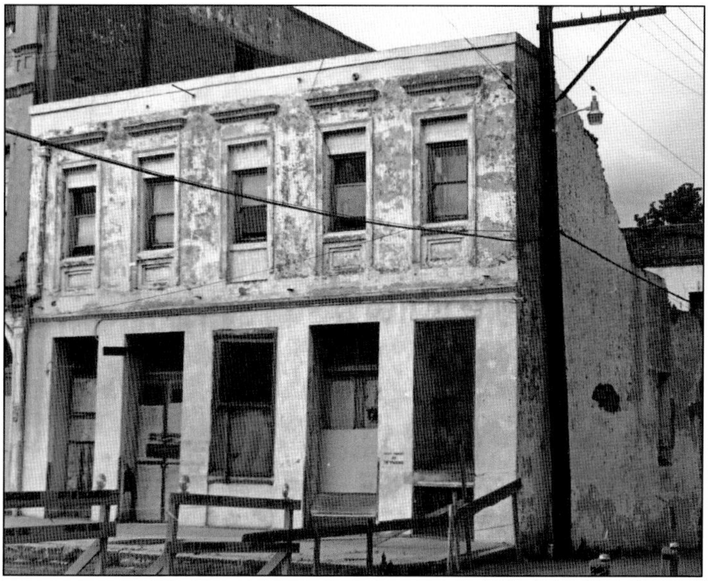

Adjacent to the Howard House is the Lady Adams Building. Named after the ship *Lady Adams*, it brought a group of German merchants to Sacramento who built the structure apparently with the aid of the ship's carpenters. Having survived the fire of November 1852, it has the distinction of being the oldest existing building in Sacramento other than Sutter's Fort. In this pre-restoration photograph, the roof had failed, collapsing a wall. (Courtesy Aubrey Neasham Collection.)

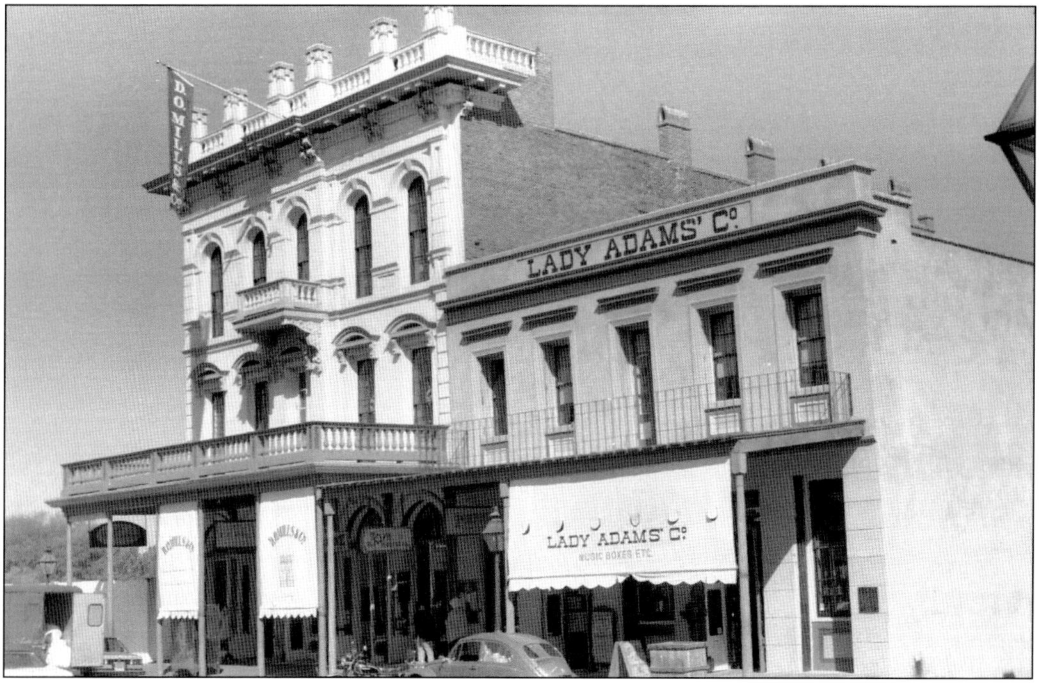

When restoration was completed on the Lady Adams and Howard House, the potential of K Street was well demonstrated. The Howard House, with some of the most complex façade elements, promoted developer confidence to take on more buildings within the district. (Courtesy Ted Leonard Collection.)

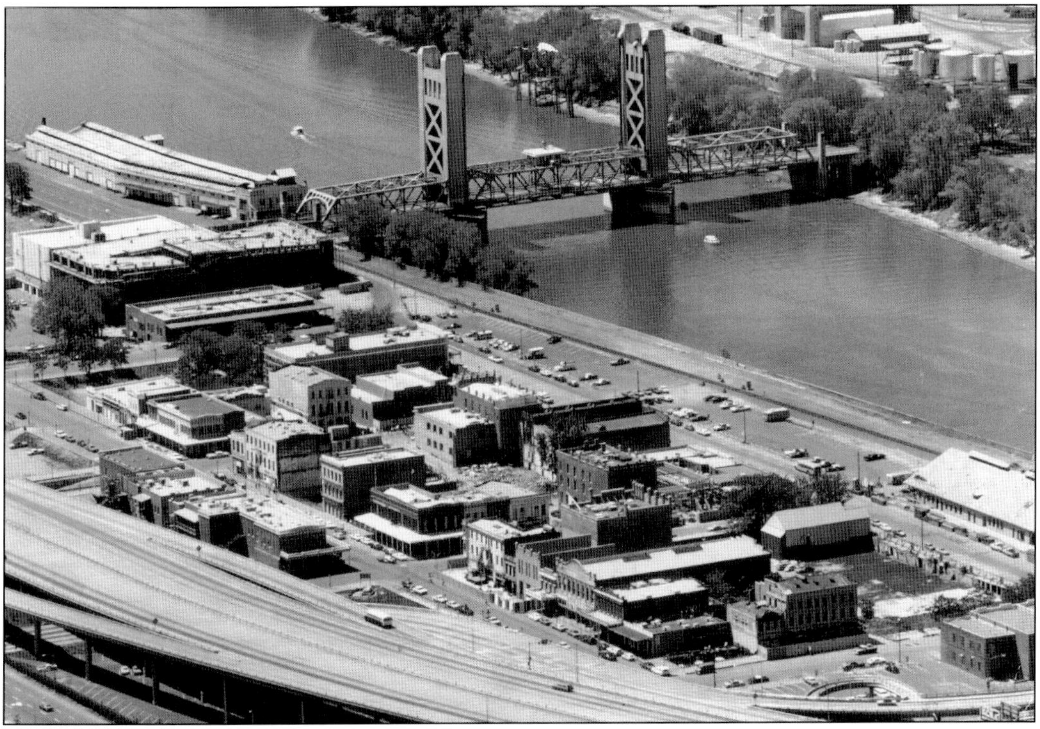

A number of buildings had been restored or reconstructed by May 12, 1976. The waterfront had been cleared earlier, and the Arcade passenger building was nearing completion. Much was yet to be undertaken. Streets, sidewalks, and waterfront docks were future dreams. (Courtesy *Sacramento Bee* Collection.)

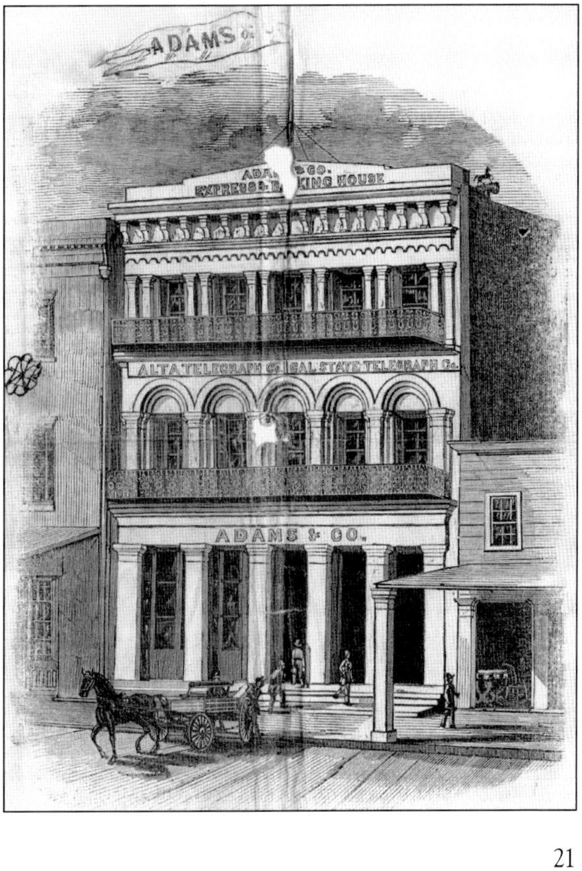

The Adams and Company Building was proclaimed to be the first granite façade building in Sacramento. With the collapse of the banking house, the building became the office of James Birch's California Combination Stage Company, which operated north to Oregon, south to Los Angeles, and east to New Orleans. The building façade stands substantially unaltered to this day, with its interior remodeled for modern use. (Courtesy Eleanor McClatchy Collection.)

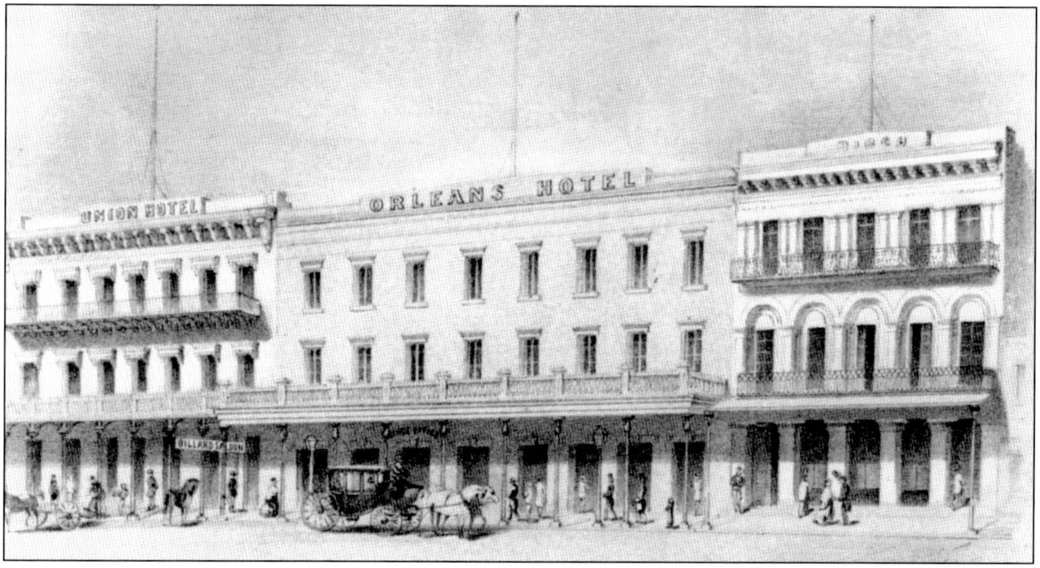

Sacramento's early Second Street was dominated by hotels and banking houses. This 1857 lithograph shows the Union Hotel on the left, the Orleans Hotel in the middle, and the banking house of Adams and Company on the right. This express company and hotels were influential in the 1850s and early 1860s. (Courtesy City of Sacramento Collection.)

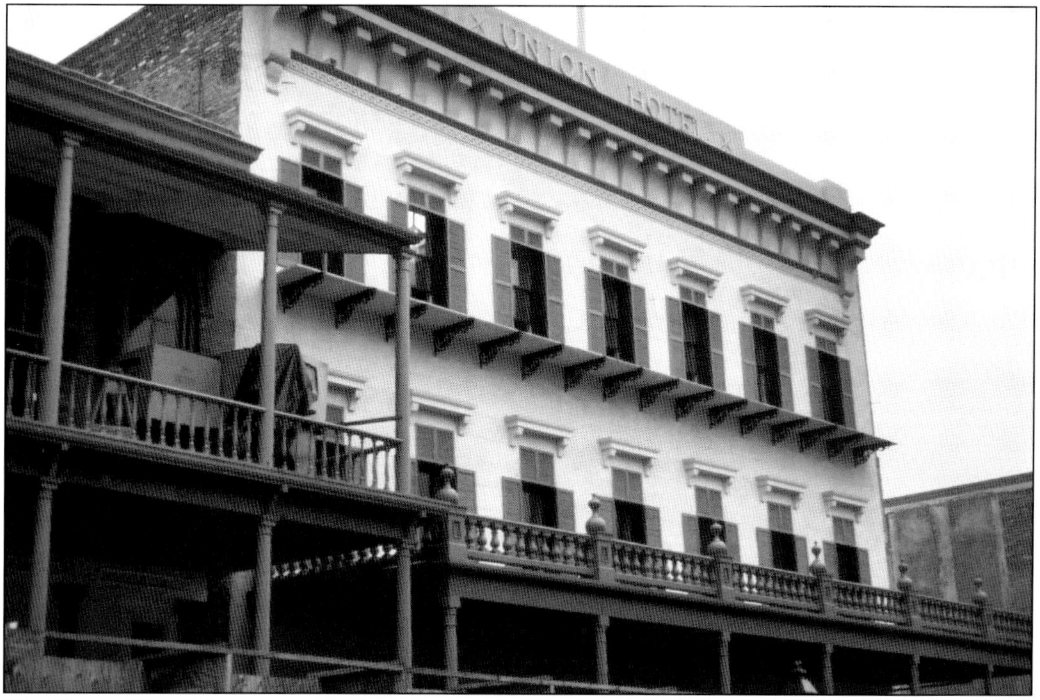

The Union Hotel's balcony was a favorite spot for political speeches. Hundreds would assemble in the street where politicians and public orators would address the crowds below for hours, without the benefit of modern amplified sound systems. This photograph shows the restored building with its reconstructed balcony. (Courtesy Ted Leonard Collection.)

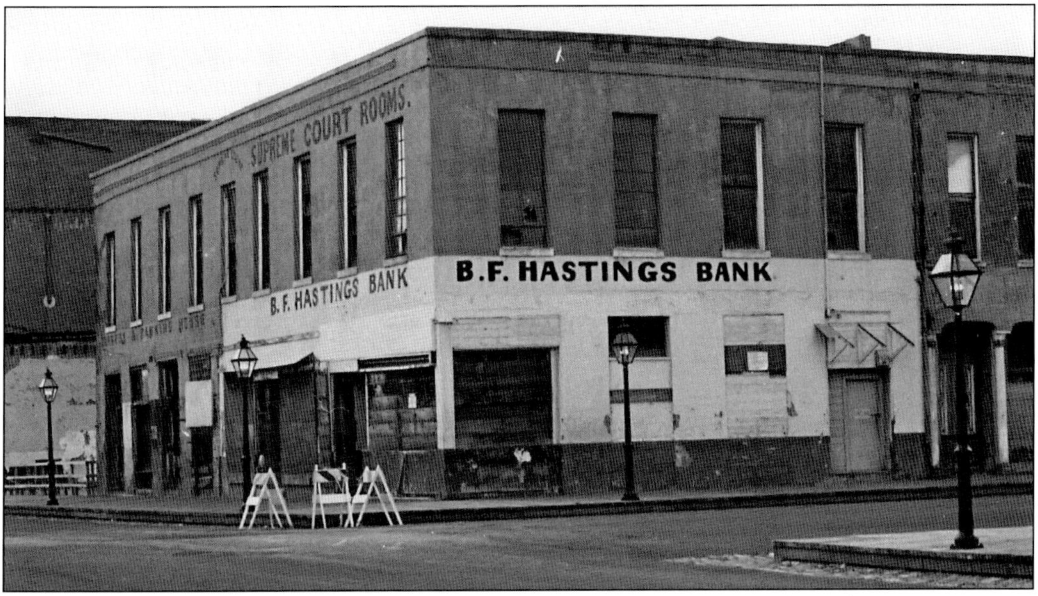

Some preservation battles were won, and others lost. In this photograph of the B. F. Hastings Building, it looks solid but dilapidated. It was the home of the California Supreme Court, Theodore Judah's office when he laid out the route of the Sacramento Valley Railroad, and the Pony Express's terminus. Some argued to tear it down and reconstruct it because of the high restoration costs, but preservationists prevailed. (Courtesy Aubrey Neasham Collection.)

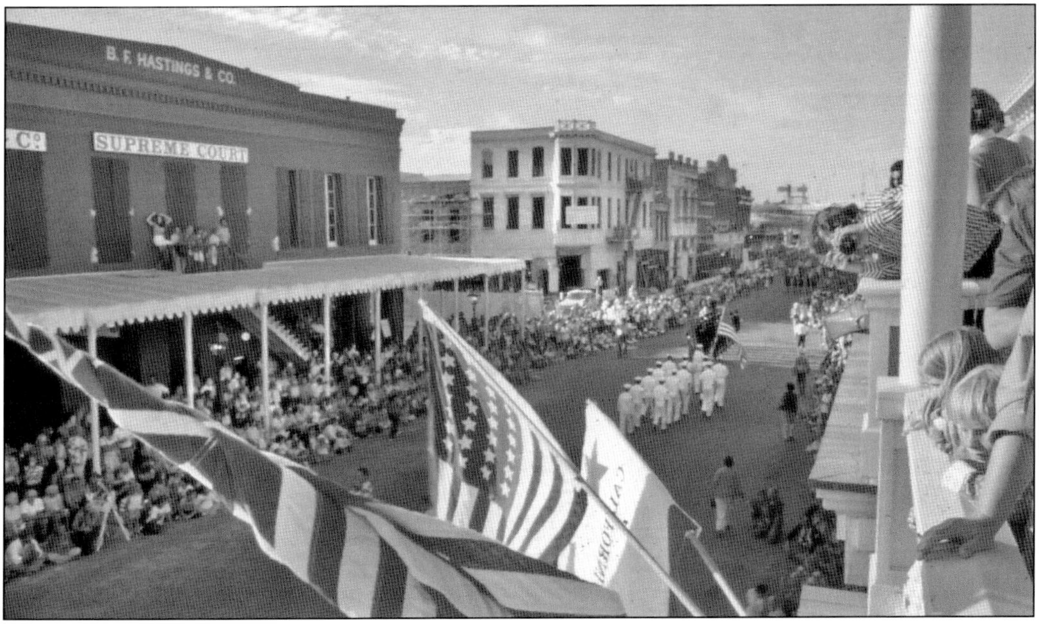

Not all buildings were as fortunate as the B. F. Hastings Building, seen here during a patriotic celebration. The Fratt Building at Second and K Streets burned and was demolished just before restoration began. Ebner's Hotel on K Street, which was a unique architectural example with a cupola on top of the three-story structure, stood vacant for many years. In spite of the efforts of preservationists, the building was demolished and has not yet been reconstructed. (Courtesy Ted Leonard Collection.)

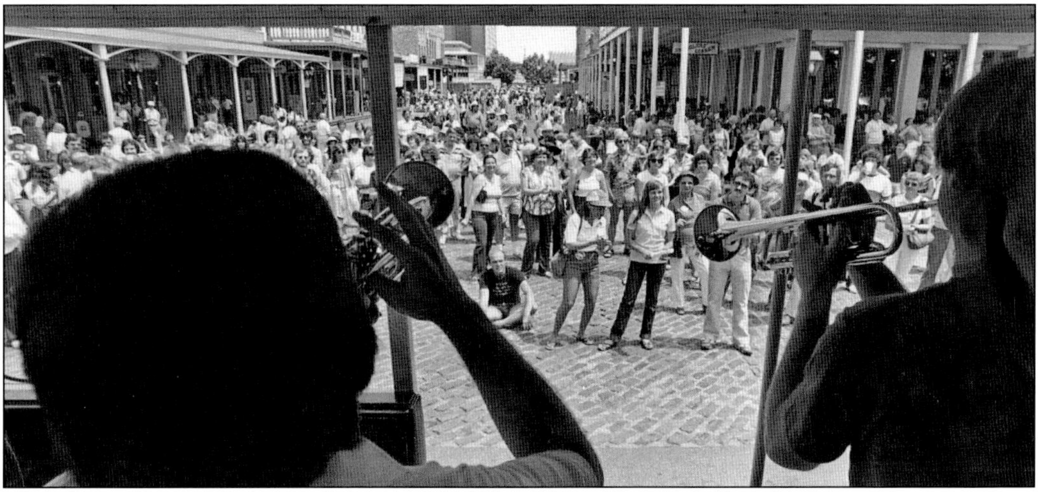

As the Old Sacramento Historic District was reclaimed, it became a premier site for festivals after its potential was demonstrated by the Sacramento Traditional Jazz Society. The Old Sacramento Dixieland Jubliee was first held in the historic district in 1974 and grew each year. Many performance venues were in buildings or enclosed "gardens," but impromptu performances took place wherever a crowd gathered. This band was playing from the "Old Town Jazz Trolley" on Front Street. (Courtesy *Sacramento Bee* Collection.)

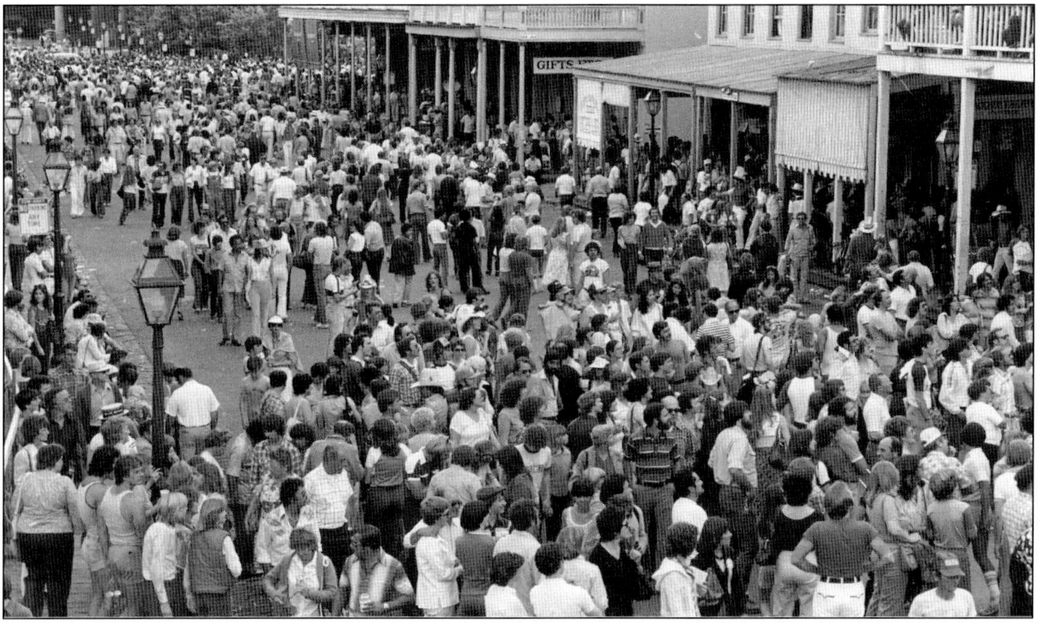

Eventually the jazz festival became so popular that everywhere in the district there was a crowd. The festival expanded beyond the historic district to the convention center, Cal Expo, and hotels throughout the Sacramento region. This May 26, 1980, photograph was taken on Second Street between J and K Streets. The *Sacramento Bee* story reported that thousands jammed the street. The bands and visitors were from around the world. (Courtesy *Sacramento Bee* Collection.)

Some festivals have a specific tie to Old Sacramento and its history. Railfair, promoted and produced by the California State Railroad Museum, has provided an opportunity to revive the community's strong railroad heritage. Locomotives and other equipment from around the world are assembled for public view. In this photograph, the Southern Pacific *Daylight* locomotive No. 8444 from Portland, Oregon, arrives for display in May 1981. (Courtesy *Sacramento Bee* Collection.)

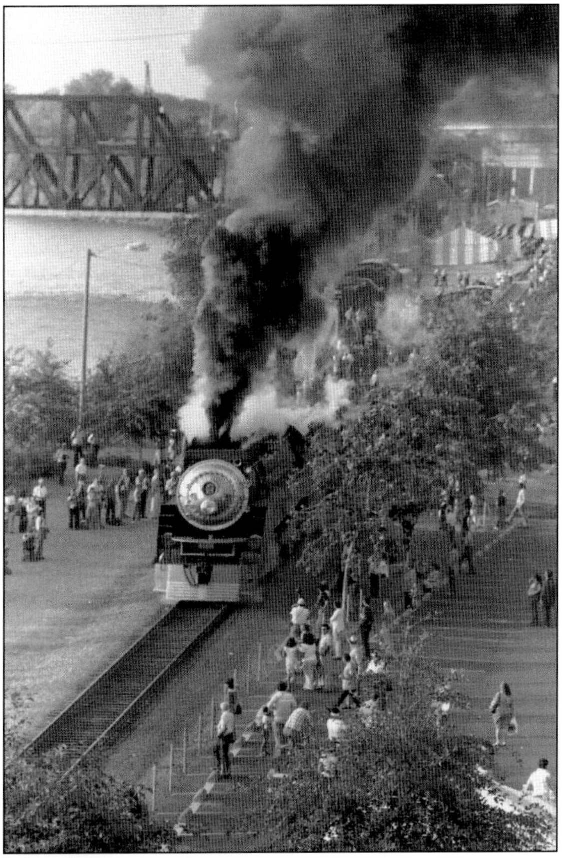

Railroads are an integral part of American culture that appeals to all ages. In this photograph, visitors to Railfair pick up their flattened coins, souvenirs smashed by the *Daylight* locomotive No. 8444. (Courtesy *Sacramento Bee* Collection.)

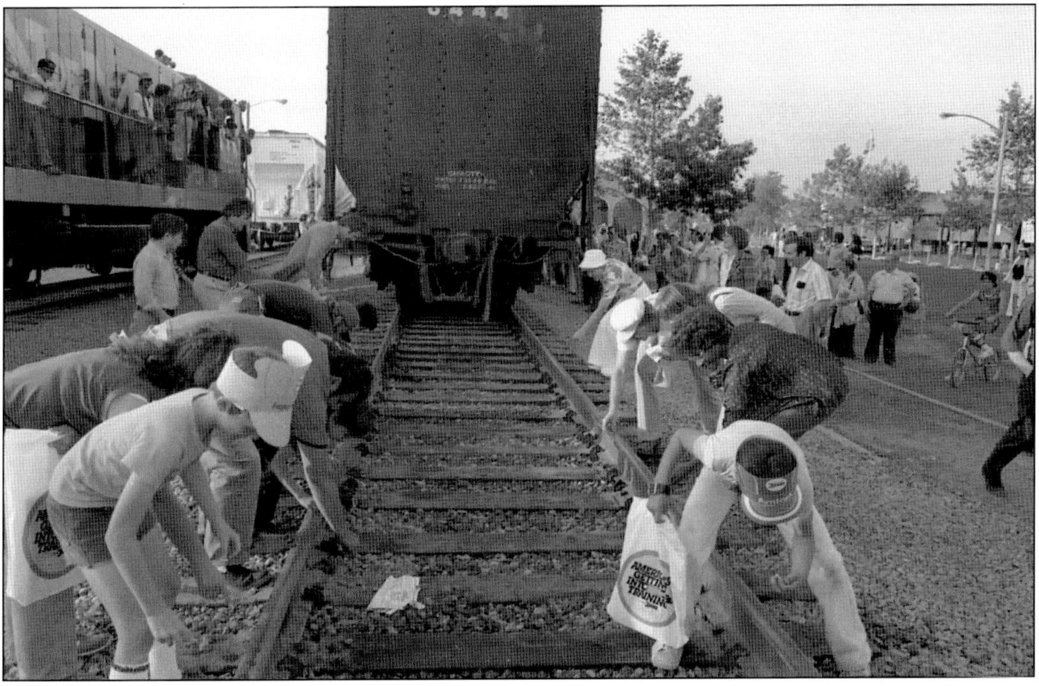

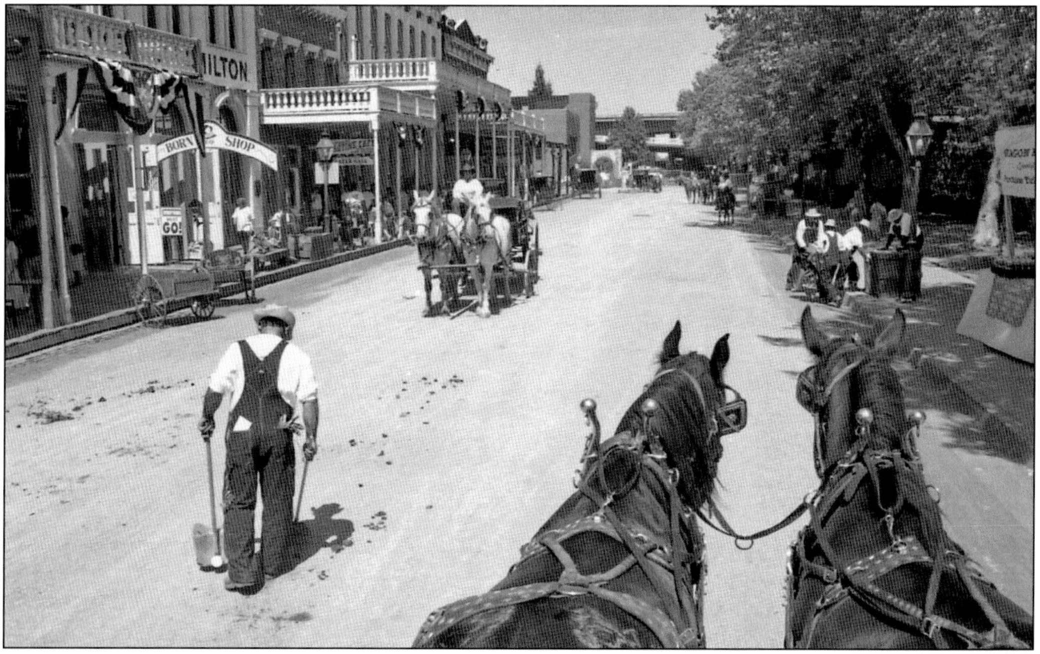

One of the signature happenings for Old Sacramento is an annual Labor Day weekend event called "Gold Rush Days." The first such festival was held in 1998 and was called the "Second Great Gold Rush." During the festival, dirt was placed over the streets and many individuals were dressed in period clothing. Even the street cleaners and garbage collectors dressed for the event and used period tools. (Courtesy *Sacramento Bee* Collection.)

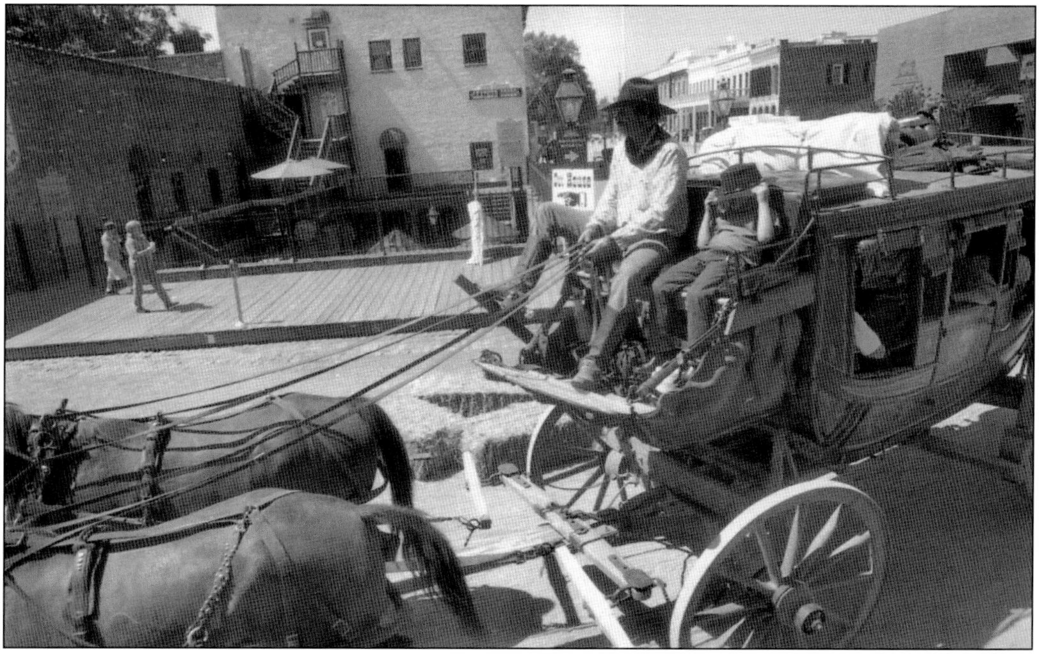

Some horse-drawn vehicles were only for ambience, while others were used as freight wagons. Others, like the stagecoach, would take visitors for short rides. A real treat for children was to ride with the stagecoach driver. (Courtesy *Sacramento Bee* Collection.)

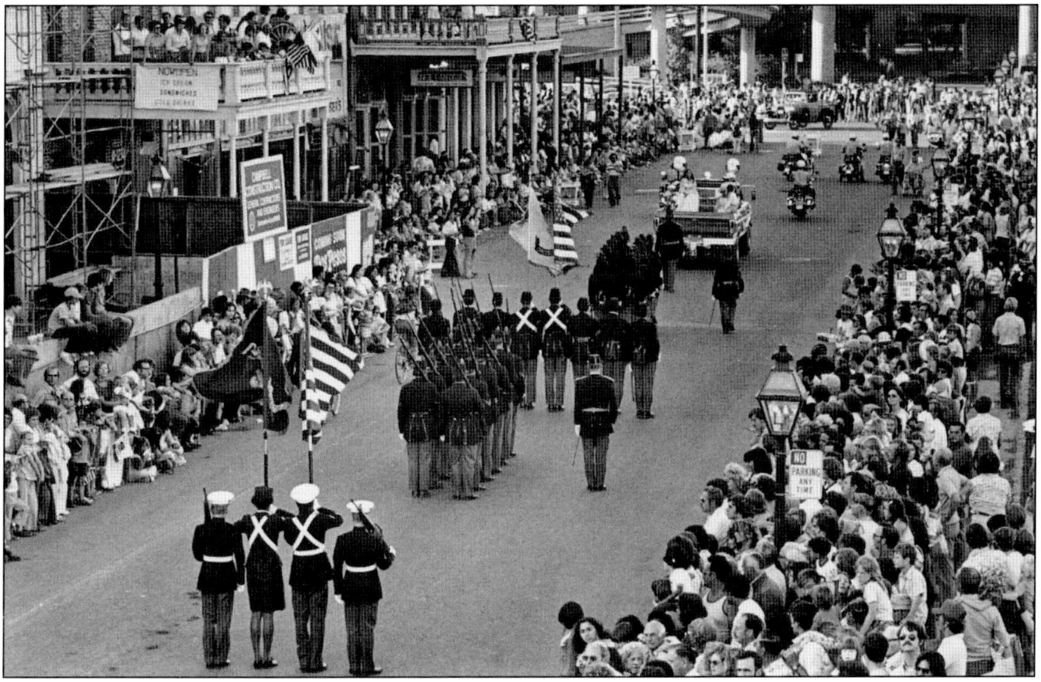

After more than a year of preparation, Old Sacramento became the local stage for the nation's bicentennial celebration. Beginning with the "Freedom Train" in 1975, the celebration continued and, by July 3, 1976, the streets were filled with celebrants. The nation's birthday in 1976, as well as in many subsequent years, was marked by a large fireworks display on the Sacramento River. (Courtesy *Sacramento Bee* Collection.)

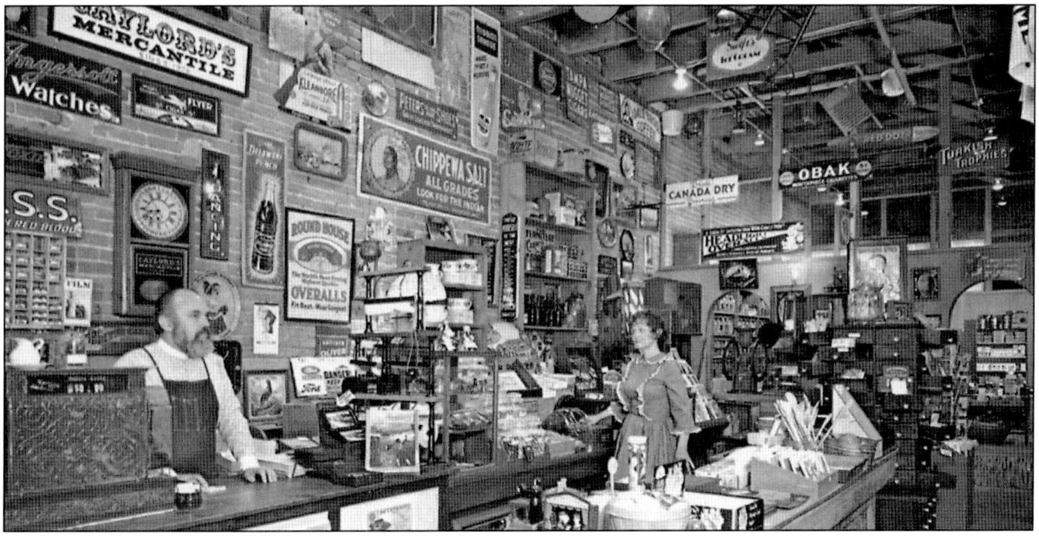

Old Sacramento is a historic district and a location for festivals and special events. Above and beyond that, it is the home for museums and many shops and businesses such as law offices, restaurants, and at times even a private investigator. Sacramento was a commercial center and Old Sacramento preserves that spirit. Gaylord's Mercantile was one of the pioneering businesses in the restored district, specializing in coffee, herbs, and antique advertising. (Courtesy City of Sacramento Collection.)

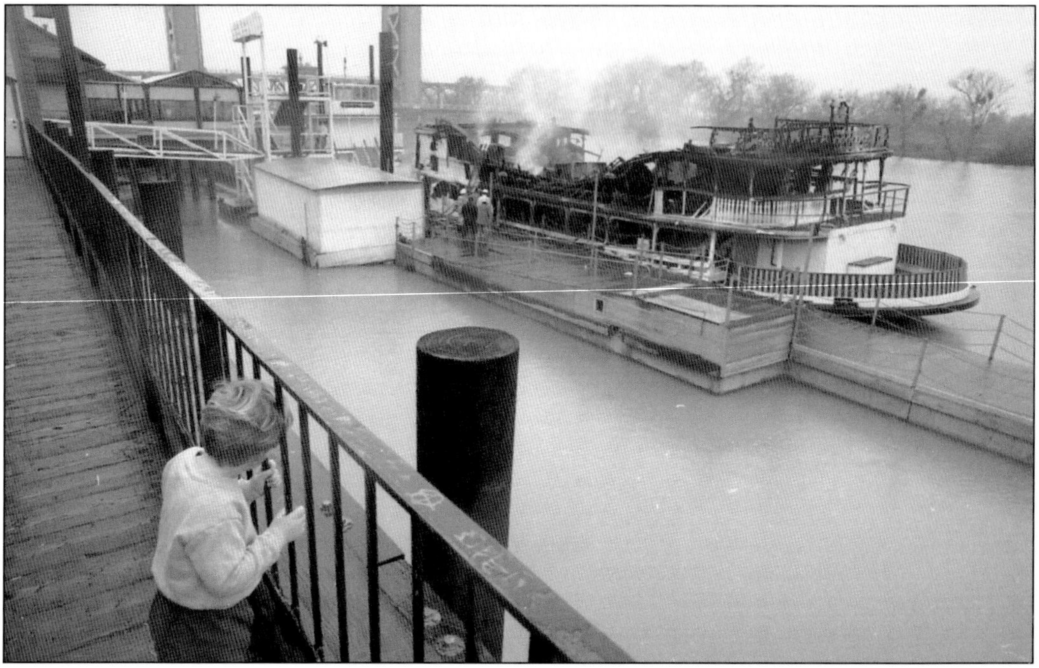

Old Sacramento has been subjected to many fires, and not all have been in the distant past. On February 3, 1996, at approximately 3:30 a.m., the fire department responded to a fire aboard the *Spirit of Sacramento* near the K Street landing. Finding the boat "fully involved," a second alarm was called and the firemen prevented the spread of the fire to the *Delta King* riverboat. (Courtesy *Sacramento Bee* Collection.)

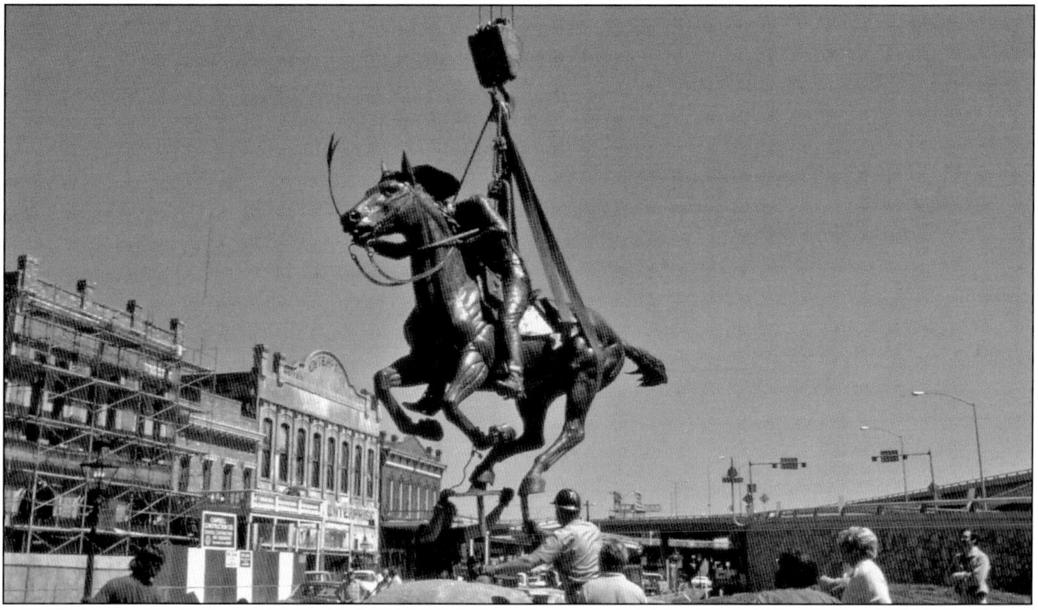

In 1976, Old Sacramento still had many years of construction ahead. However, the celebrations and activities, such as the installation of the monument to the Pony Express on the northeast corner of Second and J Streets, sent a message to the community that Old Sacramento was inviting residents and tourists to come and visit. (Courtesy Ted Leonard Collection.)

Two

Government

Service to the People

by Patricia J. Johnson

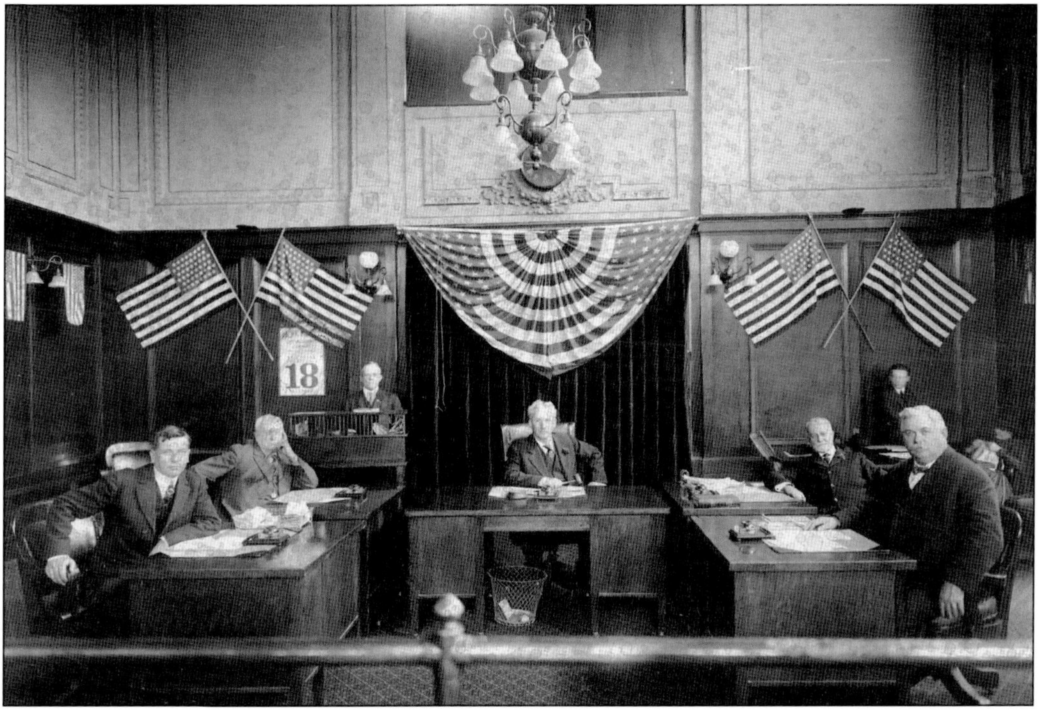

While John Sutter Jr. and Sam Brannan laid out the city in 1849, Sacramento City did not actually incorporate until March 18, 1850. As California achieved statehood in September 1850, Sacramento County became one of the original 27 charter counties and the city became its county seat. By 1854, Sacramento had developed into the permanent site for the California state capital. State government shared offices with county government until a permanent building was finished in 1874. In 1858, with city government in financial straits, it merged with county government for five years in what has been called a "marriage of convenience." The federal government made Sacramento the site of several federal courthouses. In 1917, D. W. Carmichael served as president of the city commission, later to be known as the city council. He appears in the center of this photograph. Other members of the commission were T. J. Coulter, E. W. Haynes, G. C. Simmons, and G. Turner. The commission chamber, seen here festooned in flags, was indicative of the wave of patriotism that swept the country during World War I. (Courtesy Sacramento Police Department Collection.)

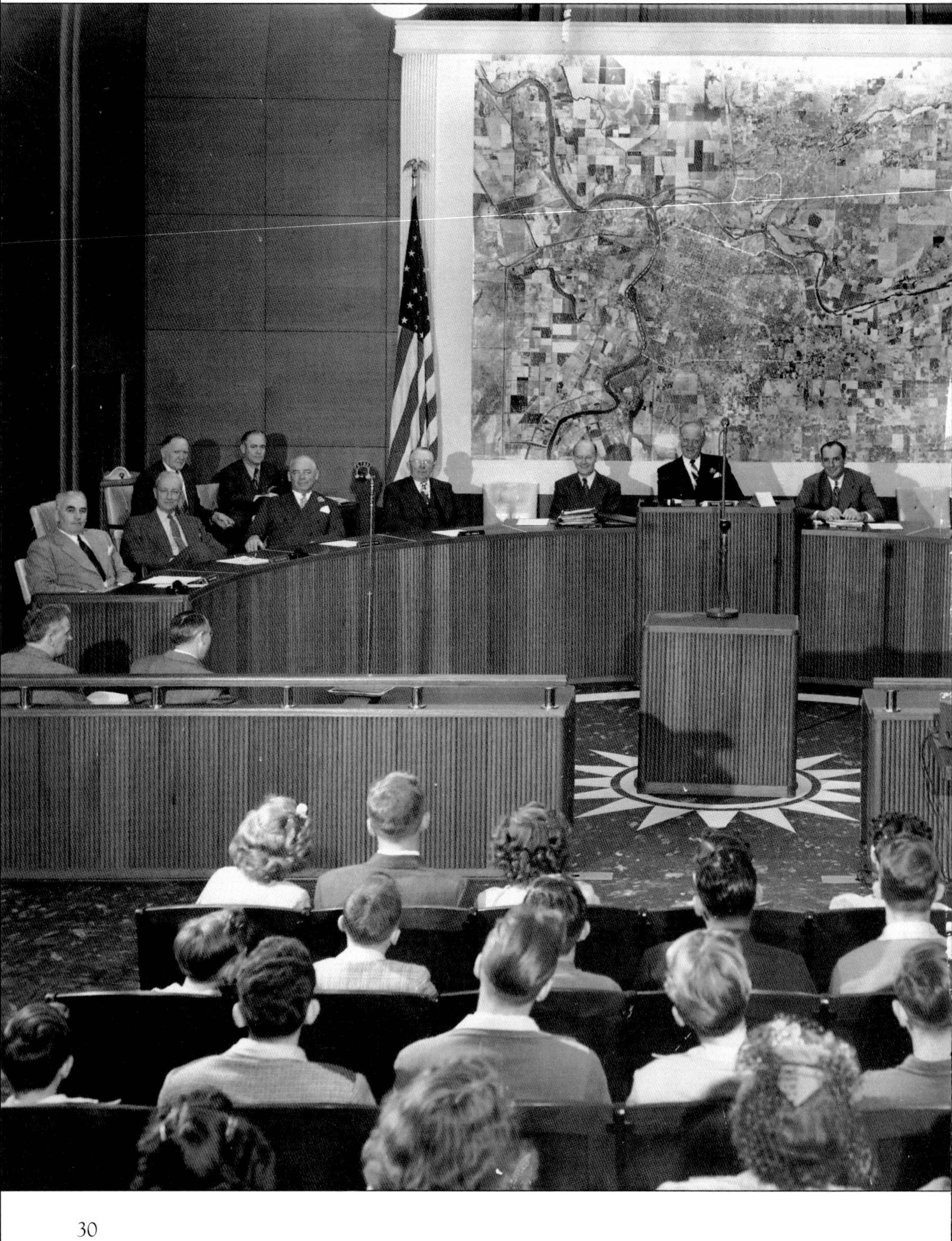

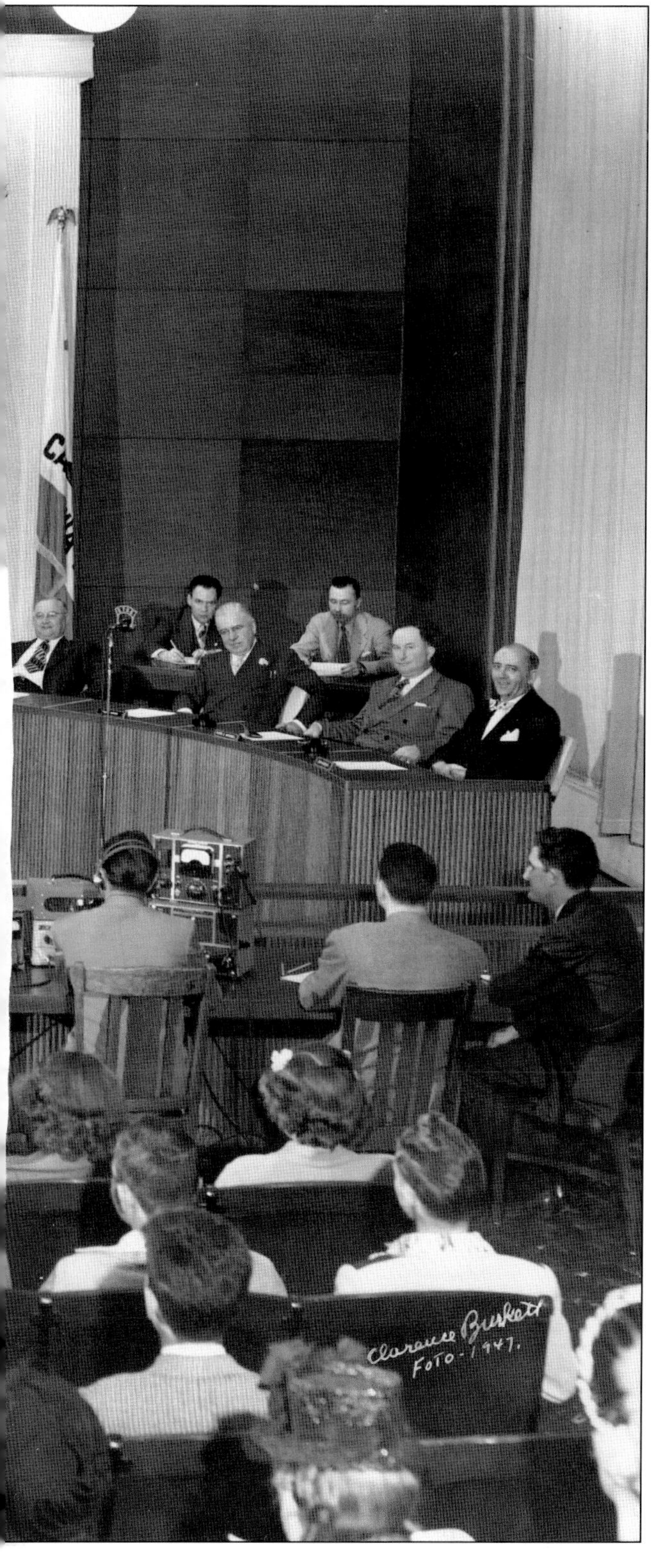

Representative governments at all levels repeat this scene over and over. In this form of government, service to the people is a basic tenet whether it is at the city, county, state, or federal level. In the mold of C-Span, the Sacramento City Council broadcast its regular meetings over radio in 1947. Note the KFBK Radio microphones in front of the council, and the technician with the headset monitoring the broadcast. In this photograph, the council conducts business before a group of school students. Seated at the dais, from left to right, are council members Paul Taylor, Roy Nielsen, George Watrous, Fred Arnold, city clerk Harry Denton, Mayor George Klumpp, City Manager Bartley Cavanaugh, and council members Ray Flint, Tom Monk, Peter Mitchell, and John Welsh. (Courtesy City of Sacramento Collection.)

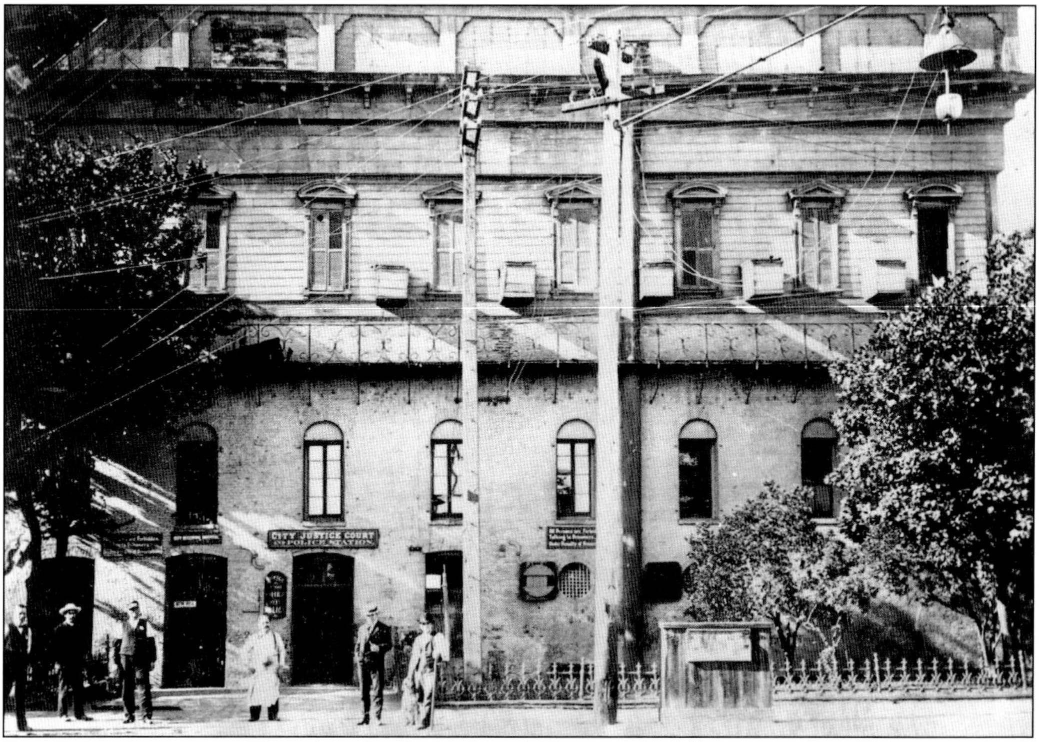

Built in 1853 and costing $120,000, the City Water Works Building at Front and I Streets served most city governmental activities. In this 1895 photograph of the building, note the signs for the offices of city justice court, receiving hospital, and police station. City offices operated here until 1909, when they moved to their interim offices at 426 J Street before moving into the new city hall at Ninth and I Streets in 1915. (Courtesy Joseph Benetti Collection.)

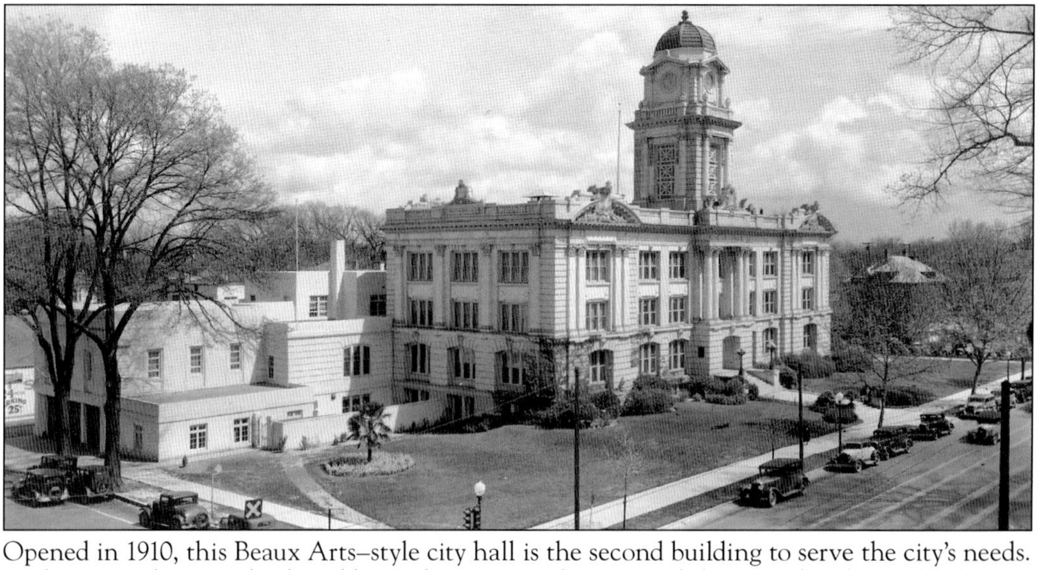

Opened in 1910, this Beaux Arts–style city hall is the second building to serve the city's needs. In this 1934 photograph, the additional annex can be seen at left. Immediately north of Cesar Chavez Plaza Park on I Street between Ninth and Tenth Streets, the building recently underwent a major renovation and earthquake-safety retrofit. (Courtesy Don Rivett Collection.)

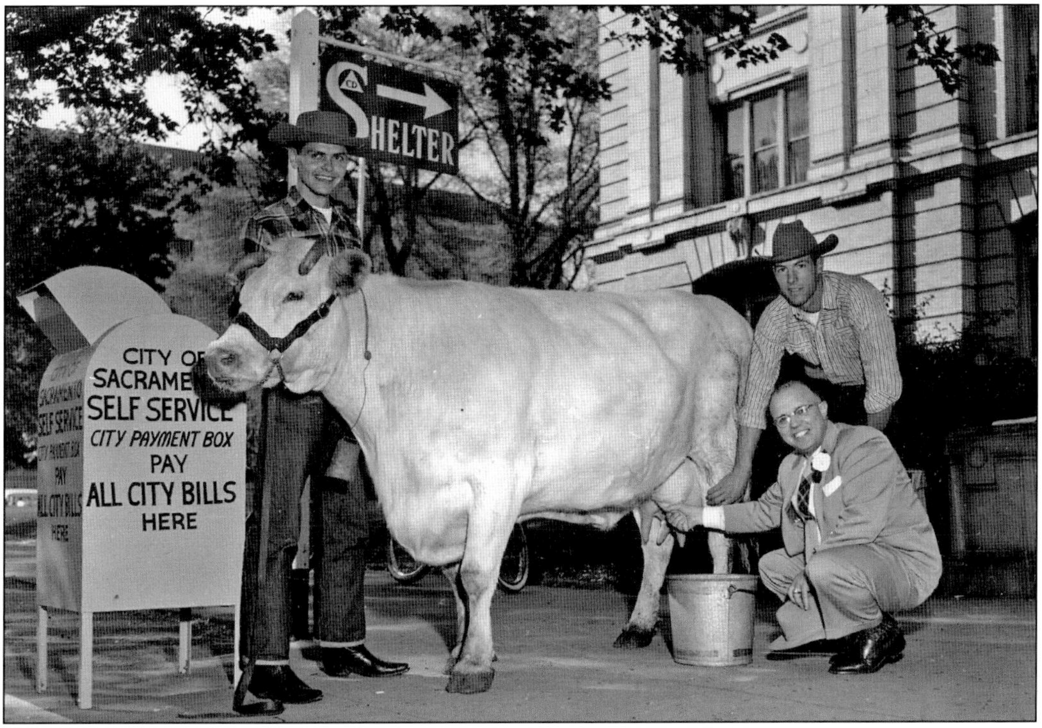

Mayor Clarence Azevedo milks a cow in front of city hall on April 19, 1956, to publicize University of California, Davis Picnic Day. Standing at the head of the cow is student Fred Boomer, and assisting the mayor is publicity chairman Don Donsing. Azevedo served as mayor from 1956 until 1960. Gone are the days when citizens could pay their city bills at the curb. (Courtesy Joseph Benetti Collection.)

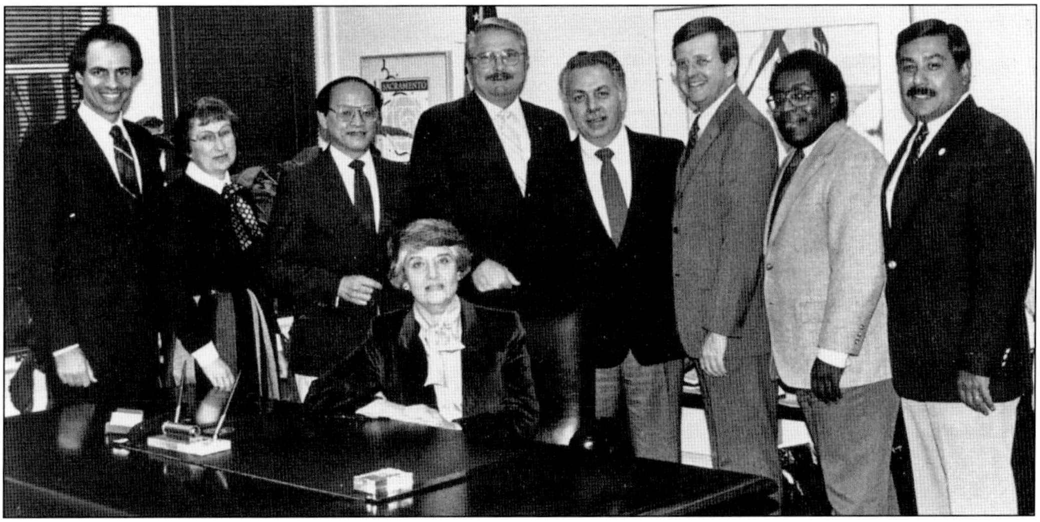

In 1985, the Sacramento City Council represented a diverse community. In this gathering of council members surrounding Mayor Anne Rudin, the first woman directly elected mayor of Sacramento, are, from left to right, David Shore, Lynn Robie, Thomas Chinn, William Smallman, Terry Kastanis, Douglas Pope, Grantland Johnson, and Joe Serna. Joe Serna would succeed Anne Rudin in 1992 and serve until his death in 1999. (Courtesy Terry Kastanis Collection.)

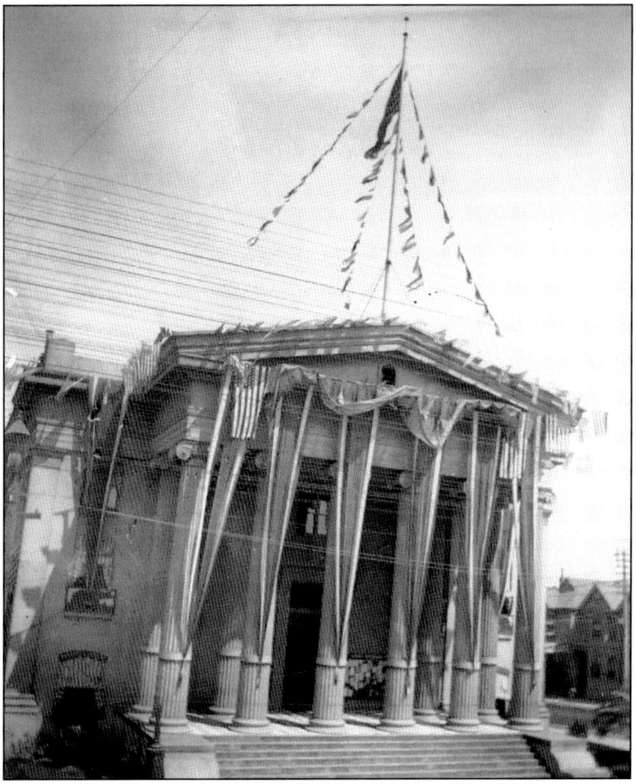

Sacramento's second county courthouse opened January 1, 1855, on the northwest corner of Seventh and I Streets, the same location as the first. The earlier structure, which served as the first state capitol, was destroyed by fire in July 1854. Designed by San Francisco architect David Farquharson and finished in three months, the new courthouse served until 1913. State officials also occupied this building until moving into the present state capitol in 1869. (Courtesy Roger Joslyn Collection.)

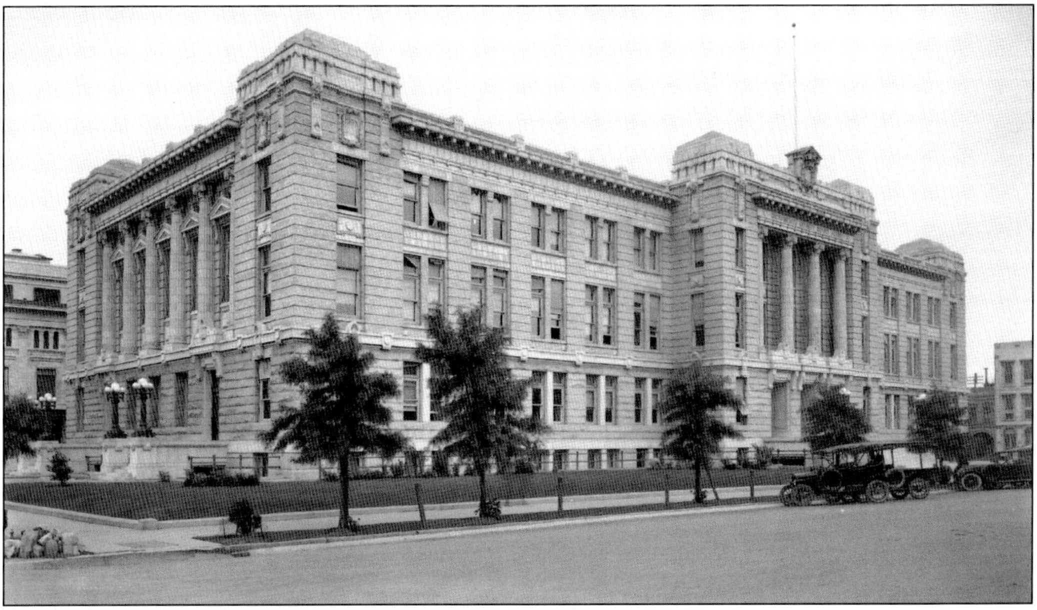

Sacramento's third courthouse would also occupy the same location at Seventh and I Streets. Completed in 1913 and serving until 1960, the third courthouse was built in a classical Beaux Arts–style and was designed by R. A. Herold, the Sacramento architect who also orchestrated the creation of Sacramento's city hall. This 1920s photograph shows the expanse of the building that included three courtrooms. (Courtesy David Joslyn Collection.)

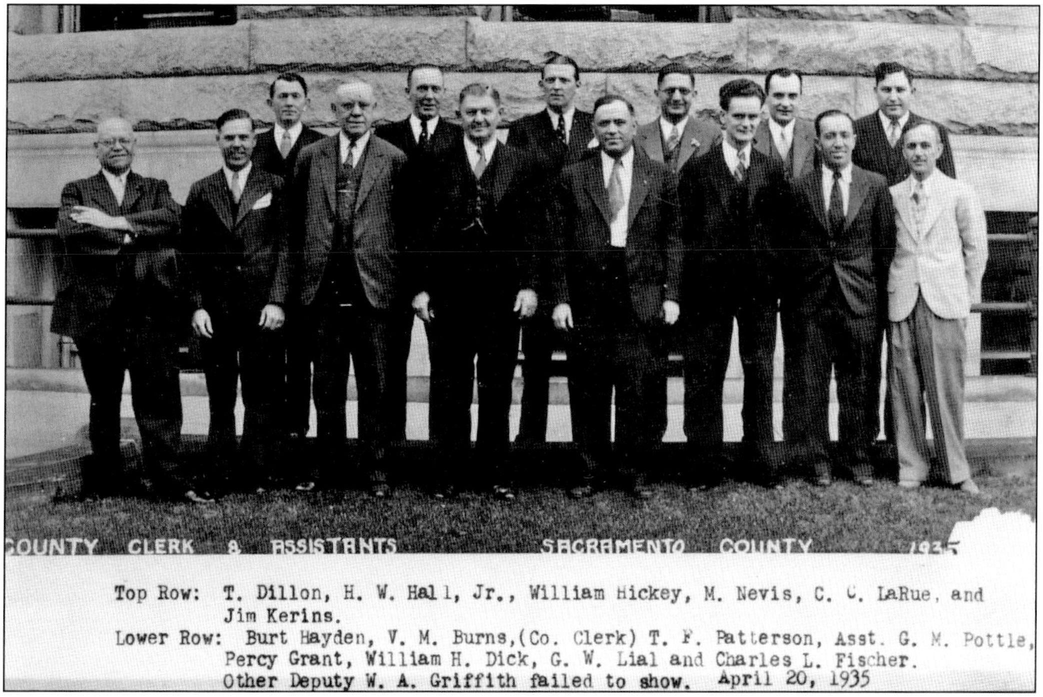

Sacramento County clerk V. M. Burns, second from the left in the front row, and his assistants pose for their photograph in 1935. The county clerk was the ex-officio clerk for the superior court, the board of supervisors, and other offices of the county. He was responsible for recording all the proceedings of these agencies. Today, there is a separate clerk for each agency. (Courtesy Frank Christy Collection.)

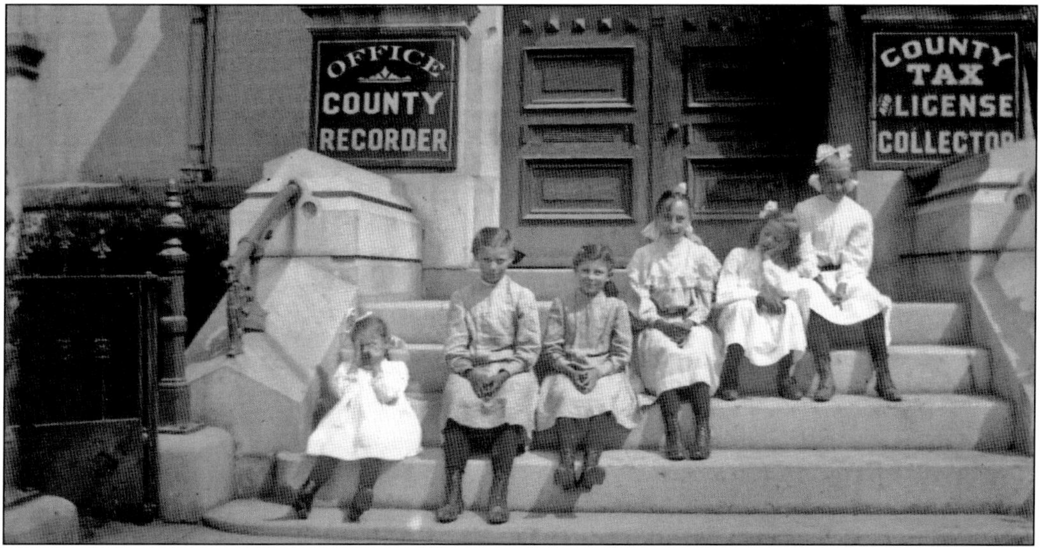

The brick Hall of Records Building was constructed in 1881–1882 on I Street and attached by an elevated bridge to the courthouse. The hall of records housed the offices of the board of supervisors, the county clerk, and the county recorder where citizens could officially record business transactions. In this photograph from the 1900s, Isabell Joslyn, fourth from the left, sits with her friends or family. (Courtesy Roger Joslyn Collection.)

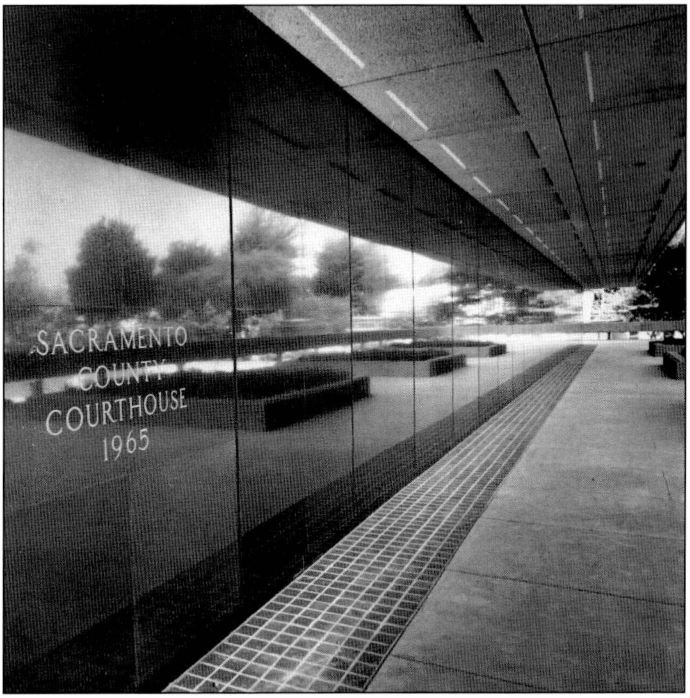

Sacramento's fourth courthouse still serves the county today. Built in 1965 at a cost of over $5 million, it moved from the previous location to its new residence at Eighth and H Streets. The new facility has 45 courtrooms as opposed to the third courthouse, which had only three. This image was taken during the opening of the building in August 1965. (Courtesy Frank Christy Collection.)

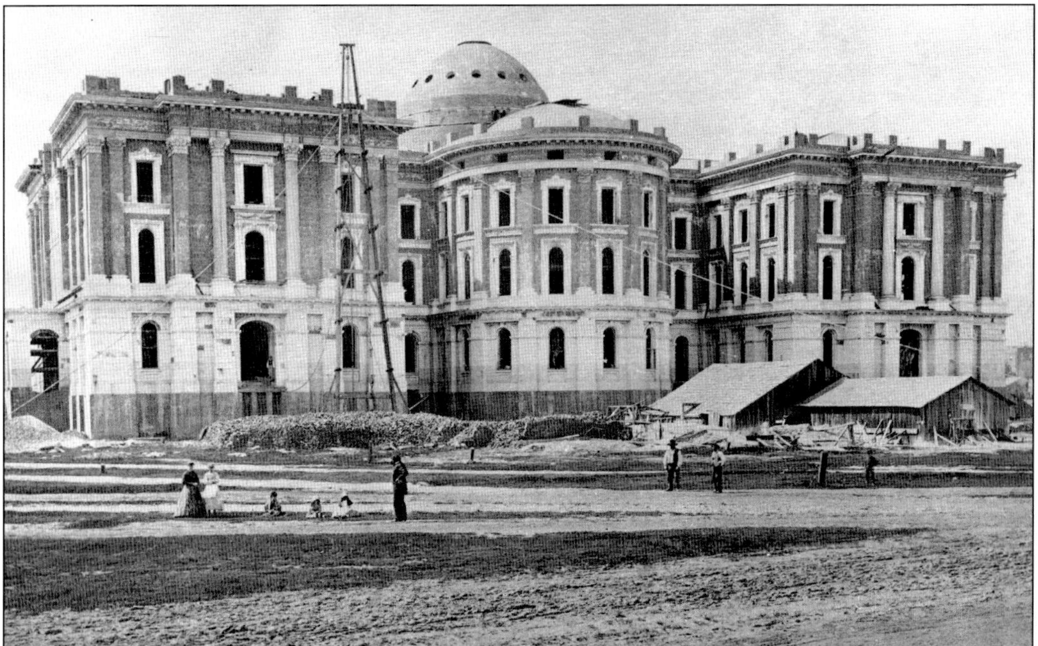

After sharing quarters with Sacramento County, the state legislature voted $300,000 in bonds in 1856 to build a new capitol. The legislature accepted plans for the building in 1860 at the Tenth, Eleventh, L, and N Street block location. While the state supreme court occupied its chambers in 1869, the building remained unfinished until 1874. This photograph, taken during construction in 1868, is from the southeast side. (Courtesy Sacramento Metropolitan Chamber of Commerce Collection.)

This is an example of a local ballot from the Civil War-era election of 1864 in Sacramento County. Note that the ballot is a "Regular Union Ticket." While not all the candidates won election, Newton Booth was selected as state senator and went on to become governor in 1871. James McClatchy, editor of the *Sacramento Bee,* was elected sheriff and served one term. (Courtesy Eleanor McClatchy Collection.)

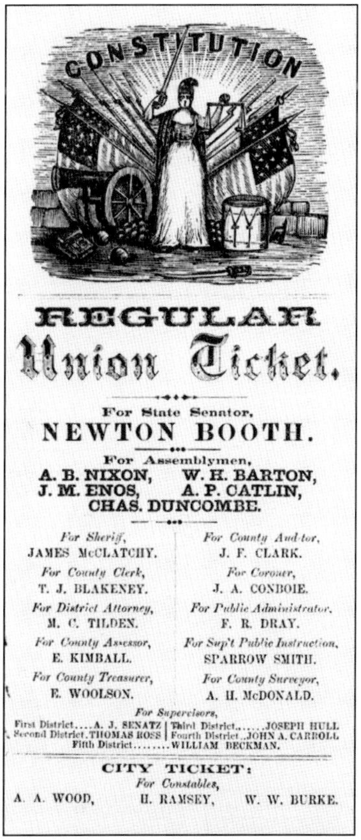

REGULAR

Union Ticket.

For State Senator,

NEWTON BOOTH.

For Assemblymen,

A. B. NIXON, W. H. BARTON,
J. M. ENOS, A. P. CATLIN,
CHAS. DUNCOMBE.

For Sheriff,
JAMES McCLATCHY.

For County Clerk,
T. J. BLAKENEY.

For District Attorney,
M. C. TILDEN.

For County Assessor,
E. KIMBALL.

For County Treasurer,
E. WOOLSON.

For County Auditor,
J. F. CLARK.

For Coroner,
J. A. CONBOIE.

For Public Administrator,
F. R. DRAY.

For Sup't Public Instruction,
SPARROW SMITH.

For County Surveyor,
A. H. McDONALD.

For Supervisors,

First District....A. J. SENATZ | Third District......JOSEPH HULL
Second District.THOMAS ROSS | Fourth District..JOHN A. CARROLL
Fifth District........WILLIAM BECKMAN.

CITY TICKET:

For Constables,

A. A. WOOD, H. RAMSEY, W. W. BURKE.

The first transmission of electricity from the Folsom Power House to Sacramento was in July 1895. On Admission Day, September 9, 1895, Sacramento held a "Grand Electric Carnival" in celebration of the achievement. Electric lights adorning the capitol and the park were a prime focus of the carnival. The Walt Disney Company would use the carnival as a historic model for its Electric Light Parade. (Courtesy California State Library Collection.)

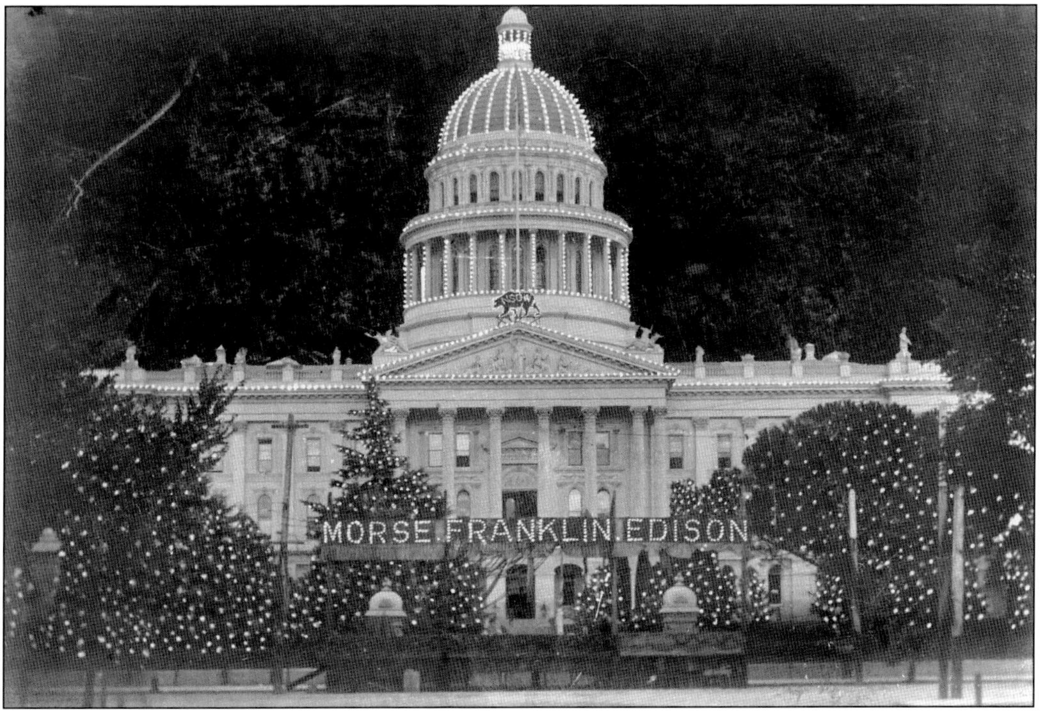

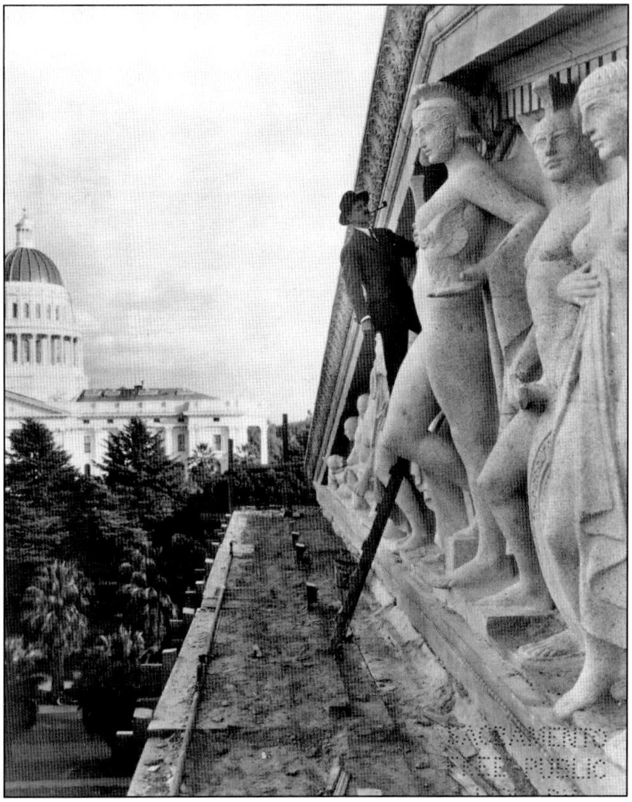

By the 1920s, the state capitol was bulging at the seams. To relieve overcrowding, the legislature voted $3 million in bonds to construct two Greek Revival-style buildings on M Street—one for state offices and the other for the state supreme court and state library. In this image, around 1928, sculptor Edward Sanford Jr. stands among the sculptures atop the library building inspecting his work. (Courtesy Sacramento Valley Photographic Survey Collection.)

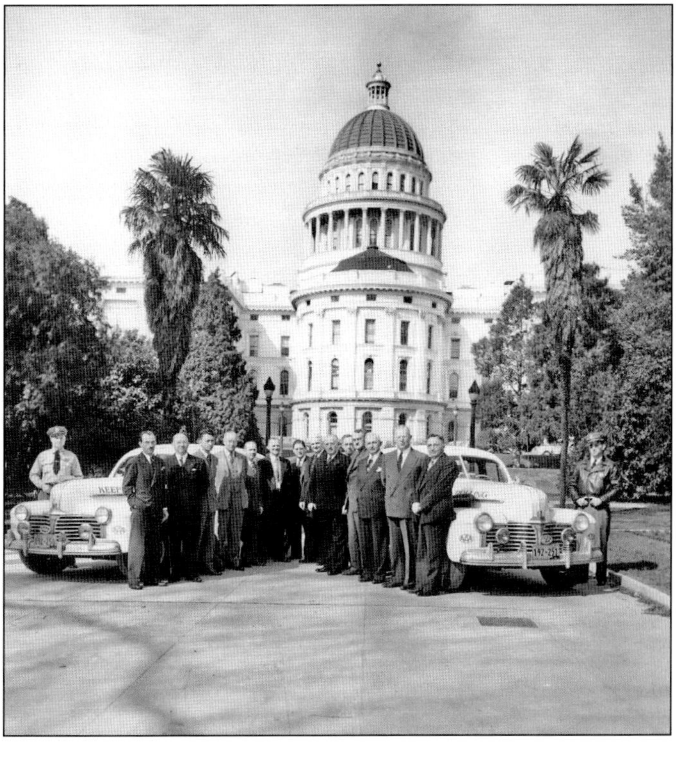

In 1944, Gov. Earl Warren, pictured second from right, and his staff pose for a group photograph on the driveway looking west at the apse on the east side of the capitol. The apse was removed during the annex expansion project that created more state offices. Appointed by President Eisenhower, Warren would serve as chief justice of the United States Supreme Court from 1953 until his retirement in 1969. (Courtesy Eleanor McClatchy Collection.)

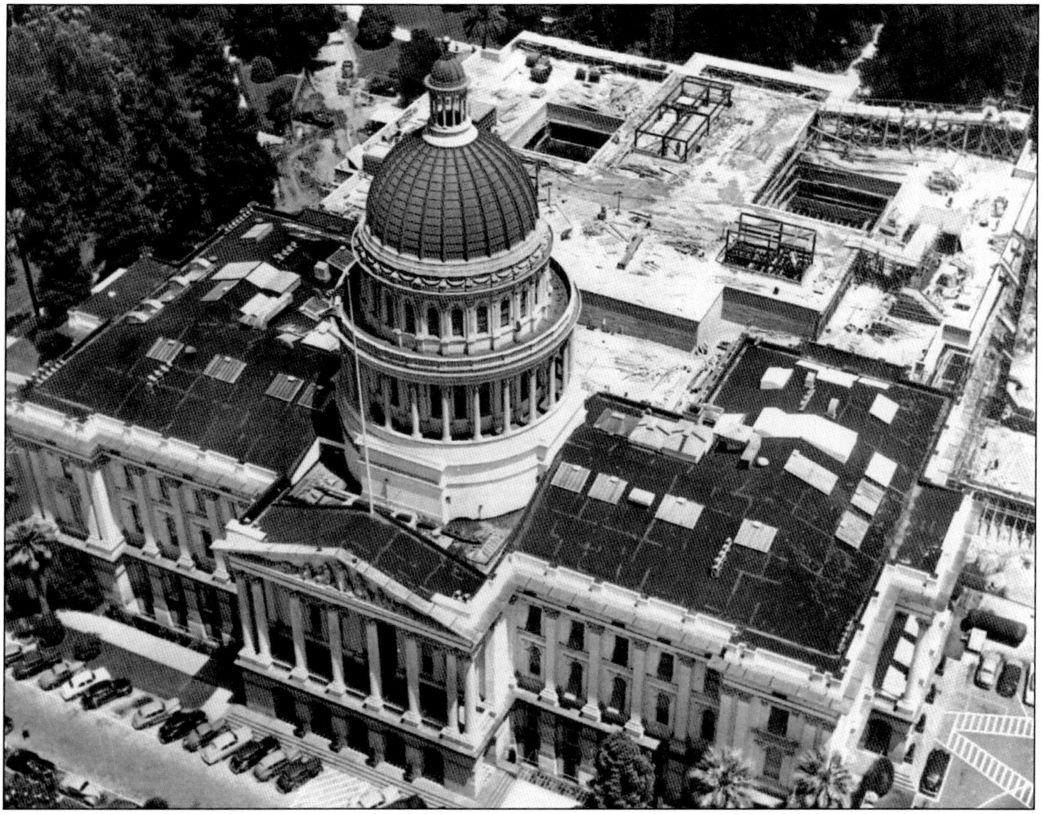

The east side of the capitol underwent remodeling to make room for an annex that would provide more offices. Construction crews removed the apse in 1949. The annex took two years to complete and cost $7.25 million. It contains eight acres of floor space and is over five stories high. This photograph looks east toward the progress of the annex addition in June 1950. (Courtesy Ralph Shaw Collection.)

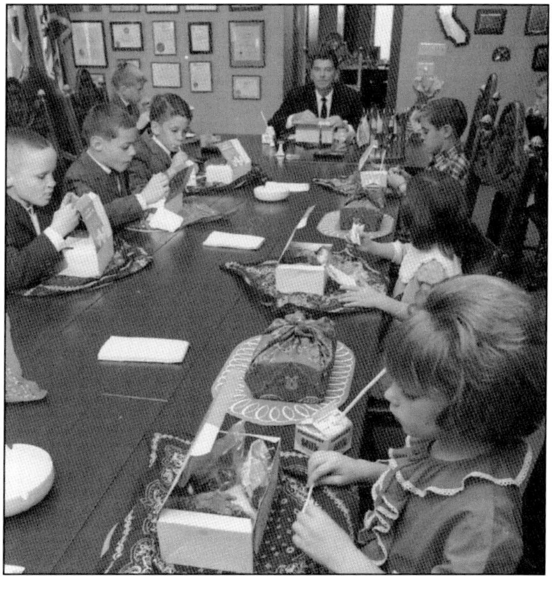

Lunch with the governor was a special treat. Gov. Ronald Reagan hosted a group of children from the one-room Buck Meadow School at Groveland in Tuolumne County on November 10, 1967. The students were treated to a box lunch in the governor's outer office at the capitol. Teacher Diane Clark arranged the tour of the capitol with the students and received VIP treatment. *Sacramento Bee* photographer Richard Gilmore captured the event. (Courtesy *Sacramento Bee* Collection.)

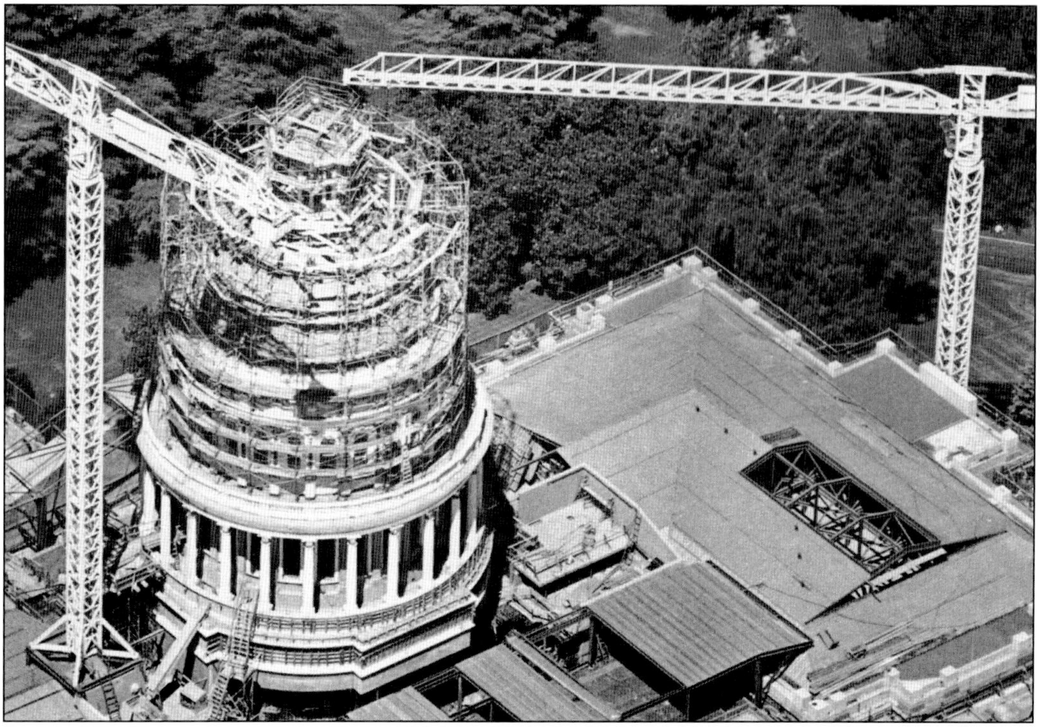

To bring the state capitol up to earthquake safety standards, California undertook a six-year restoration project. Shrouded in scaffolding, engineers used a unique process that strengthened the dome and all the floors in place. Costing more than $68 million, the capitol reopened in January 1982 with a weeklong gala celebration. *Sacramento Bee* photographer Dick Schmidt took this photograph in August 1979. (Courtesy *Sacramento Bee* Collection.)

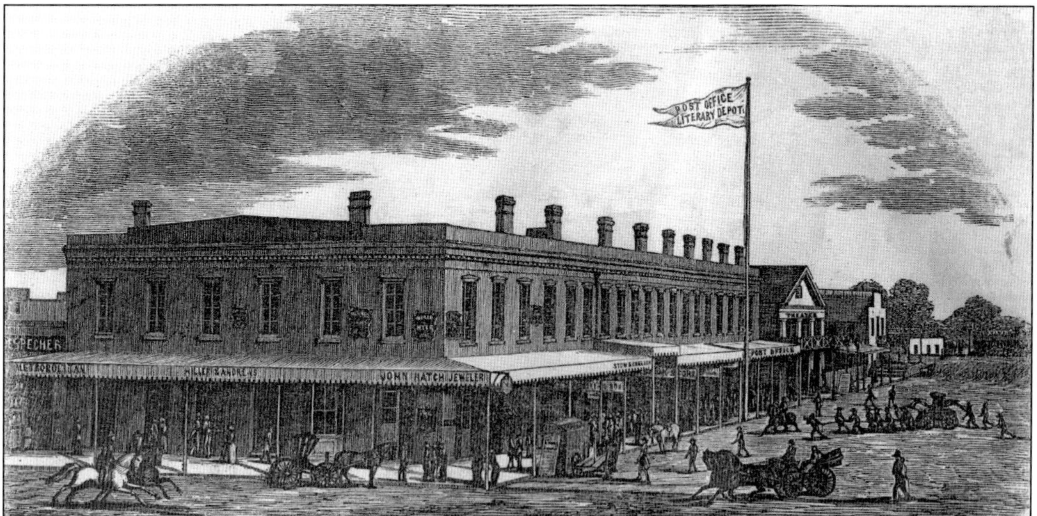

Sacramento's first post office opened in July 1849 and was aboard the store ship *Whiton*, docked at the Embarcadero. It soon set up on dry land in Read's Building on Third Street between I and J Streets on the Overton Block. This 1853 rendering shows how bustling Sacramento was in the early gold-rush era. (Courtesy California State Library Collection.)

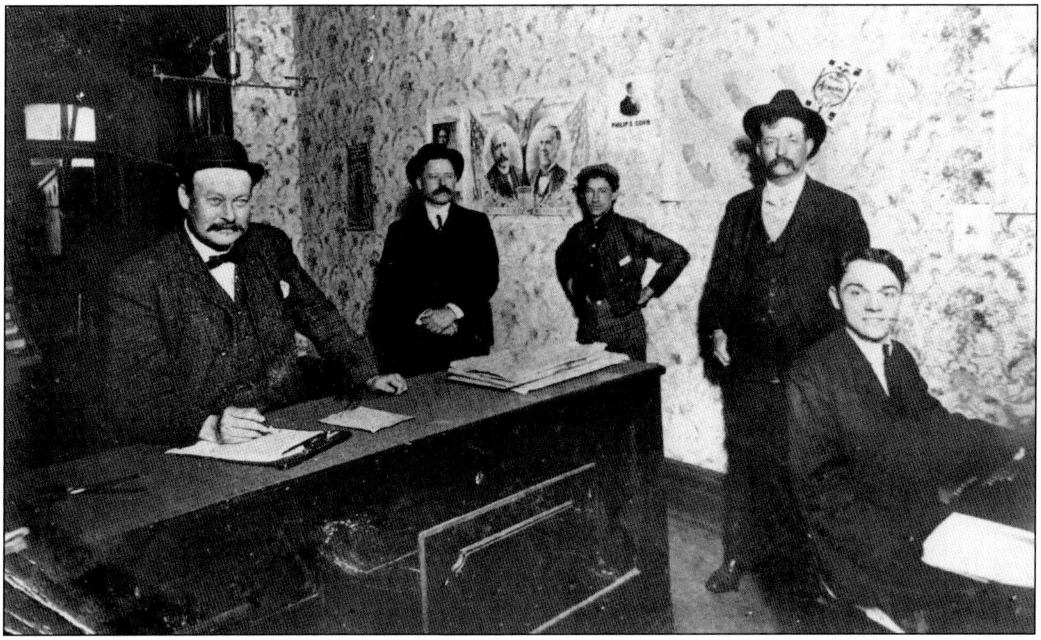

This was a typical polling place in 1900 at Eleventh and K Streets in Sacramento. The day that Pres. William McKinley was elected to a second term, these men were at the precinct's poll. At left, standing behind the desk, is Winfield J. Davis. Seated, at right, is John H. Gilpin, and standing behind him is Bing C. Brier. The other men are unidentified. (Courtesy Eugene Hepting Collection.)

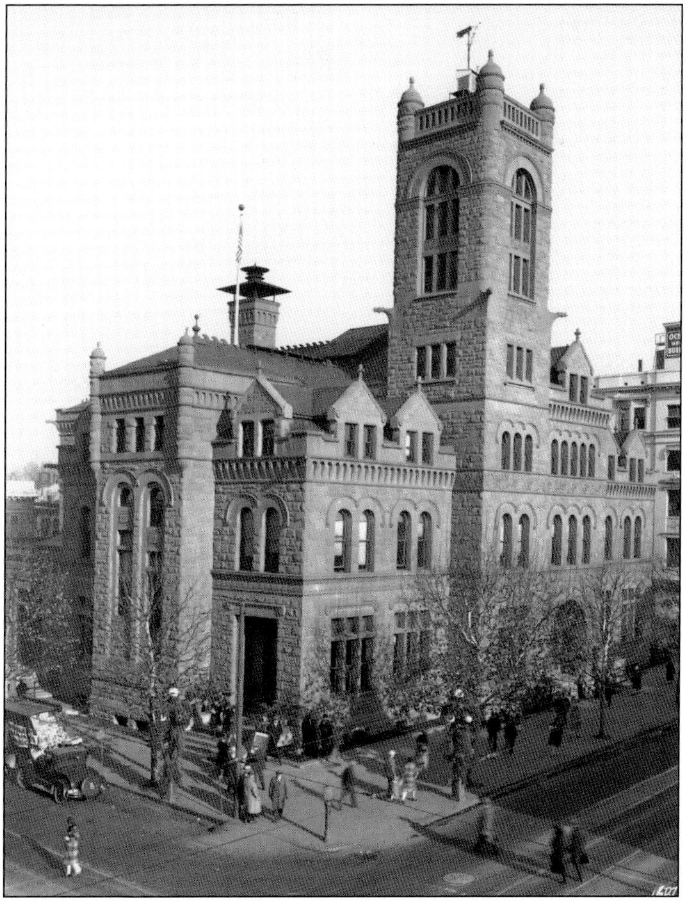

The "pink" post office, built of sandstone, stood on the corner of Seventh and K Streets. Constructed on the site where St. Rose of Lima Catholic Church flourished from 1854 through the 1880s, the dedication for the post office was held February 22, 1894. This landmark building, pictured here in the 1920s, was reproduced for postcards, calendars, and other K Street views. (Courtesy David Joslyn Collection.)

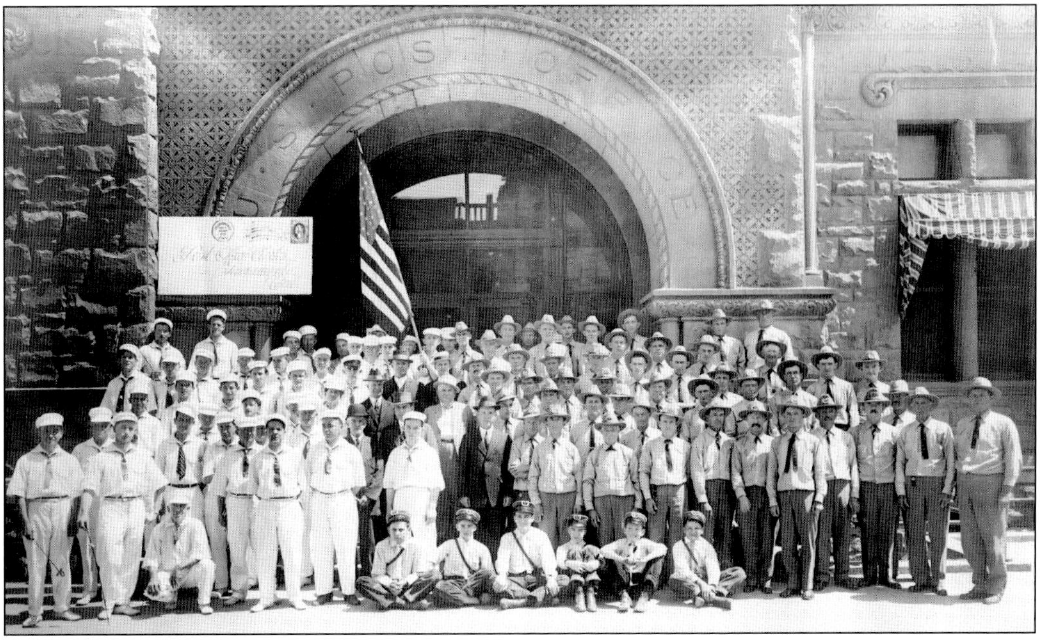

In this close-up photograph of the "pink" post office, Wesley Thomas (front row, left) poses with his fellow employees on July 4, 1915. The sandstone post office was victim of the wrecking ball in 1967 with the K Street Mall Redevelopment Project. Today it is the site of the St. Rose of Lima Park, used as an ice-skating rink in the winter. (Courtesy Edwin Beach Collection.)

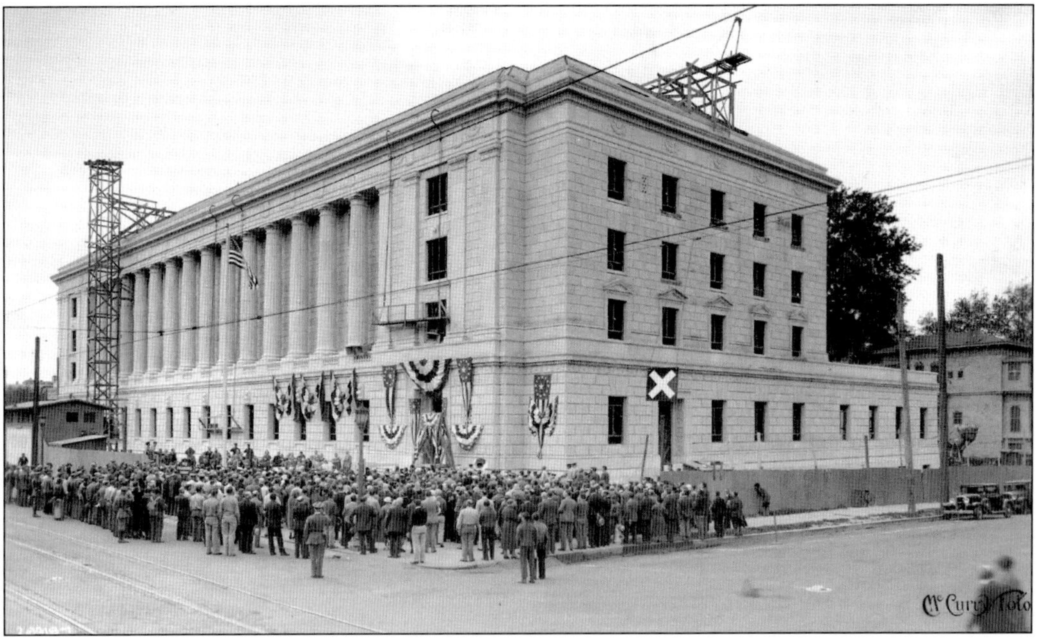

The cornerstone-laying ceremony for the new federal post office and courthouse between Eighth and Ninth on I Street occurred April 29, 1933. Costing over $1.3 million, it opened later in 1933 and housed over 30 federal offices and courtrooms. Constructed during the height of the Depression, it is just one example of the many federal projects to employ Sacramentans. It remains a post office today. (Courtesy Frank Christy Collection.)

Three

PUBLIC SAFETY

TO PROTECT LIFE AND PROPERTY

BY DYLAN MCDONALD

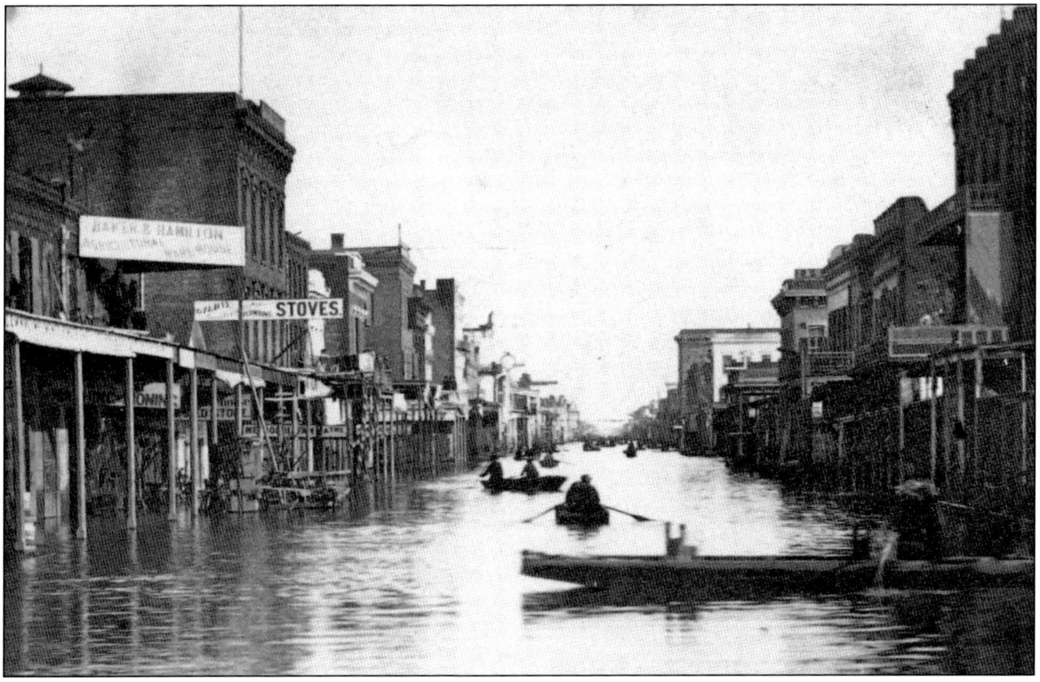

Sacramento City endured numerous challenges during its early years—floods, fires, epidemics, and riots, to name a few—yet its citizens answered with creative solutions, thereby shaping the city's character. Located at the confluence of two rivers, the fledgling capital often fell victim to devastating floods, enduring high waters in 1850, 1852, 1853, 1861, and 1862. Photographer Charles Weed captured the flood of January 1862 through a series of stereocards, including this one, showing J Street looking east from the levee. Business and political leaders decided a massive engineering project to raise the city streets and a system of levees would help to best the Sacramento and American Rivers. When fires in 1852 and 1854 destroyed much of the bustling business district, Sacramentans quickly rebuilt. It would be one of the many times the city's downtown would undergo a massive transformation. Volunteer fire units first organized in 1850, the same year the first elected town marshal took office. As the city grew, a professional police and firefighting force became a necessary part of public safety efforts. (Courtesy Don Rivett Collection.)

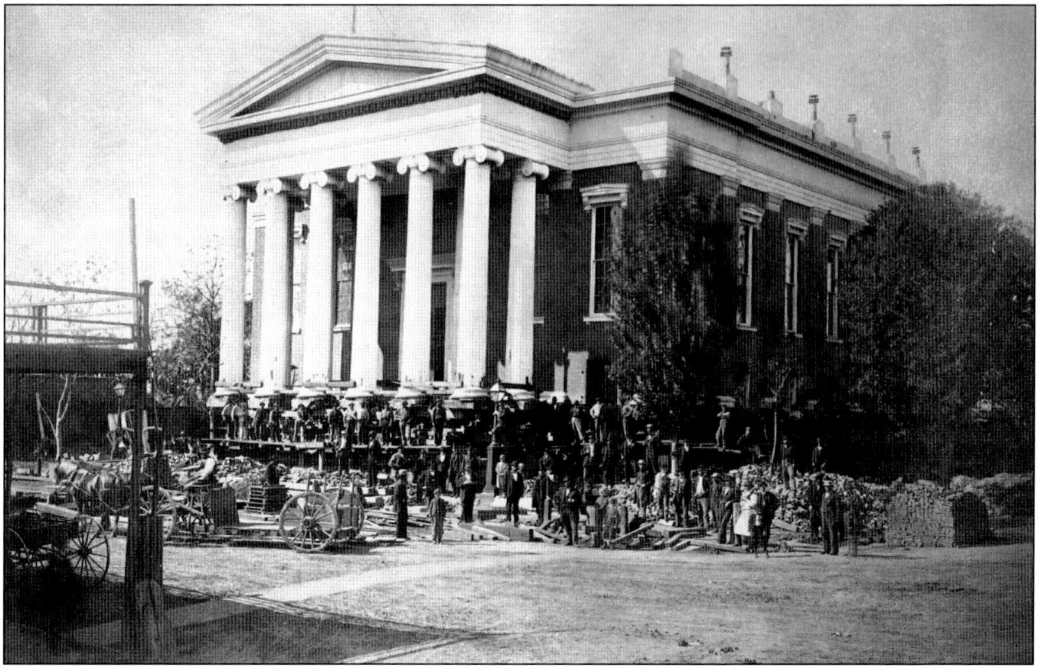

Hoping to avoid floodwaters, Sacramentans began raising streets and lifting buildings in the 1860s, earning the nickname of a "city on stilts." On March 22, 1870, the partnership of Turton and Knox received the bid to lift the county courthouse at a cost of $16,900. It took 400 jackscrews to elevate the building that once stood at the northwest corner of Seventh and I Streets. (Courtesy California State Library Collection.)

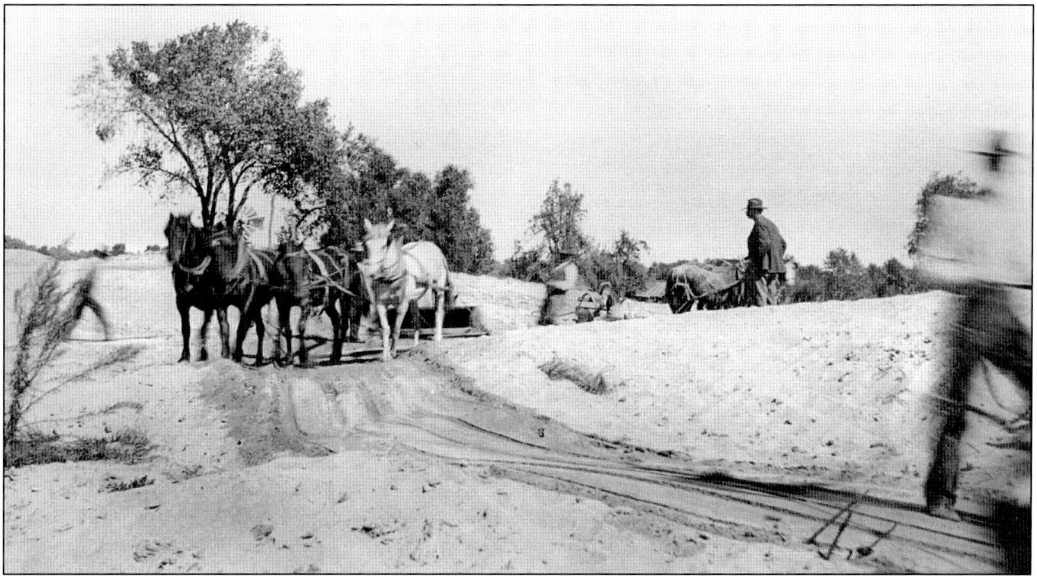

Building and maintaining levees in Sacramento dates to 1850 and proved a constant task. Here teams of mules and men work with Fresno scrapers along the Sacramento River levee, near the site of the Pacific Gas and Electric power station in September 1911. Pulled by teams, the scrapers easily lifted and transported dirt, thereby completing the backbreaking levee projects in much shorter time. (Courtesy Bob McCabe Collection.)

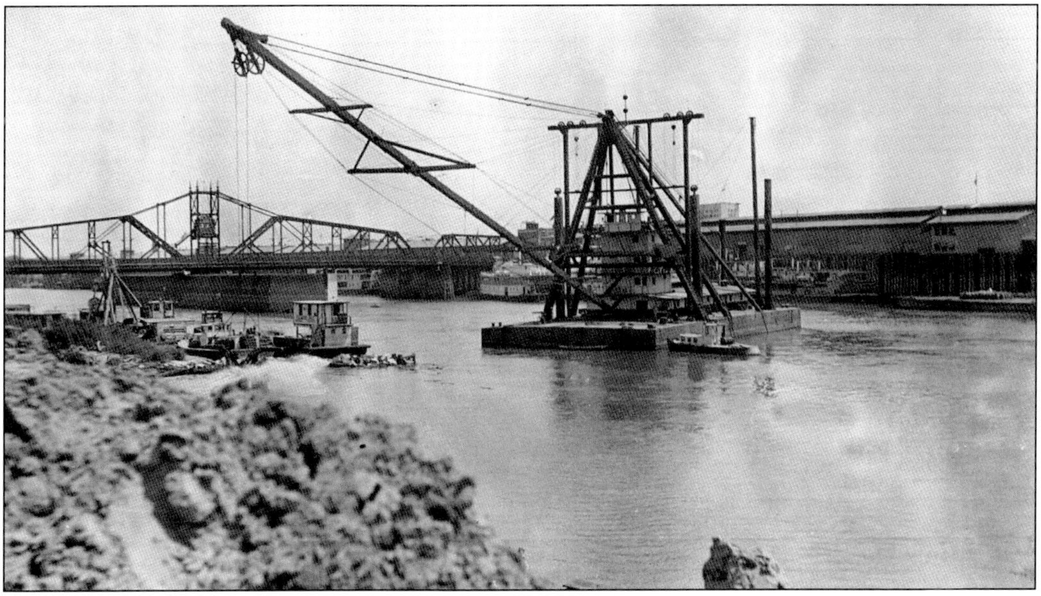

A large floating clamshell dredge operates in the Sacramento River just below the M Street Bridge. Taken from the west bank of the river on the Yolo County side in July 1917, the photograph captures the boom lowering its bucket into the water. Dredging the river bottoms not only provided the needed material for levee construction and maintenance, but it also aided navigation in these same channels. (Courtesy Ralph Shaw Collection.)

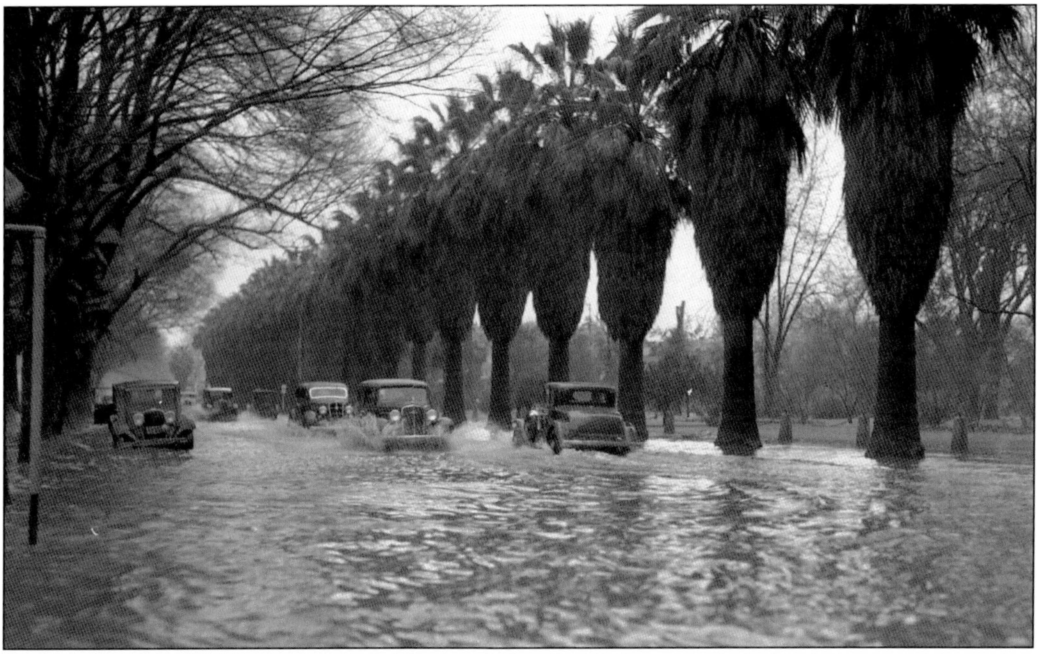

A drive past Capitol Park proves challenging after floodwaters overwhelm L Street in this 1930s photograph. Keeping water out was not the only concern—proper drainage produced difficulties as well. After heavy rains in April 1935 caused the drains in the state capitol to back up and flood the basement, state employees worked to save important records and documents from harm, including the original state constitution. (Courtesy *Sacramento Bee* Collection.)

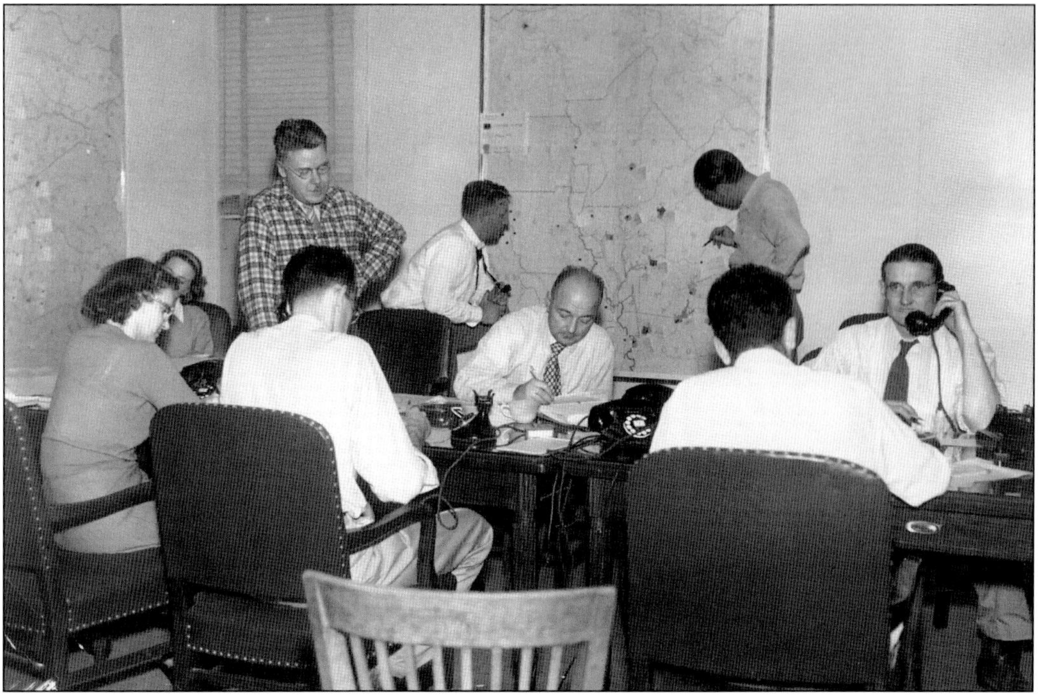

After a series of storms swept through Northern California in late 1950, swelling rivers throughout the region, the U.S. Army Corps of Engineers at one point went into continuous flood operations for over 126 hours. Corps personnel monitored the flood control system at this Sacramento nerve center, dispatching alerts, personnel, and equipment. Their offices were located in the Wright Building on Eighth Street and the Federal Building on I Street. (Courtesy *Sacramento Bee* Collection.)

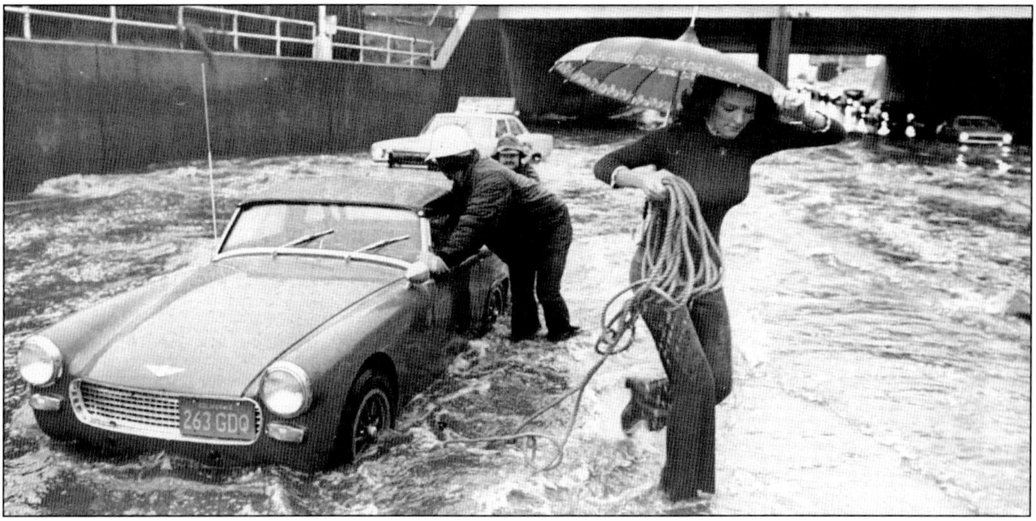

Sacramento Bee photographer Harlin Smith captured this scene at the Twelfth and C Streets underpass during a January rainstorm in 1973. Miguel Reyes and Duane Menard prepared to push the stalled car out of the way of traffic, while Genienne Bonner carried a tow rope through the flooded street. This underpass would routinely flood during heavy storms, causing havoc on this major arterial roadway. (Courtesy *Sacramento Bee* Collection.)

On the night of November 4, 1852, a devastating fire broke out on the north side of J Street, near Fourth Street, devouring seven-eighths of the city. The *Democratic State Journal* published this diagram to show readers the extent of the damage, noting key buildings lost while others mysteriously were unscathed. It was not the first time, nor the last, such destruction would visit Sacramento. (Courtesy Eleanor McClatchy Collection.)

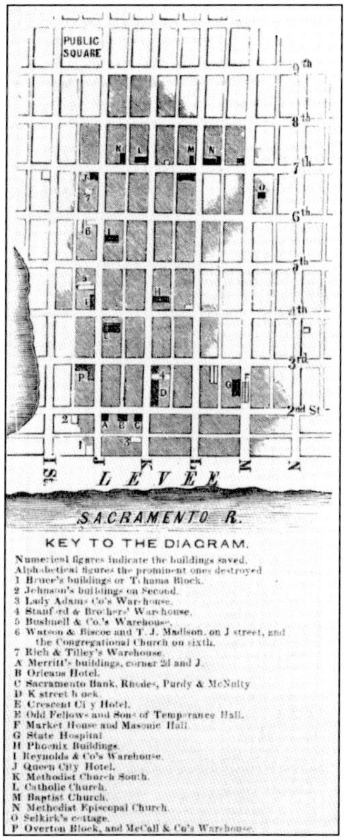

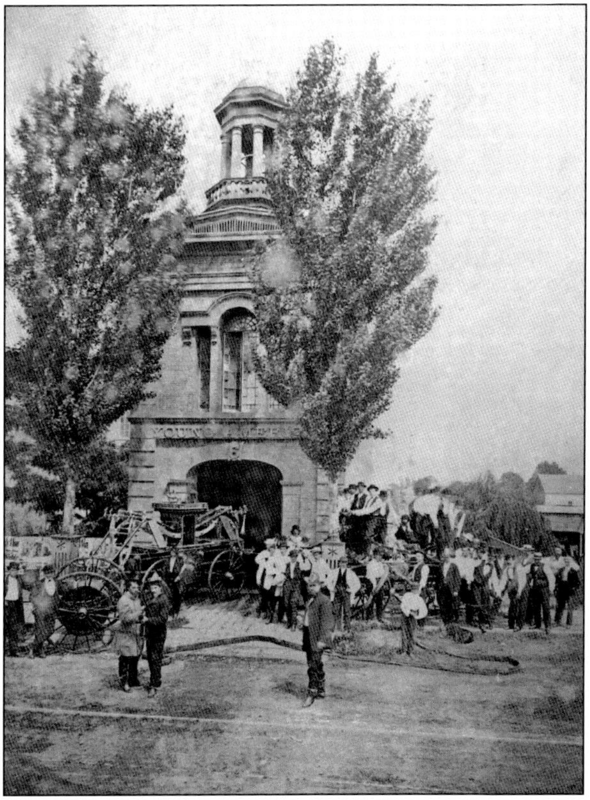

Organized on June 21, 1855, Engine Company No. 6, Young America, helped protect the city's third ward. The volunteer members gathered in front of the firehouse, located on the east side of Tenth Street, between I and J Streets, with their engines and hose cart. The two-story brick building had its cornerstone laid January 1, 1858; its bell later rang for the first Pony Express rider. (Courtesy California State Library Collection.)

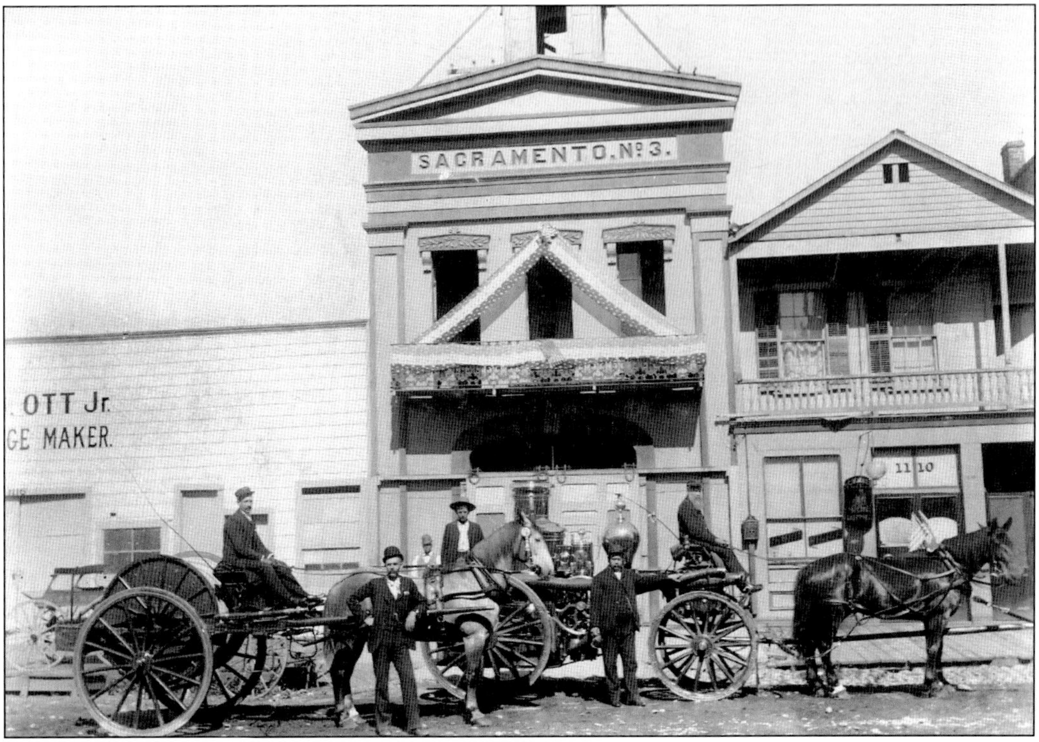

The age of volunteers passed in 1872 when a legislative act created a paid fire department in Sacramento. This photograph from the early 1890s includes Frank C. Yager (left), the driver for Station No. 3's hose cart. Yager worked for the department over for 25 years, eventually serving as assistant fire chief. The others pictured are unidentified. Today, the station on Second Street is home to the Firehouse Restaurant. (Courtesy Miriam Butler Collection.)

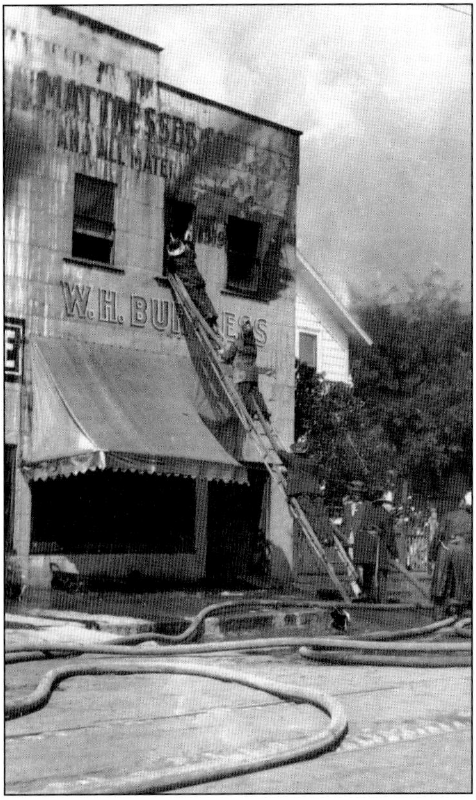

A fire gutted the William H. Burtless Mattress Factory on May 25, 1911. The blaze started around 2:30 p.m., producing heat so intense firefighters had difficulty approaching the two-story building at 1319 J Street. Nearby homes and businesses also suffered damage. While tackling the blaze, a wall fell on fireman William Uhl, splitting his scalp. The total loss was estimated at $20,000. (Courtesy Gene Scott Collection.)

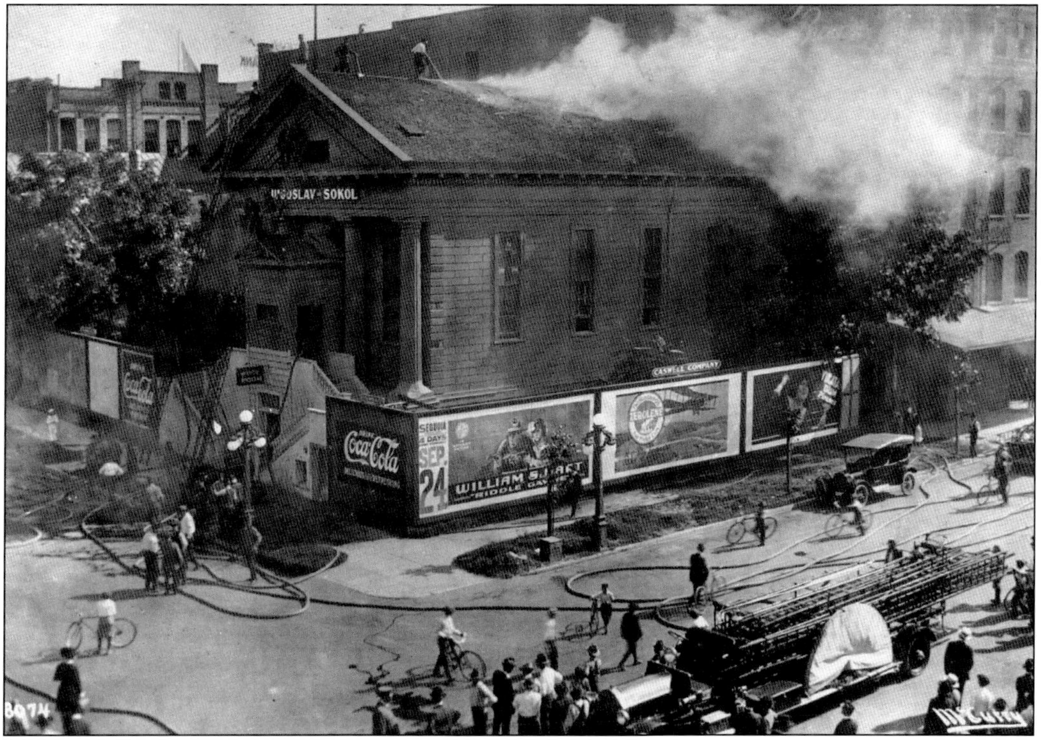

The Fraternal Hall Association's building, formerly Serra Hall, at Sixth and L Streets, caught fire on September 20, 1919, due to a defective flue. Firefighters are pictured chopping through the roof and upper façade of the structure in order to battle the flames. The total loss was estimated at $600, including the damage done to the adjoining Breuner's Warehouse. (Courtesy City of Sacramento Collection.)

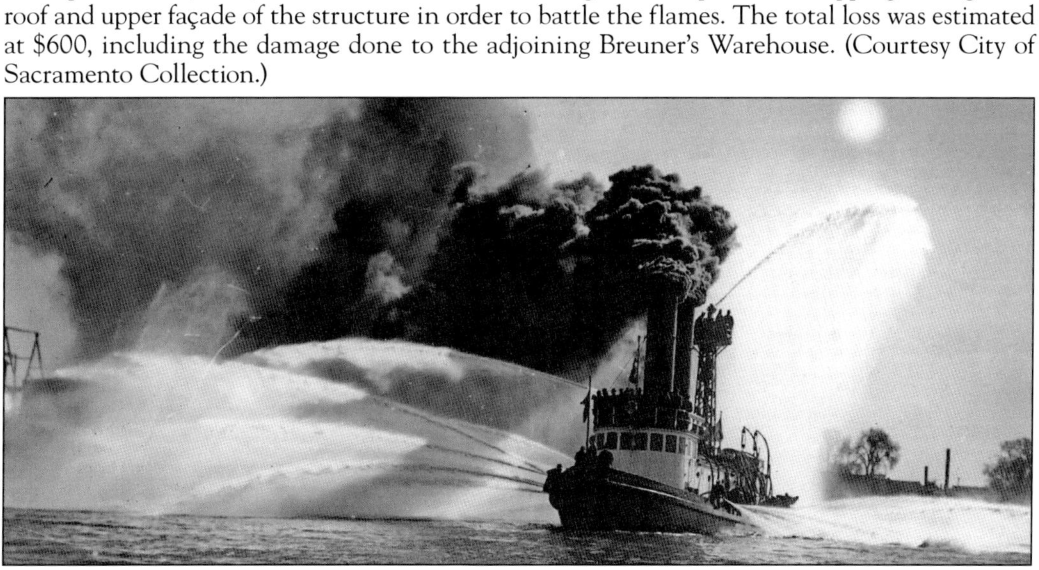

On February 15, 1911, with Gov. Hiram Johnson and other dignitaries aboard, the fireboat *Dennis T. Sullivan* of the San Francisco Fire Department demonstrates its capabilities. The fireboat pumped over 10,000 gallons a minute onto this controlled fire along the Embarcadero, above M Street. Named after the department chief who died during the 1906 earthquake, the boat journeyed up the Sacramento River to show to the state legislature the need for such firefighting equipment. (Courtesy Joseph Benetti Collection.)

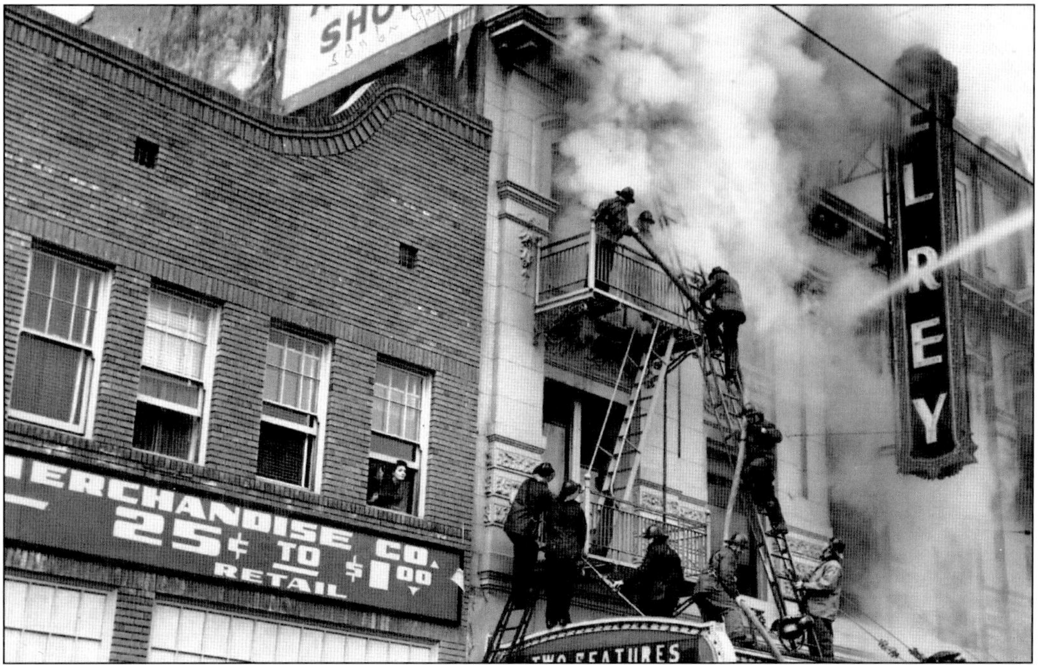

With nearly 100 theatergoers inside, the El Rey Theater at 519 J Street caught fire on February 21, 1941. Causing $50,000 in damage and injuring three firefighters, the fire attracted thousands of onlookers, including the two women visible in the window next door. The intense fire billowed smoke across downtown for over two hours and cracked the building's façade, forcing firefighters to retreat at one point. (Courtesy Eugene Hepting Collection.)

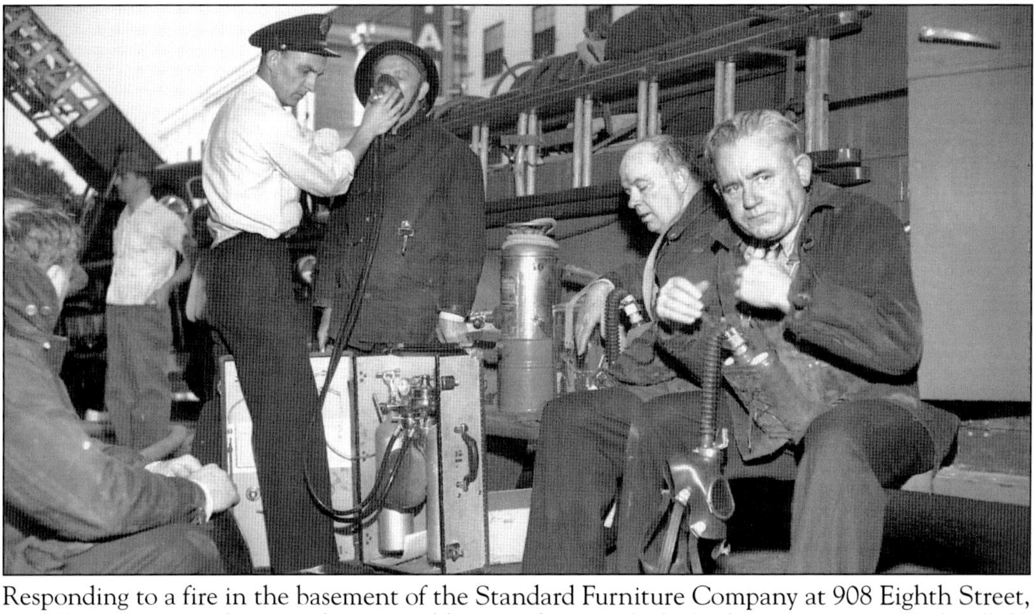
Responding to a fire in the basement of the Standard Furniture Company at 908 Eighth Street, firefighters negotiated cramped quarters, blistering heat, and a lack of oxygen. W. C. Harden (left) assists Fireman Jess Schrunk with an oxygen inhalator, while Tom Diese and F. E. Womble rest before returning to action. *Sacramento Union* photographer Joseph Benetti captured the scene during the three-alarm fire on May 25, 1950. (Courtesy Joseph Benetti Collection.)

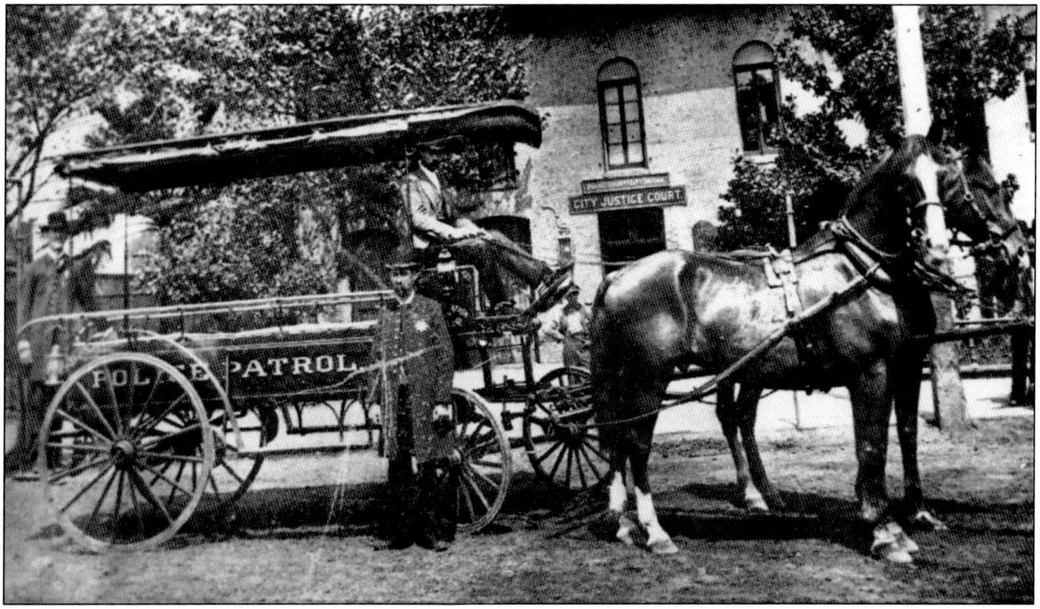

A 1901 photograph in front of the police station at Front and I Streets shows the Sacramento Police Department's first vehicle. Dubbed the "Black Maria," this 1895 horse-drawn patrol wagon doubled as a prisoner transport and an ambulance. Fifteen years later, a motorized patrol wagon replaced it. The wagon's patrolmen are driver John Fitzgerald, with William Talbot on the rear platform and William Rutherford standing. (Courtesy Noel LaDue Collection.)

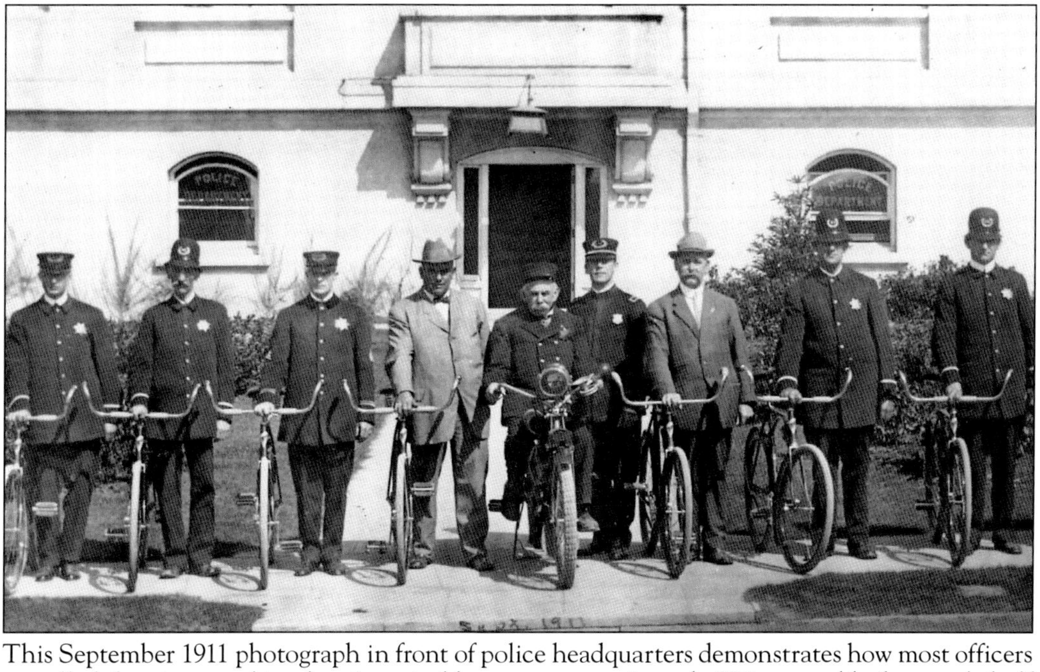

This September 1911 photograph in front of police headquarters demonstrates how most officers patrolled the city—on bicycles. A typical beat was approximately 200 square blocks, nearly half of the city. With no radios, communications were via police call boxes. To the right of the one-cylinder motorcycle is likely Ed M. Brown, the department's first motorcycle officer, who enforced the citywide 15 mile-per-hour speed limit. (Courtesy Sacramento Police Officers Association.)

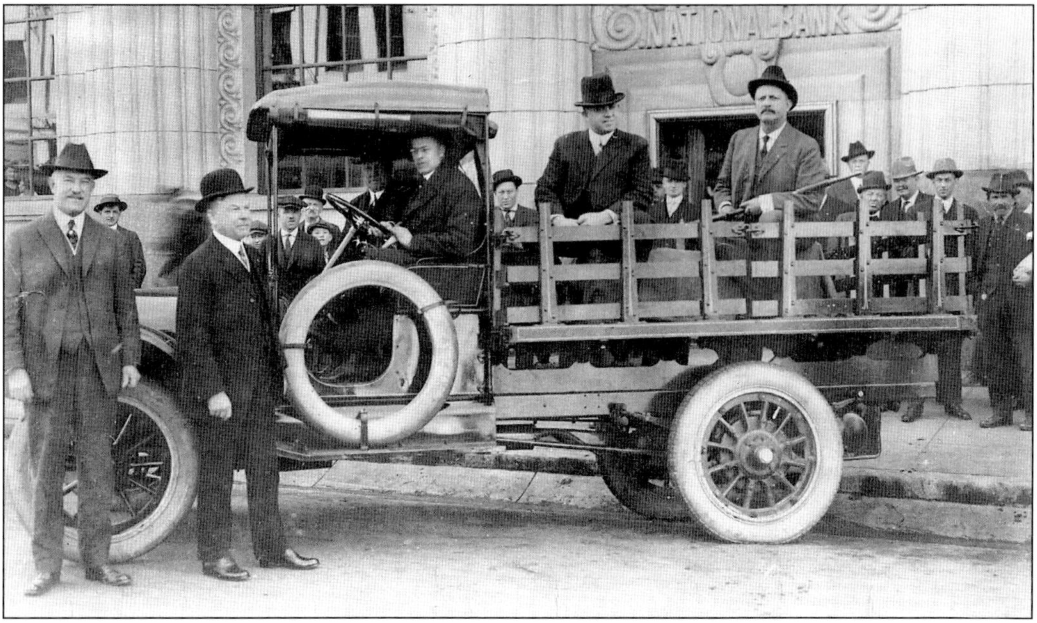

Police escort a transfer of $1 million from the Capital National Bank at the southeast corner of Seventh and J Streets, *c.* 1920. Bank president Alden Anderson, a former California lieutenant governor, is second from the left. Arthur Ryan, the unarmed officer in the back of the truck, would eventually serve as an inspector within the department. (Courtesy Sacramento Police Department Collection.)

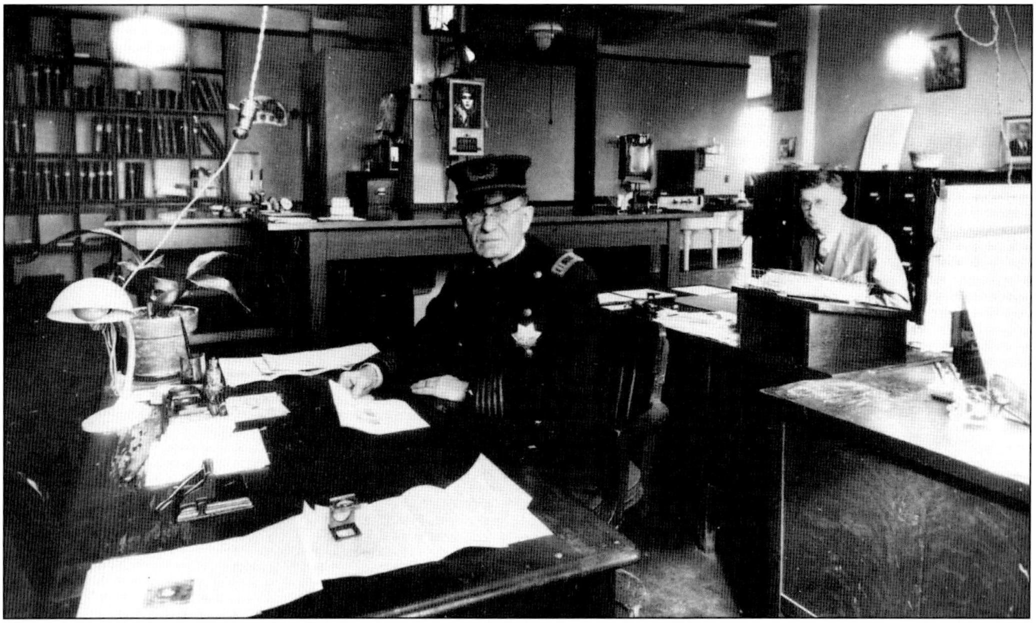

At their desks, Capt. Max P. Fisher (left) and Leslie Cox are pictured working to identify offenders, *c.* 1925. Known nationwide for his pioneering efforts in criminal recognition, Fisher started the department's identification bureau in 1899. By 1935, the bureau had collected over 100,000 fingerprints, sharing them with other state and federal bureaus. Cox himself would later serve as head of the bureau after Fisher's retirement in 1932. (Courtesy Noel LaDue Collection.)

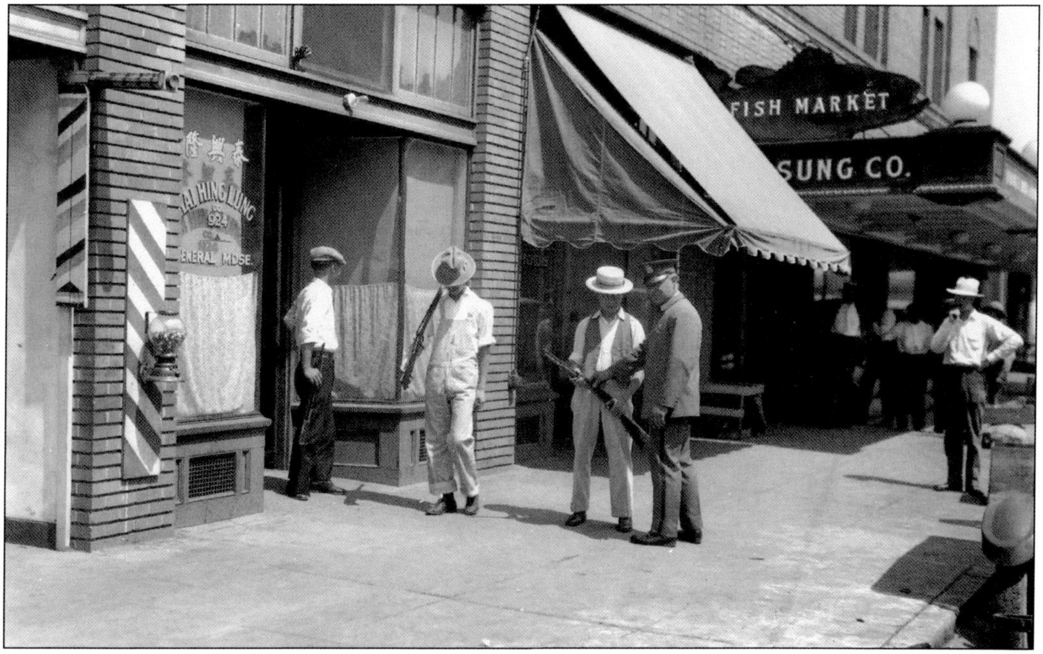

A police officer begins to disarm three guards in front of the Hai Hing Lung General Merchandise Store at 924 Third Street in Sacramento's Chinatown, *c.* 1934. Feuds between rival factions within the Chinese community at times required the police to step in and help negotiate truces, even occasionally standing watch over threatened businesses during these disputes. (Courtesy David Joslyn Collection.)

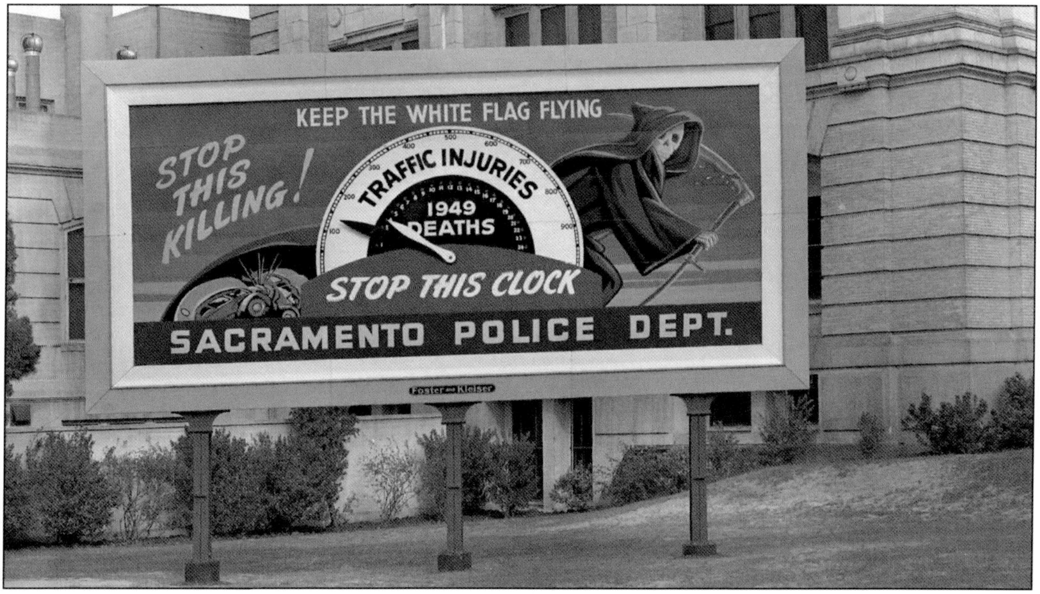

As part of a public safety campaign, this eye-catching billboard, situated on the west side of city hall on I Street, cautions drivers about their driving habits. The police department's sign ominously tallies automobile accident fatalities for 1949; the final number would be 25. With Sacramento's growing population, automobiles were rapidly increasing in number, then having one of the highest per capita automobile-registration ratios in the world. (Courtesy Ernest Myers Collection.)

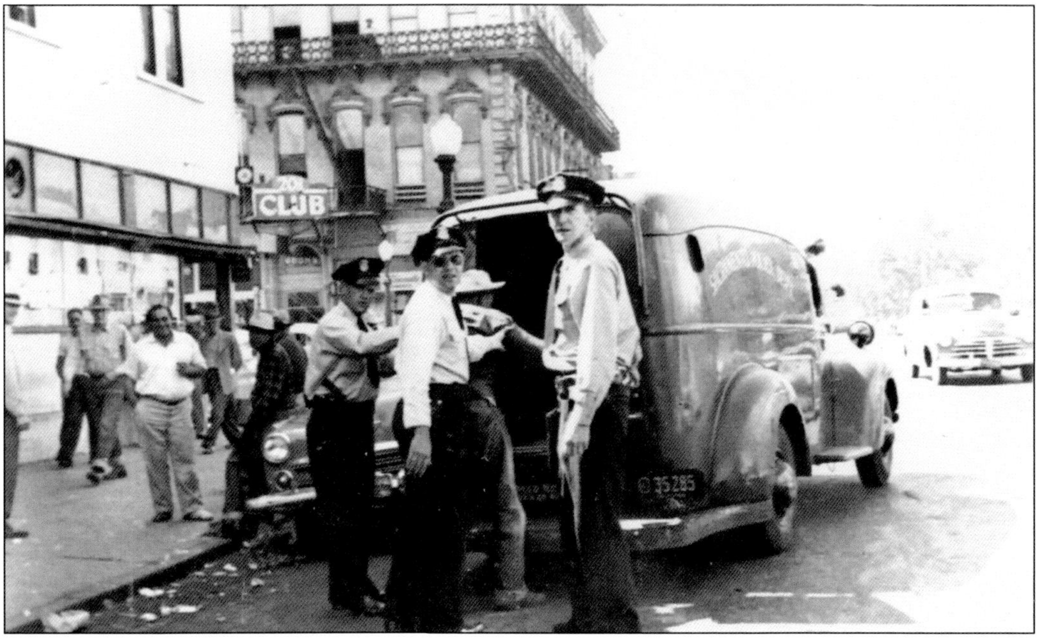

Officers Bob Reynolds, Gene McKnight, and Gene Babbit assist an inebriated man into the back of the department's paddy wagon outside the 201 Club at the corner of Second and K Streets, *c.* 1955. Sacramento's West End, with its transitory population and numerous bars and flop houses, drew its share of police patrols. The area became the focus of the city's redevelopment efforts. (Courtesy Noel LaDue Collection.)

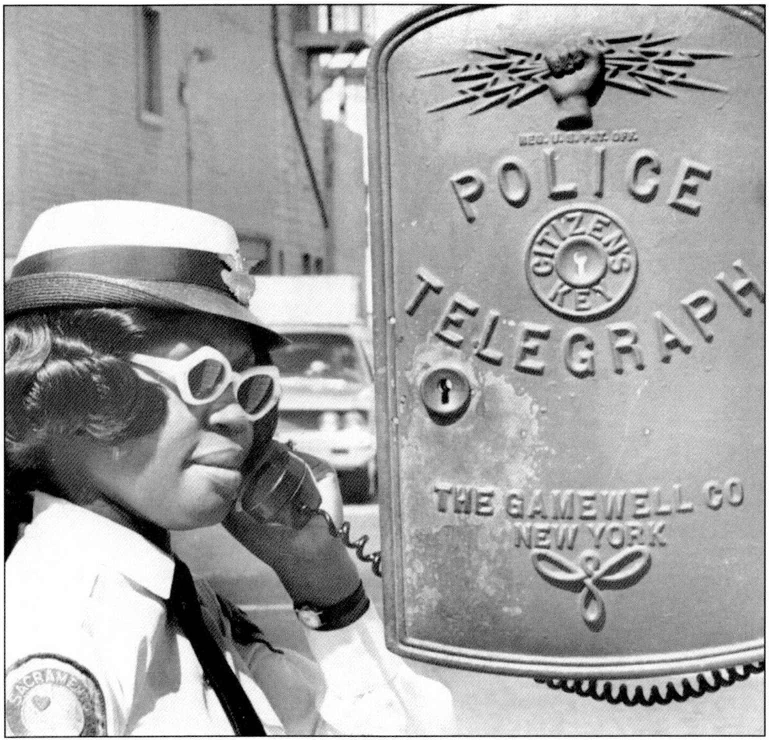

Winifred Simmons checks in with dispatch via this police call box while working her downtown parking enforcement beat on October 24, 1970. Covering nearly 32 city blocks and averaging between 25 to 50 tickets a day, these members of the police force had to be "good humored, able to turn the other cheek and rugged enough to walk long distances," all while monitoring parked cars and meters. (Courtesy *Sacramento Bee* Collection.)

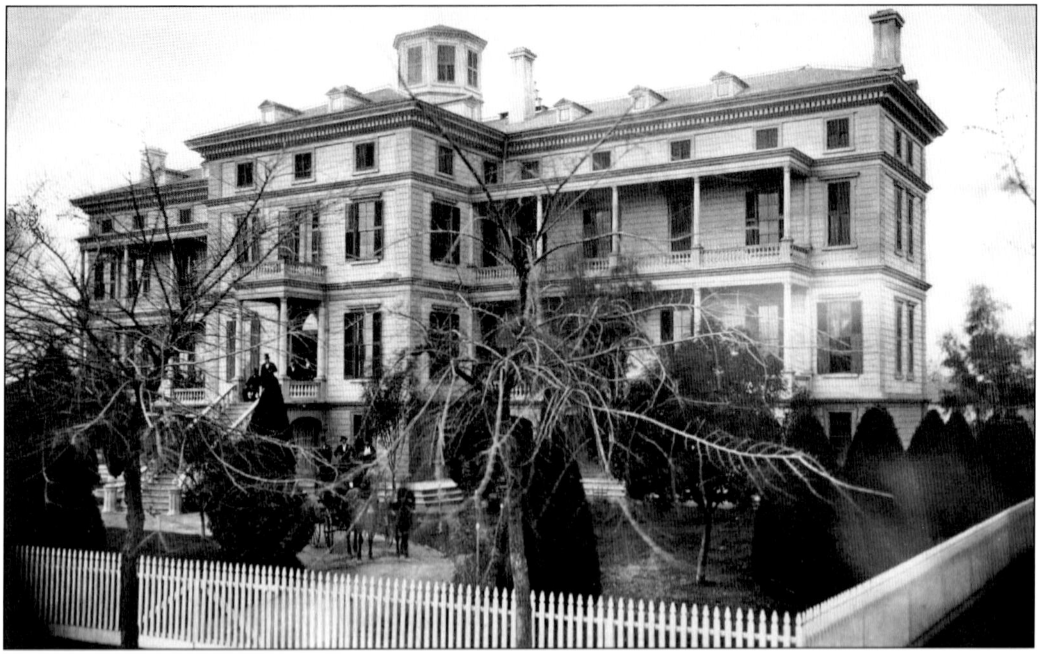

The Central Pacific Railroad Company built a 125-bed hospital for its employees at the southwest corner of Thirteenth and C Streets in 1870 for $64,000. The hospital was the first of its kind, funded through dues charged to all "white" railroad employees at a rate of 50¢ a month. The hospital, pictured here *c.* 1875, boasted of its modern improvements done to help its patients. (Courtesy David Joslyn Collection.)

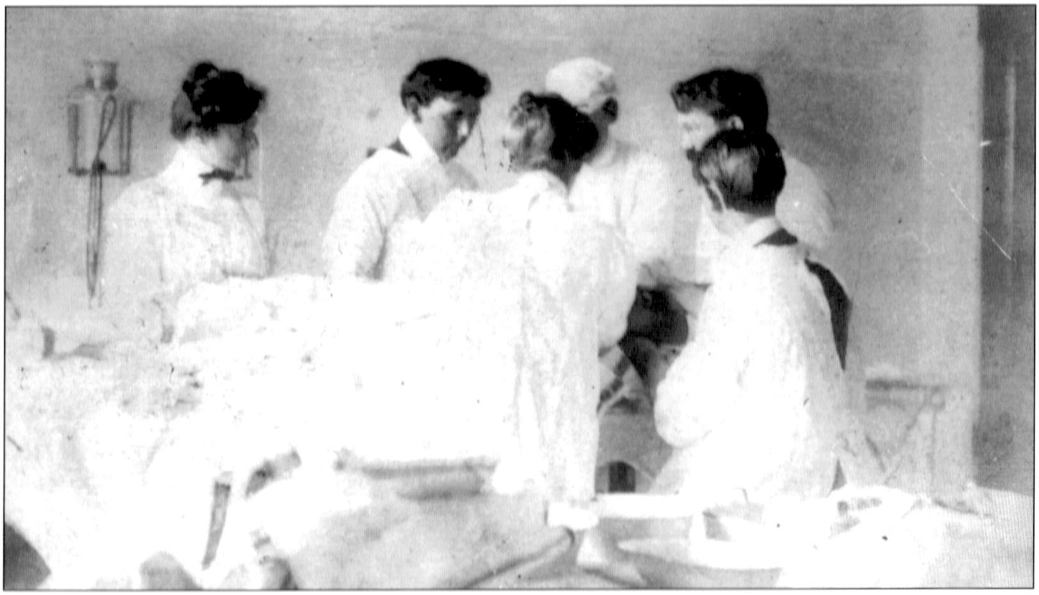

Under the direction of chief surgeon Dr. Thomas W. Huntington, the railroad hospital established the first antiseptic operating room on the West Coast in 1882 and performed the first operation for appendicitis in California in 1891. This *c.* 1890 scene of the hospital's operating room shows Dr. Huntington during surgery, assisted by G. W. Stevenson and Stanley Reckers. (Courtesy Sacramento–El Dorado Medical Society Collection.)

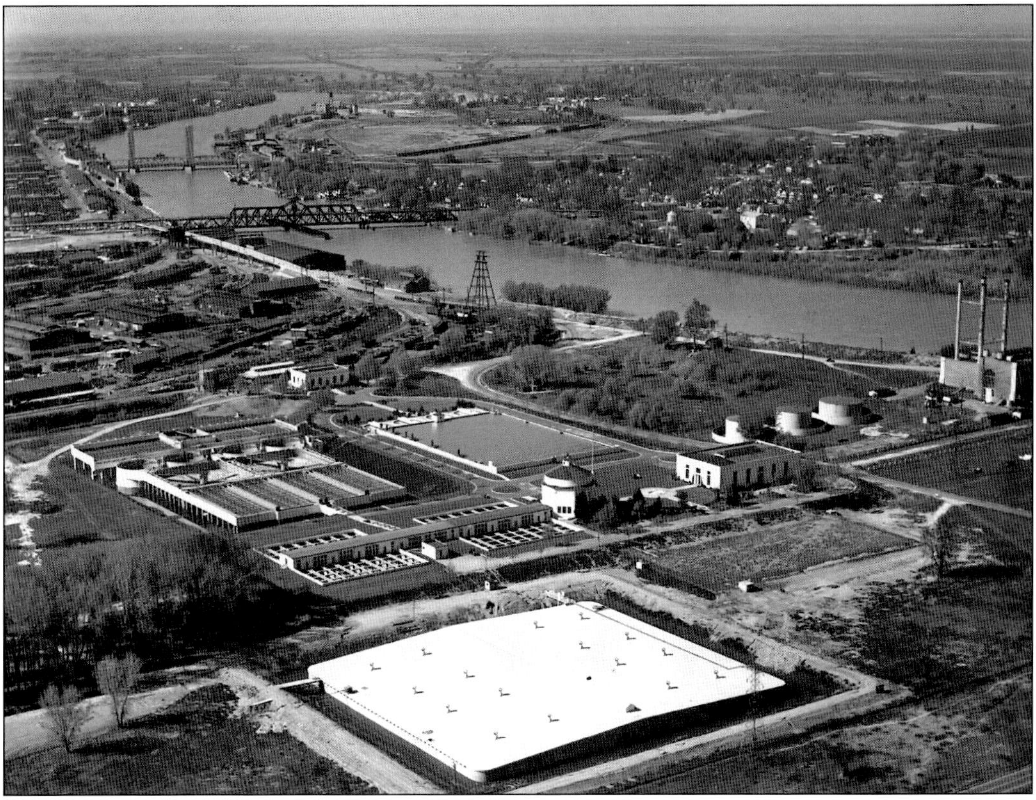

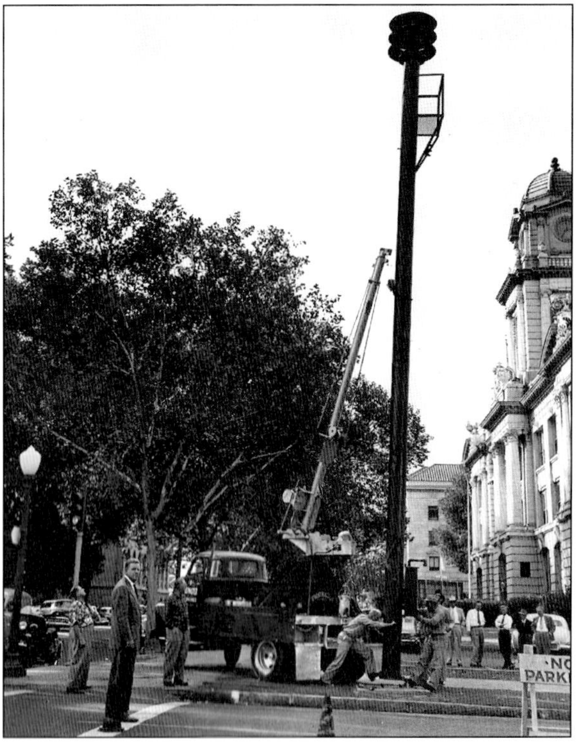

A three-day "clean water celebration" surrounded the opening of the Sacramento River Water Treatment Plant in early 1924. This aerial photograph from the 1940s shows the plant, built near the confluence of the Sacramento and American Rivers. Since 1854, the city has provided a safe and reliable supply of water via both rivers. Still in operation, the plant currently produces about 110 million gallons a day. (Courtesy Don Rivett Collection.)

Workers install one of the city's 1,500-pound air-raid sirens on the grounds of city hall at the corner of Tenth and I Streets, c. 1952. The civil defense sirens were capable of being heard over a mile away as they emitted a 60-second warbling tone. The threat of bombings during World War II, and later potential nuclear attacks, prompted the installation of these warning systems. (Courtesy City of Sacramento Collection.)

Four

TRANSPORTATION

GETTING THERE IS HALF THE FUN

BY CARSON HENDRICKS

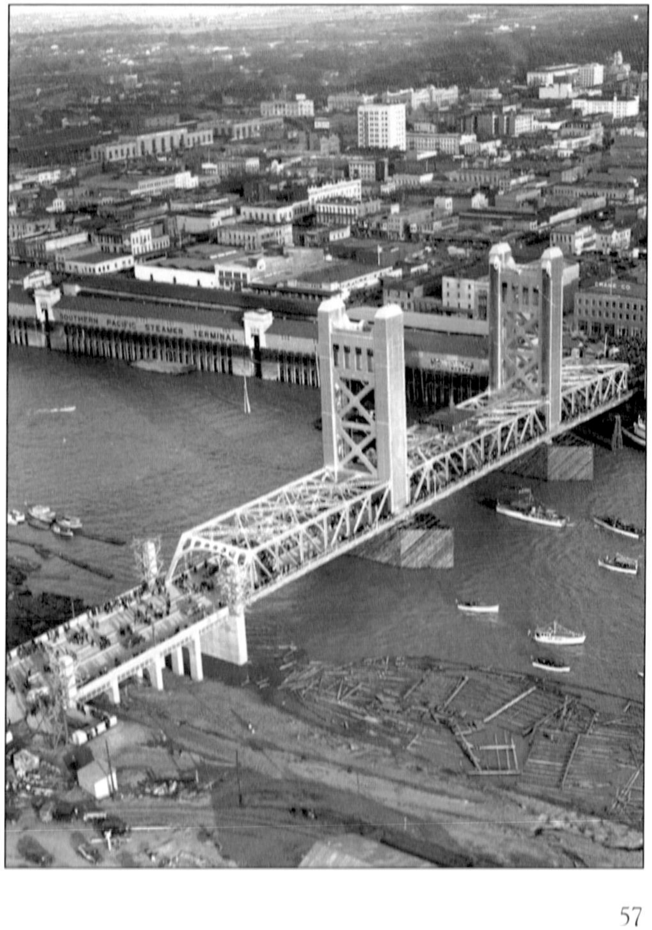

The Tower Bridge was opened with great fanfare on December 15, 1935. It was built at an original cost of $994,000 and replaced the old M Street Bridge. Considered to be the "gateway to Sacramento," it was appropriate to the growing status of Sacramento as the capital of California. In the 20th century, transportation loomed large as a major issue to be confronted. Well into the 1900s, steamships and trains were the best way to travel to other cities. Early in the 1900s, Sacramento had an extensive trolley-car system. By the 1940s, this gave way to the automobile, whose requirements forever changed the face of the city. Except for a small portion that became Old Sacramento, Interstate 5 cut off access to the river that was responsible for the city's explosive early growth. A throwback to the original trolley system, Regional Transit's light rail made its appearance in the mid-1980s. (Courtesy *Sacramento Bee* Collection.)

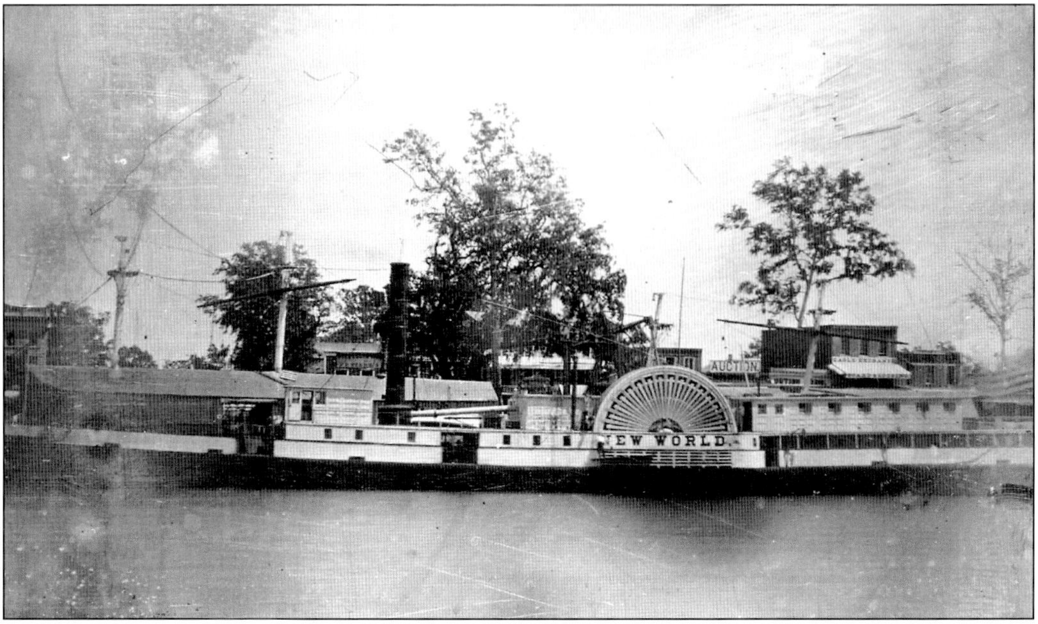

The steamship *New World* arrived at Sacramento's Embarcadero in 1850. This is the earliest known daguerreotype taken of Sacramento. This ship was "borrowed" in New York and sailed to Sacramento. The person blocking the letter "N" is actually painting the name on the ship, as the boat left New York in haste to get to the gold fields. (Courtesy Mead Kibbey and Setzer Foundation Collection.)

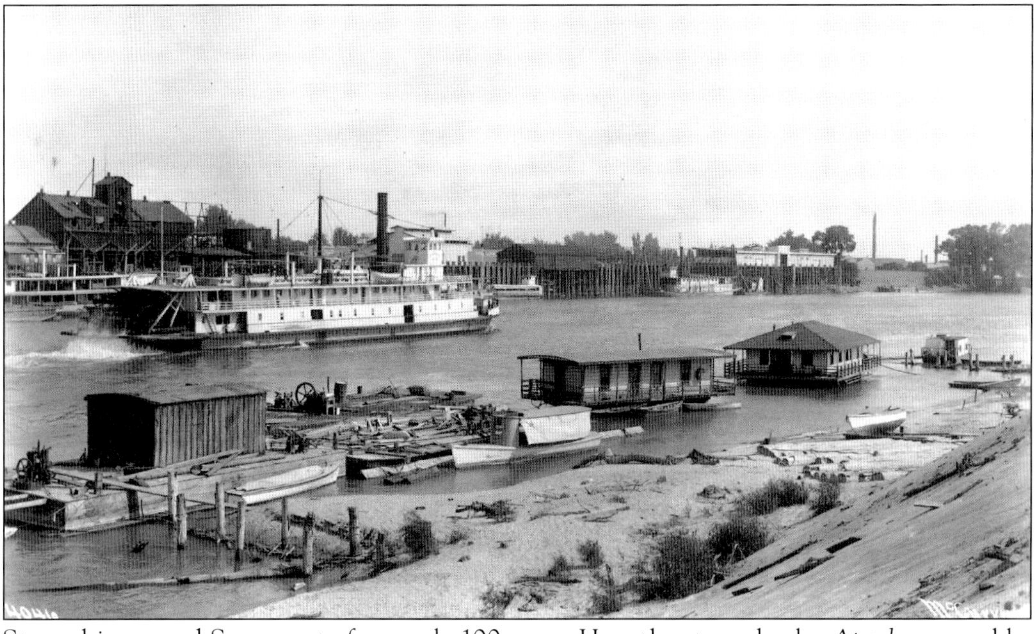

Steamships served Sacramento for nearly 100 years. Here the sternwheeler *Apache*, owned by the Southern Pacific Company, heads south out of Sacramento in 1910. In addition to railroads, the Southern Pacific Company was the major operator of passenger and cargo vessels serving Sacramento and Northern California. There were also many other smaller companies involved in river shipping. (Courtesy California State Library Collection.)

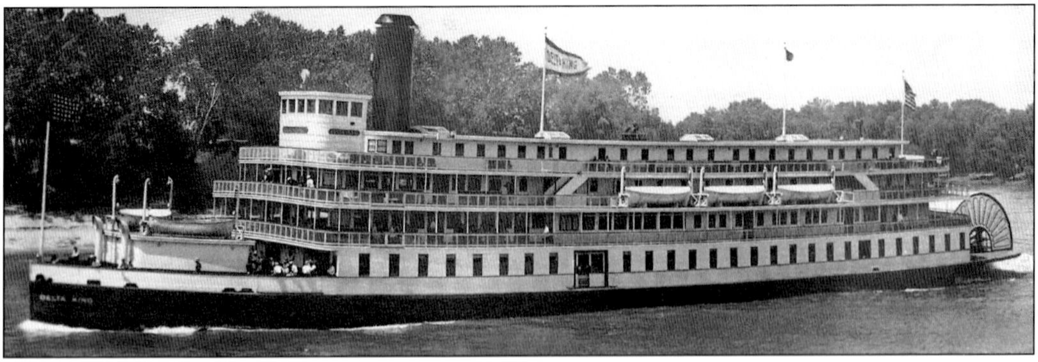

The *Delta King*, and its sister ship the *Delta Queen*, is the largest, most expensive, and the best known of all the ships to serve Sacramento. Built in 1926, it plied the Sacramento River until 1940. After nearly being lost to developers in San Francisco, it now serves Sacramento as a hotel, restaurant, and theater in Old Sacramento. Many consider it symbolic of Old Sacramento. (Courtesy R. F. Reynolds Collection.)

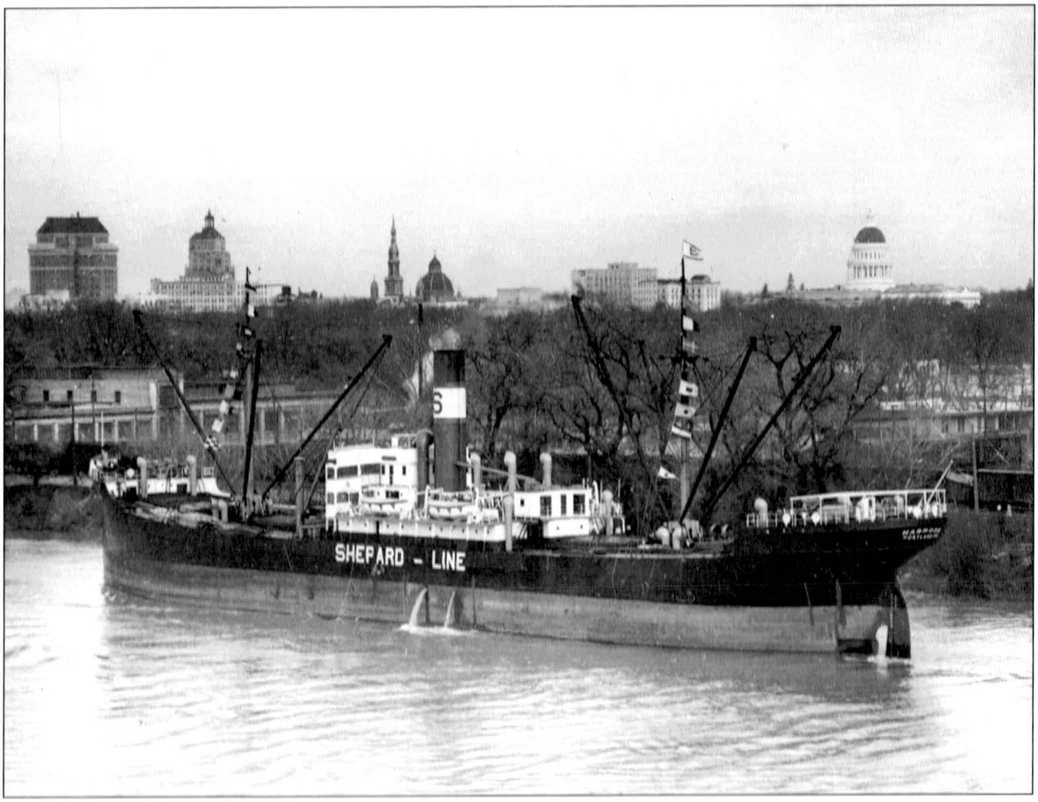

The freighter *Harpoon*, the flagship of the Shepard Line, arrives in Sacramento in early March 1934. With a displacement of 10,000 tons and a load of 400 tons, it was then the largest ship to make the trip up the Sacramento River. Proving that ocean-going ships could call in Sacramento, it eventually led to the Port of Sacramento being established. (Courtesy Sacramento Metropolitan Chamber of Commerce Collection.)

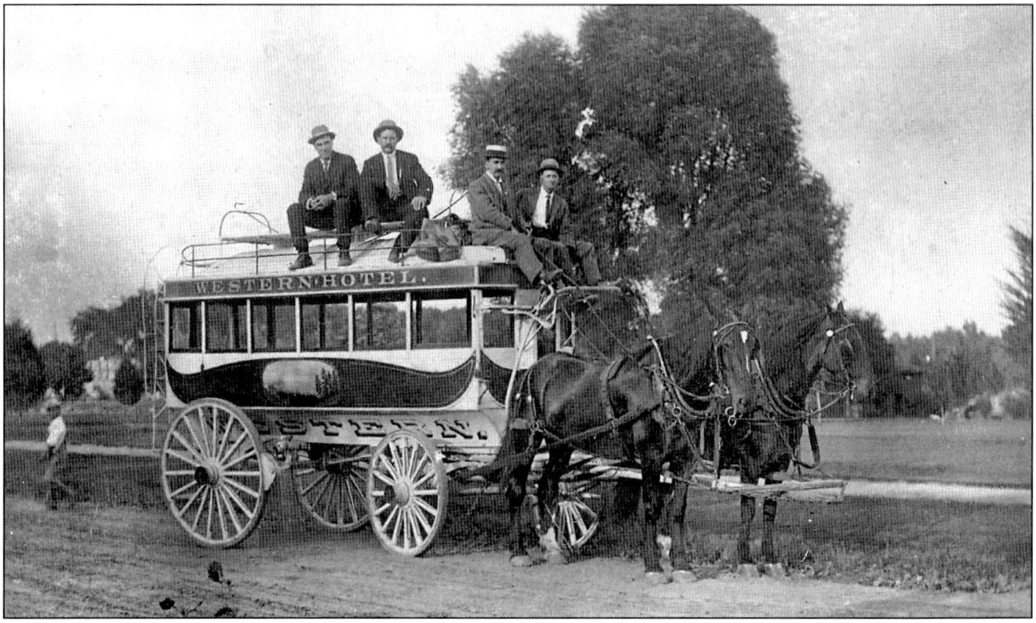

Horse-drawn wagons and carriages were the main mode of local ground transportation into the early 1900s. The Western Hotel had its own version of a courtesy van, as pictured here. This was used to transport clients to and from the train depot and steamship docks. The men are unidentified and the exact date is not known, but it is probably around 1890. (Courtesy Sacramento Public Library Collection.)

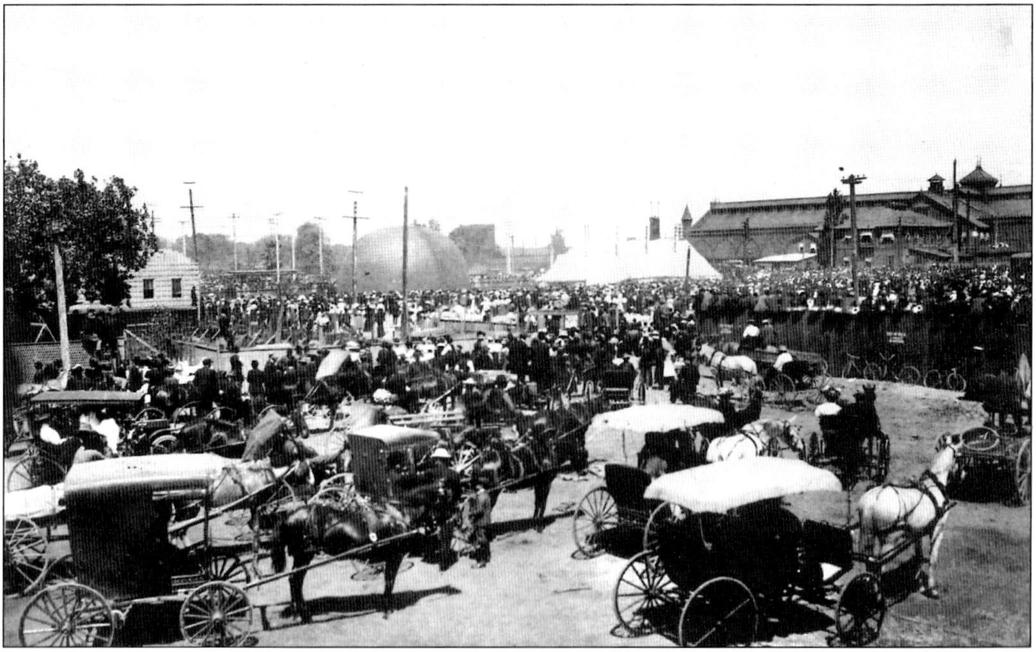

As evidenced here, horse-drawn carriages were quite popular. This *c.* 1900 image shows a hot-air balloon being inflated in front of the Central Pacific Railroad Station. On November 17, 1896, an airship, probably a balloon, made a night passage over Sacramento to the wonderment of the community as recorded in the *Sacramento Bee.* (Courtesy Ann Romani Collection.)

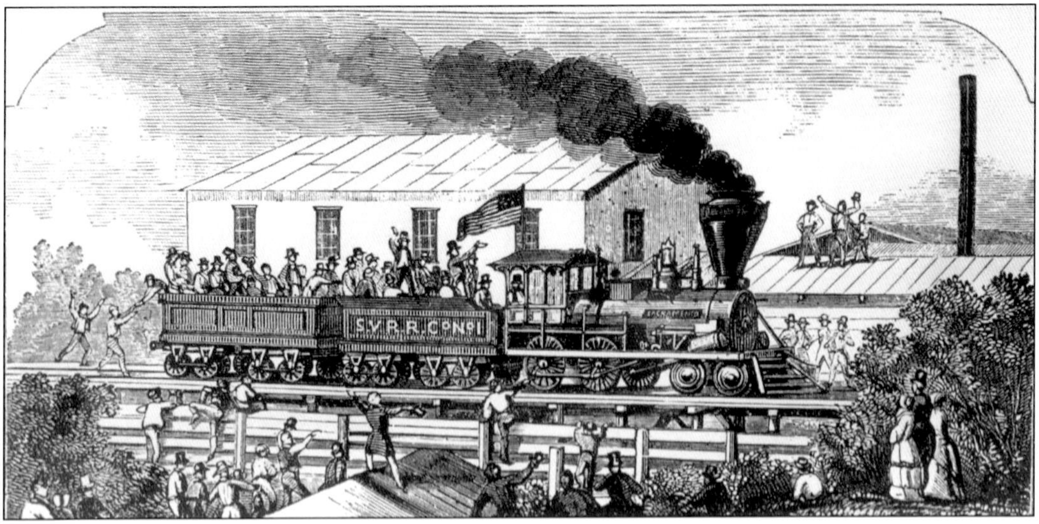

This illustration depicts the initial run of the Sacramento Valley Railroad (SVRR) on August 17, 1855. The SVRR was the first railroad west of the Mississippi River. The line ran from downtown Sacramento to Folsom. In 1865, it was purchased by the Central Pacific Railroad. This image appeared in the *Pictorial Union* on January 1, 1856. (Courtesy Southern Pacific Company Collection.)

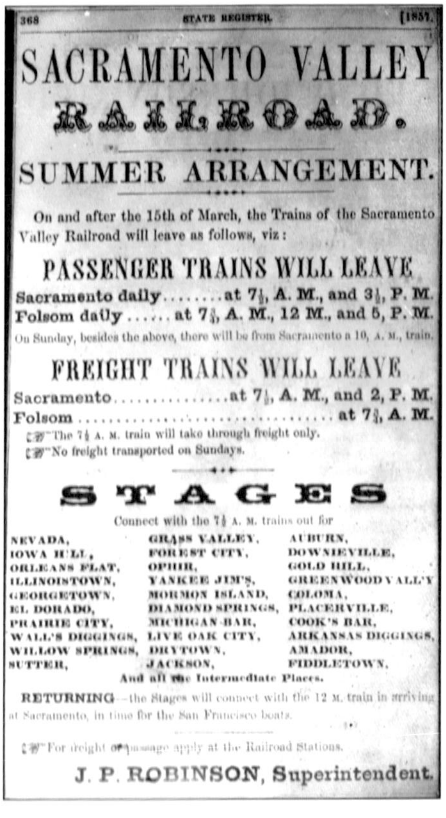

368 STATE REGISTER. [1857.

SACRAMENTO VALLEY RAILROAD.

SUMMER ARRANGEMENT.

On and after the 15th of March, the Trains of the Sacramento Valley Railroad will leave as follows, viz:

PASSENGER TRAINS WILL LEAVE

Sacramento daily .... **at 7½, A. M., and 3½, P. M.**
Folsom daily ...... **at 7¾, A. M., 12 M., and 5, P. M.**

On Sunday, besides the above, there will be from Sacramento a 10, A. M., train.

FREIGHT TRAINS WILL LEAVE

Sacramento .... **at 7½, A. M., and 2, P. M.**
Folsom .... **at 7¾, A. M.**

☞ The 7½ A. M. train will take through freight only.
☞ No freight transported on Sundays.

STAGES

Connect with the 7½ A. M. trains out for

NEVADA,	GRASS VALLEY,	AUBURN,
IOWA HILL,	FOREST CITY,	DOWNIEVILLE,
ORLEANS FLAT,	OPHIR,	GOLD HILL,
ILLINOISTOWN,	YANKEE JIM'S,	GREENWOOD VALL'Y
GEORGETOWN,	MORMON ISLAND,	COLOMA,
EL DORADO,	DIAMOND SPRINGS,	PLACERVILLE,
PRAIRIE CITY,	MICHIGAN BAR,	COOK'S BAR,
WALL'S DIGGINGS,	LIVE OAK CITY,	ARKANSAS DIGGINGS,
WILLOW SPRINGS,	DRYTOWN,	AMADOR,
SUTTER,	JACKSON,	FIDDLETOWN,

And all the Intermediate Places.

RETURNING—the Stages will connect with the 12 M. train in arriving at Sacramento, in time for the San Francisco boats.

☞ For freight or passage apply at the Railroad Stations.

J. P. ROBINSON, Superintendent.

This is an early 1857 schedule for the Sacramento Valley Railroad. The railroad was designed and built by Theodore Judah, who later surveyed the route of the transcontinental railroad over the Sierra Nevada Mountains. Even though it was purchased in 1865, the SVRR operated under that name until 1877, when it was incorporated into the Southern Pacific Railroad. (Courtesy California State Library Collection.)

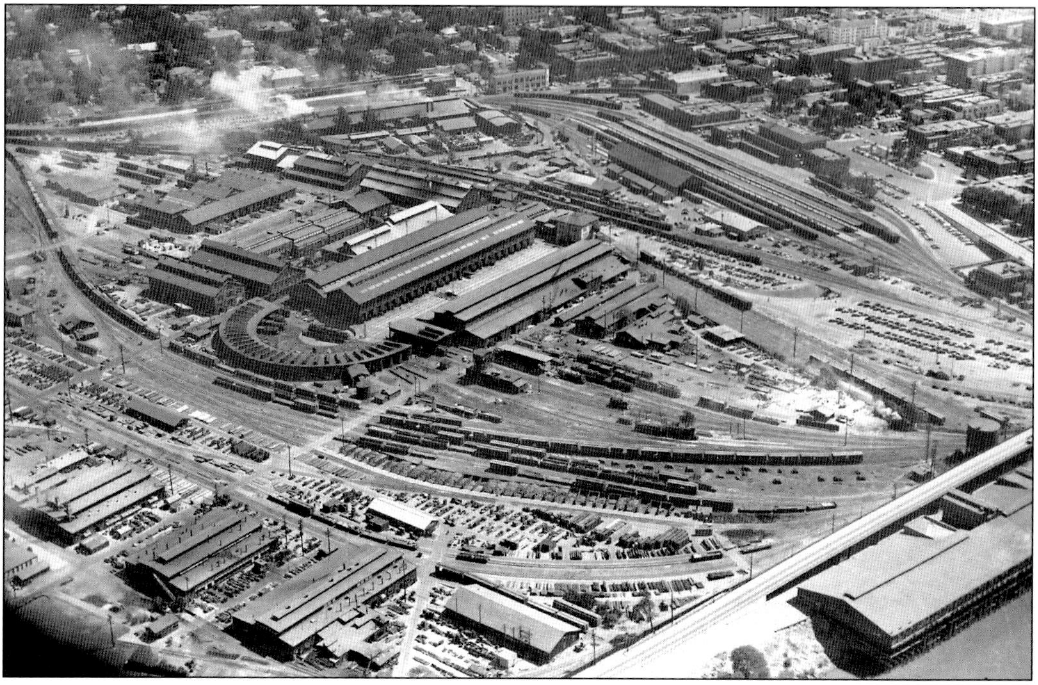

Looking to the southeast, this is a *c.* 1940 aerial photograph of the Sacramento Shops of the Southern Pacific Railroad. For years Southern Pacific was the city's largest employer and the economic engine for the area. They were known for taking good care of their employees, even building a state-of-the-art hospital in the late 1800s. This image shows the extent of their operation at its height. (Courtesy Jeff Redman Collection.)

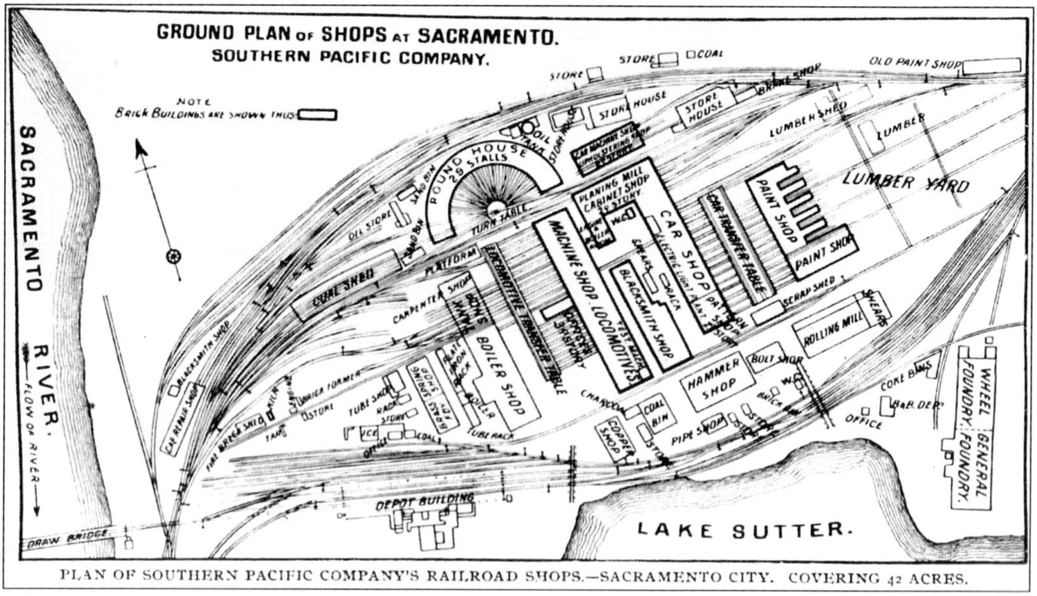

PLAN OF SOUTHERN PACIFIC COMPANY'S RAILROAD SHOPS.—SACRAMENTO CITY. COVERING 42 ACRES.

This map of the Sacramento Shops of the Southern Pacific Railroad originally ran in the 1895 book, *Sacramento County and its Resources*. Most of the original shops indicated here are identifiable in the above photograph. It is important to note how much larger the operation is in the 1940s compared to the 1890s. (Courtesy City of Sacramento Collection.)

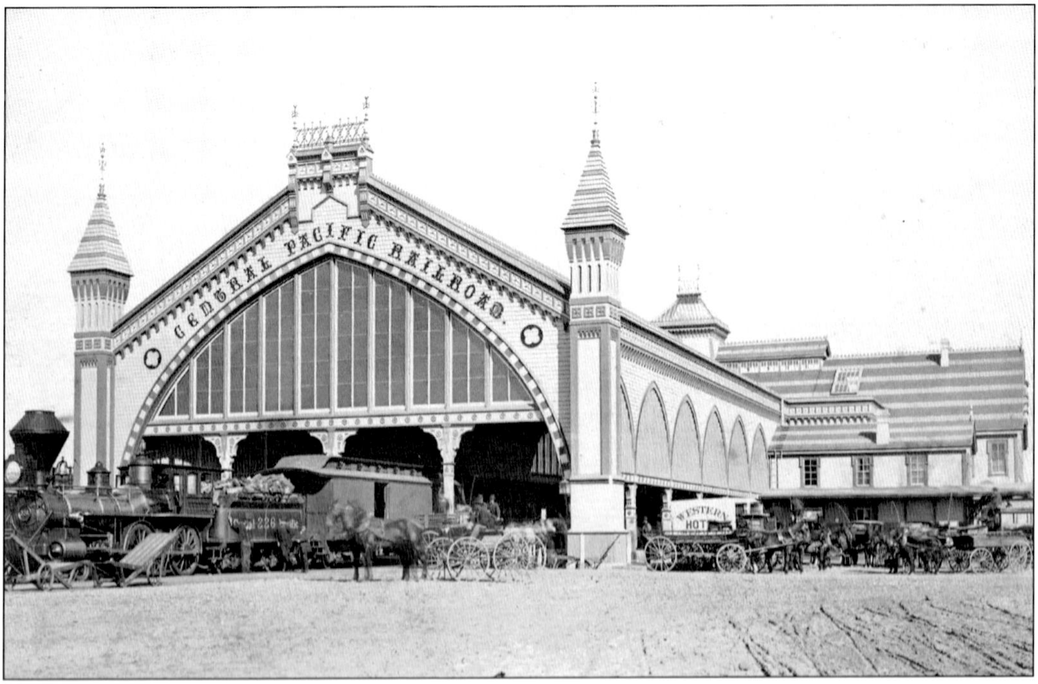

The Central Pacific Railroad Depot opened in 1879. The exact date of this image is unknown, but it was taken very shortly after the depot opened, probably in early 1880. It was built to replace the first depot on Front Street on land reclaimed from Sutter Slough. It was torn down and replaced by the current depot in 1925. (Courtesy A. R. Phillips Jr. Collection.)

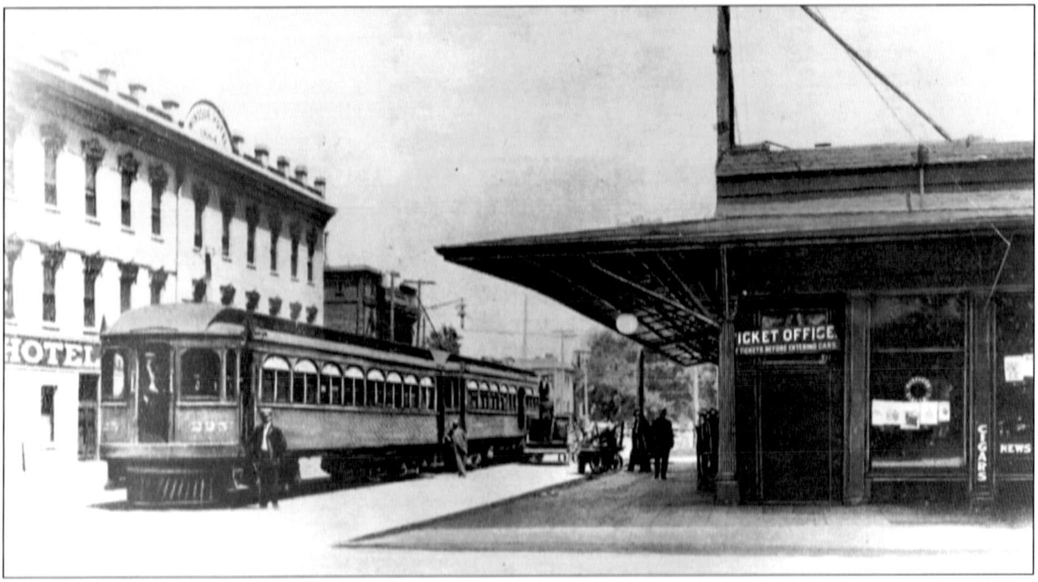

The depot for the Northern Electric Railway (NER) is pictured at the corner of Eighth and J Streets, around 1909, shortly after it opened. Completed in 1907, the NER served Northern California, making it possible to ride from Chico to Oakland on the same car. The Sacramento Northern acquired the NER in 1925. Sacramento banned interurban railroads from running on city streets in 1960. (Courtesy Eugene Hepting Collection.)

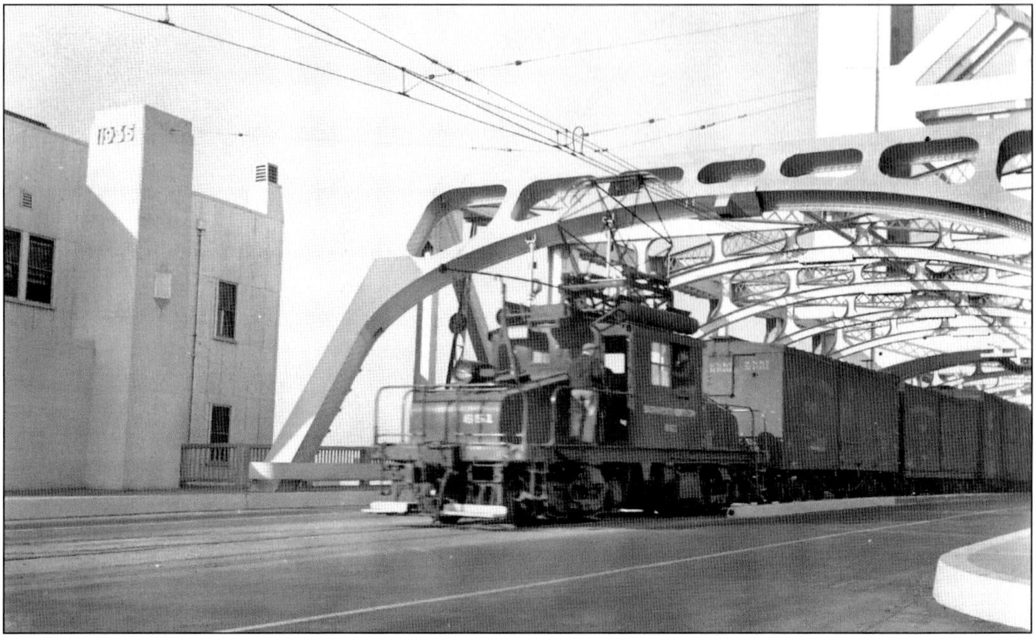

The Tower Bridge was built in part to accommodate the Sacramento Northern Railway (SNR). This photograph from November 11, 1936, shows Engine No. 651 and several boxcars of the SNR crossing the bridge into Sacramento. The railway ceased interurban passenger service on October 31, 1940, due to increased competition from buses and the rising popularity of automobiles. Freight service continued for some years. (Courtesy Florence Henderson Collection.)

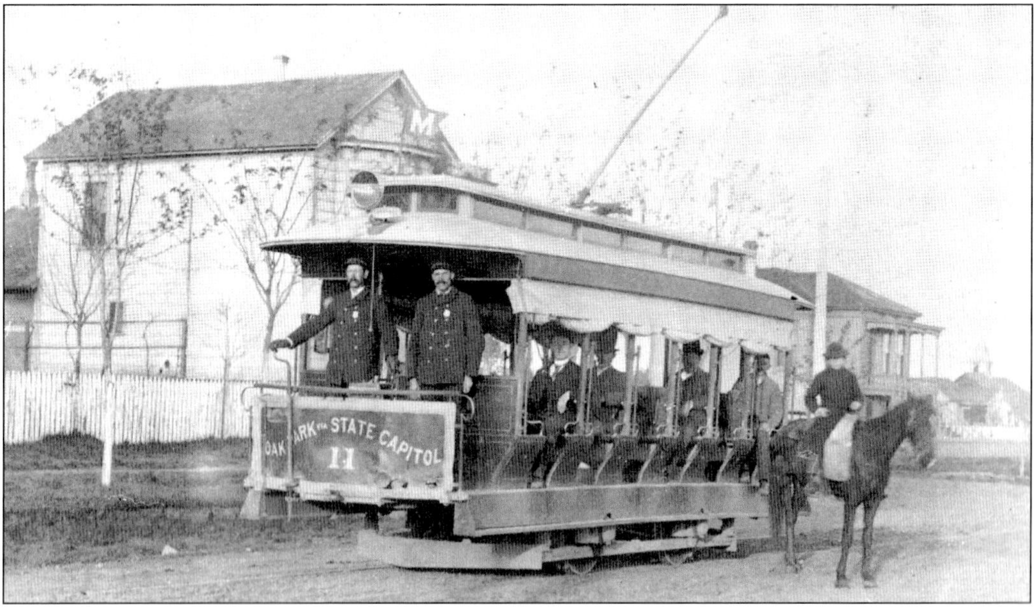

Sacramento once had a fairly extensive trolley-car system, first with horse-drawn carriages in 1858 and later with horse cars on tracks. An electric system started in 1890, using steam-generated power, converting in 1895 to hydroelectric power generated at the new Folsom Power House. This c. 1900 image shows Car No. 11 on the M Street Line, running from the Southern Pacific Depot to Oak Park. (Courtesy California State Library Collection.)

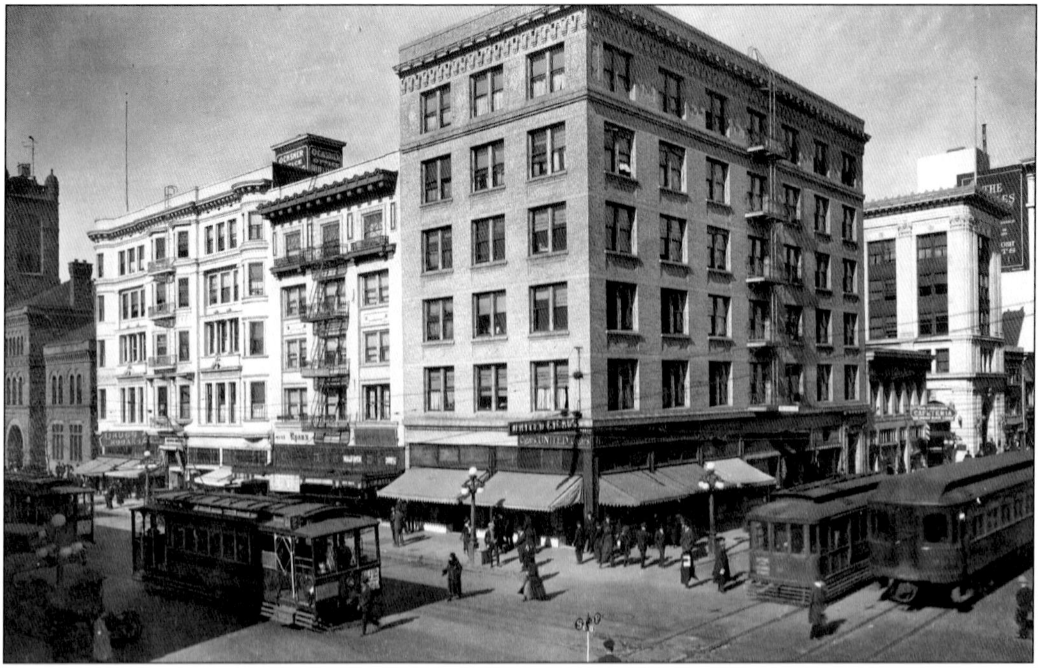

The corner of Eighth and K Streets in 1912 demonstrated the height of the streetcar and interurban systems. The car to the left is the Twenty-first Street line, on K Street. To the right, on Eighth Street, is a car from the Sacramento Traction Company and a car from the Sacramento Northern. All three systems used the same tracks. (Courtesy David Joslyn Collection.)

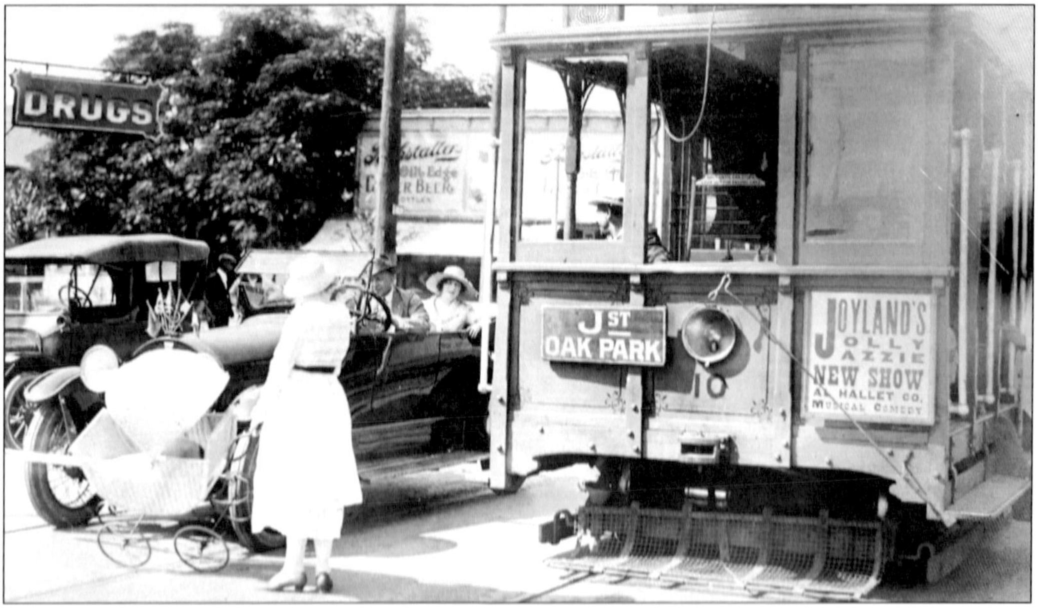

Depicting the hazards of modern transportation, this image shows Gladys McGowen's baby carriage being struck by an automobile. It appears she hurried around the back of the No. 10 streetcar on J Street and then crossed the second set of tracks without looking. This photograph was probably staged as a safety campaign as there is no baby in the carriage. (Courtesy Eugene Hepting Collection.)

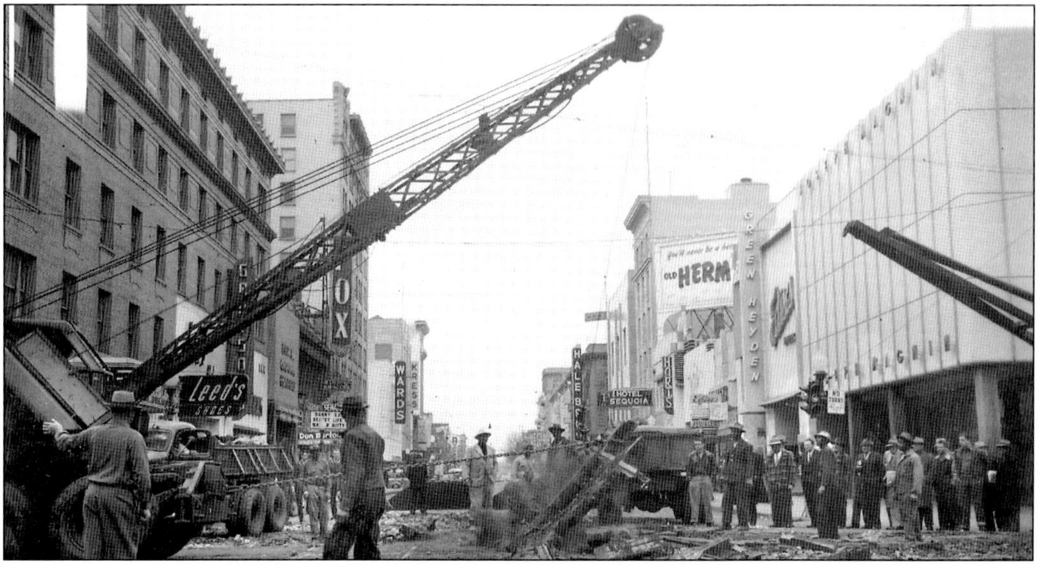

Despite streetcars being part of the landscape for nearly 90 years, the system was dismantled starting in January 1947. It was decided to give automobiles nearly exclusive use of the streets, which led to many parking garages being built. The tracks were literally ripped up, as pictured here at the corner of Tenth and K Streets on February 15, 1948. (Courtesy Eugene Hepting Collection.)

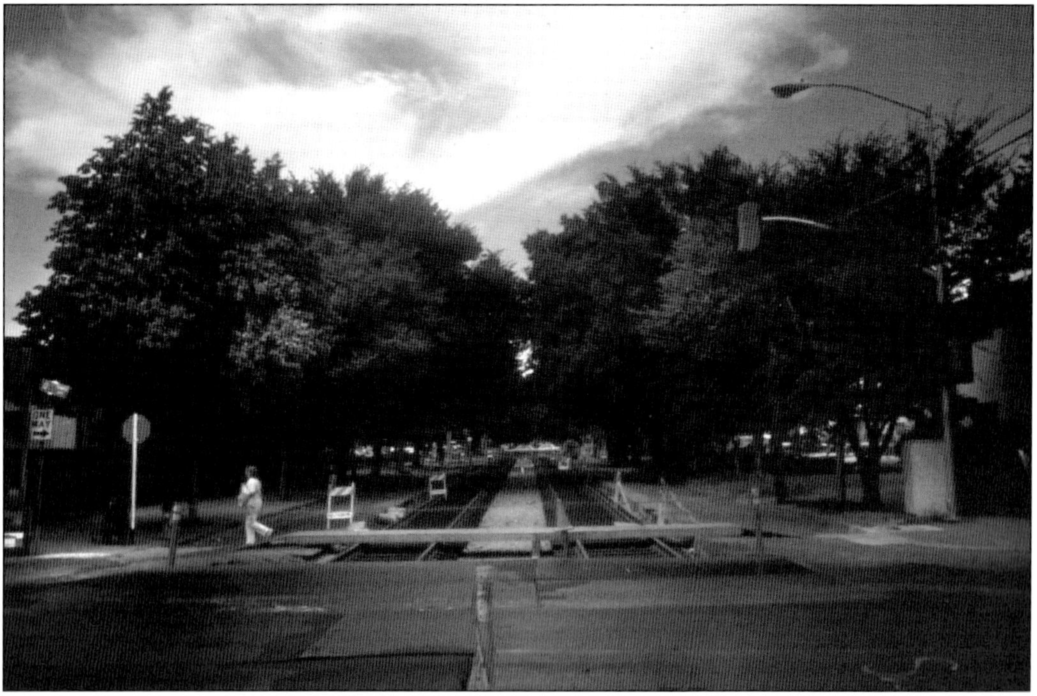

Streetcars made a comeback of sorts some 40 years after the last lines were ended. Here, at the corner of Twelfth and Q Streets, the new light-rail system is being installed. A temporary sidewalk is used to cross Twelfth Street around 1985. The pedestrian K Street Mall, opened in 1972 from Seventh to Twelfth Streets, was completely changed to accommodate the system. (Courtesy Thomas Prittie Collection.)

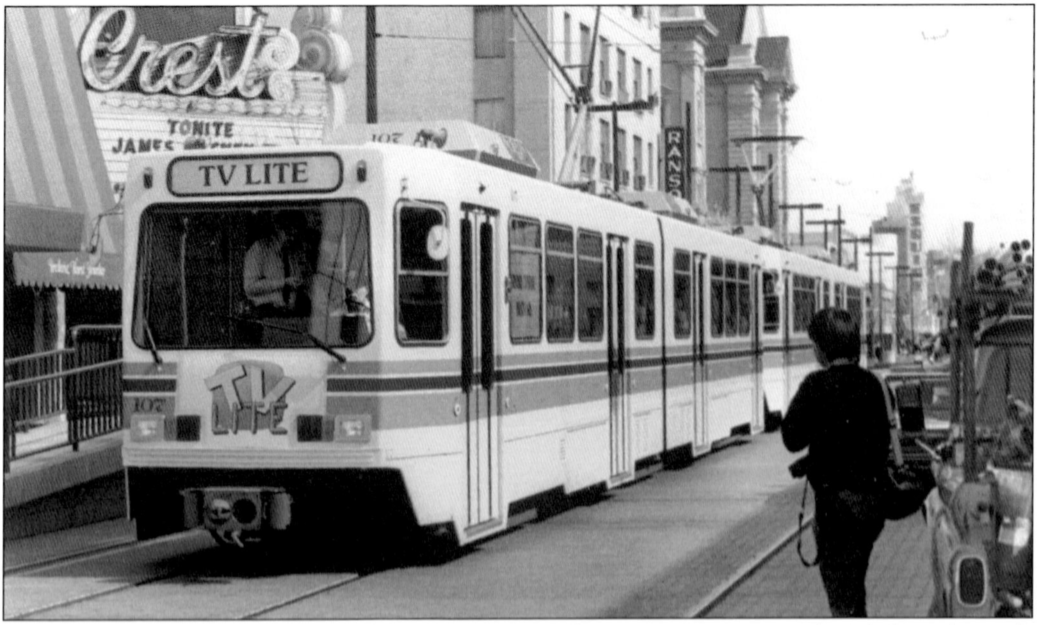

Although not as extensive in the downtown area as the previous system, today's light rail travels much farther out of downtown into the county. A train is pictured stopped in front of the Crest Theater on K Street in 1986, when the new light rail opened with great fanfare. The new system's tracks stand on what was once a series of large concrete fountains and planters along the K Street Mall. (Courtesy *Suttertown News* Collection.)

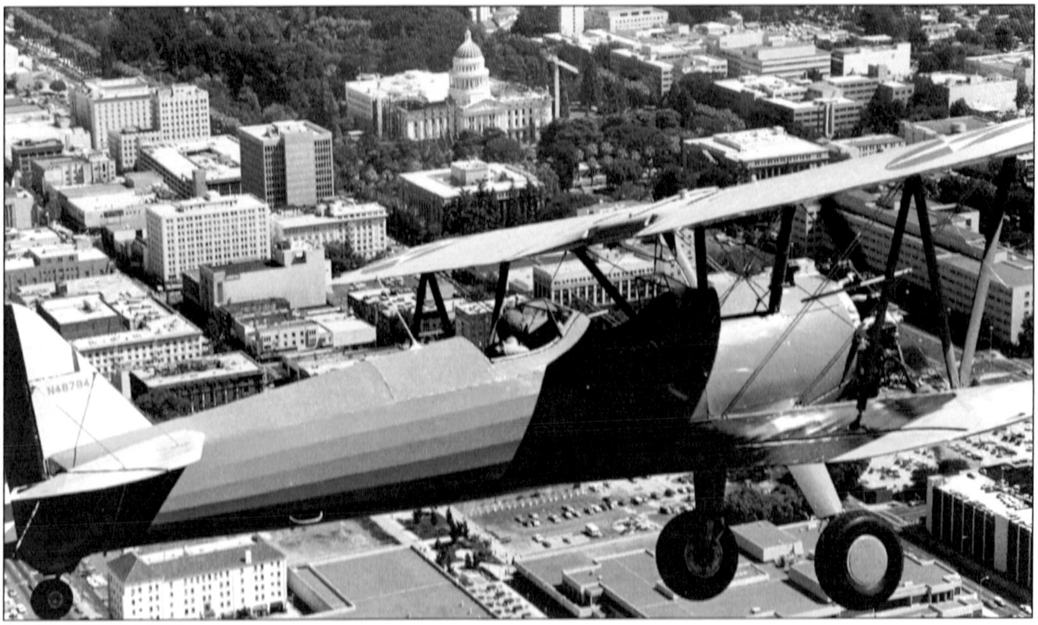

Airmail deliveries for Sacramento began in August 1927. On August 24, 1977, the event was commemorated by pilot Steve William, seen here flying over downtown. He took off from Reno, Nevada, and arrived at Sacramento Executive Airport at 12:17 p.m., exactly 50 years after the first delivery. Airmail delivery was an important milestone for Sacramento, as it was much faster than ground distribution. (Courtesy *Sacramento Bee* Collection.)

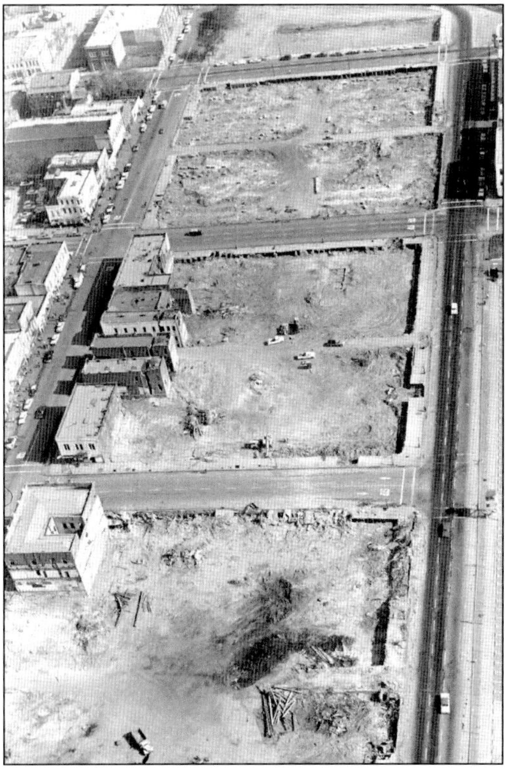

This aerial image shows the area cleared for construction of Interstate 5 along Third Street. The area to the left of the clearing will become Old Sacramento. This photograph illustrates again how dramatically the downtown area changed in just a few years due to concerns about transportation. The photograph was taken April 6, 1960. (Courtesy *Sacramento Bee* Collection.)

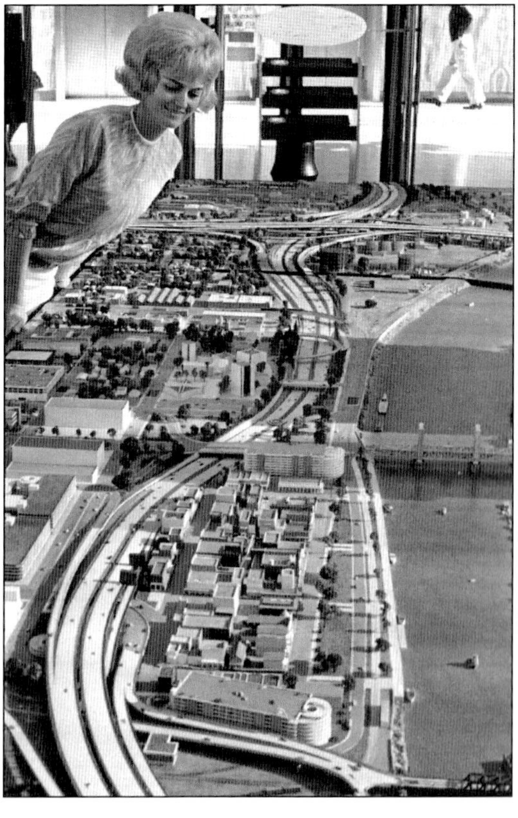

Imogene Price, a secretary at Crocker Citizens Bank at 400 Capital Mall, looks at a model of Interstate 5 on display in the building's lobby. While the freeway model was accurate, the plan for the riverfront was changed considerably. The recreated Embarcadero is part of the railroad museum complex, which stands where the parking garage is located in the model, next to the I Street on-ramp. (Courtesy *Sacramento Bee* Collection.)

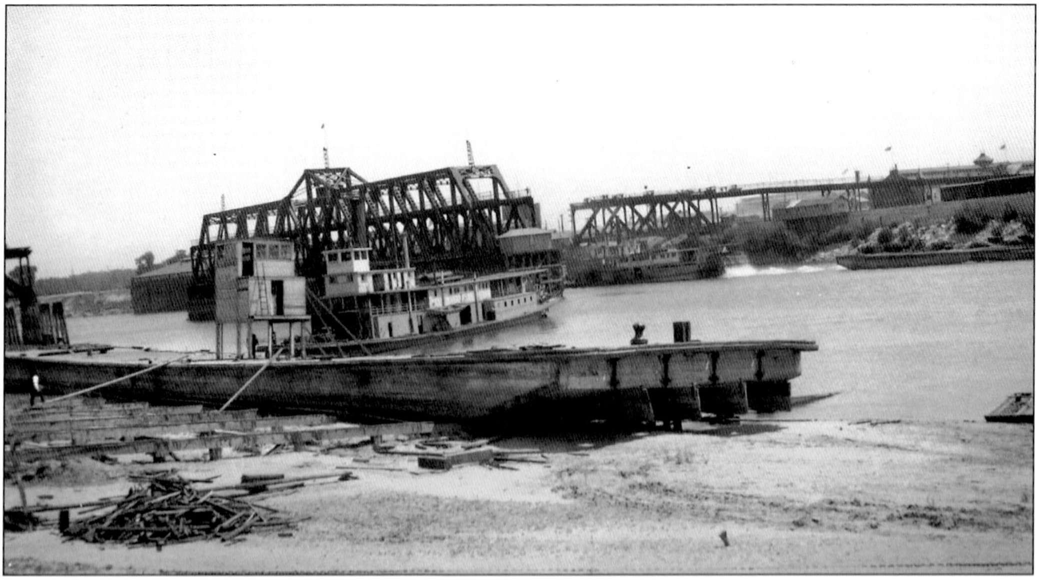

The current I Street Bridge was built in 1911 to replace the previous one and handle railroad traffic while not impeding river traffic. The first bridge, built in 1858, replaced a ferry and increased traffic along Front Street. In this 1917 image from the West Sacramento side of the river, the bridge is opened to allow the sternwheeler *Jacinto* to pass. (Courtesy Ralph Shaw Collection.)

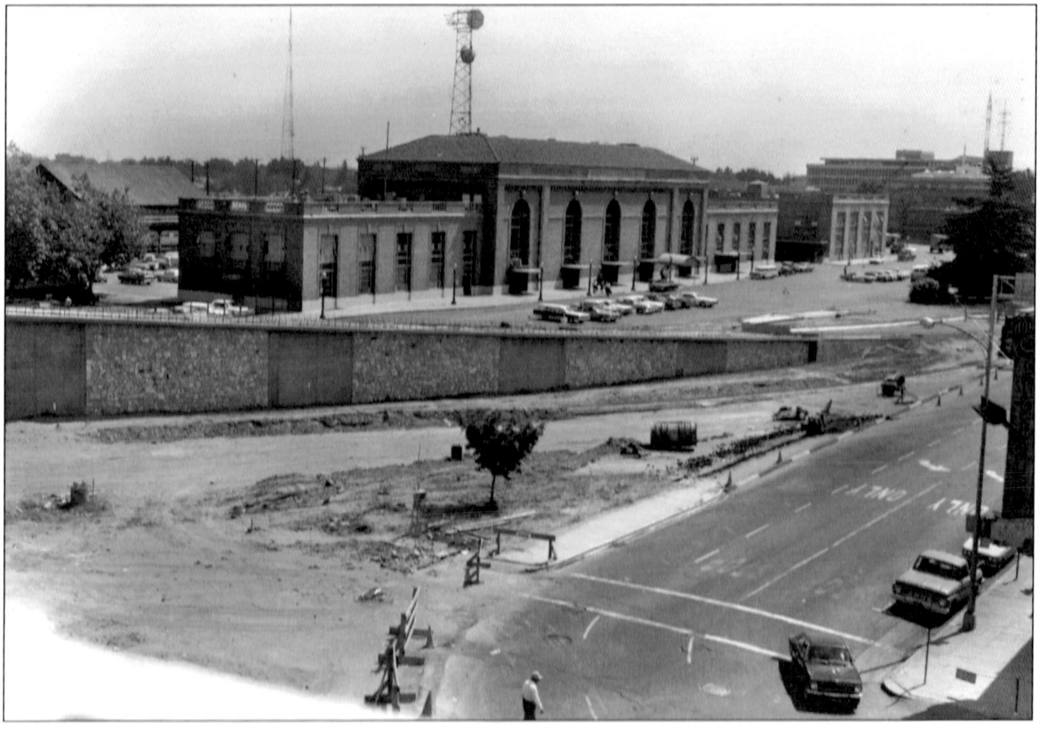

With the Southern Pacific Depot in the background, the on-ramp from I Street to Interstate 5 is under construction, *c.* 1965. By this time, the freeway system was well on its way to replacing rail as the main form of transportation in and around Sacramento, as this photograph demonstrates. (Courtesy City of Sacramento Collection.)

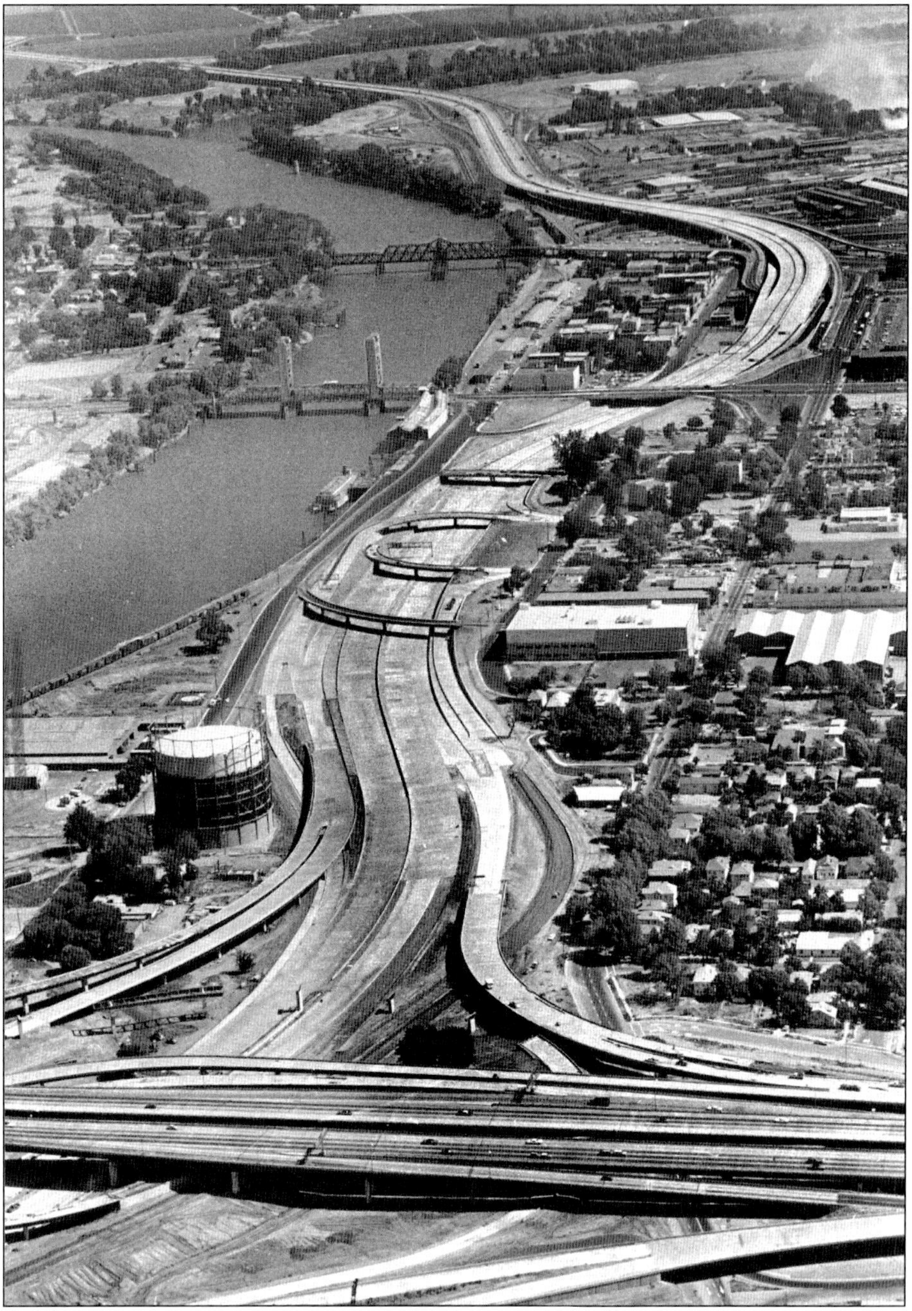

The nearly completed Interstate 5 Freeway on August 3, 1970, shows how thoroughly the West End of Sacramento changed. The *Sacramento Bee* reported that Macy's required nearby freeway access as one condition to opening a store. There were many other reasons for the project, which included economic considerations such as Macy's, Sacramento's position as the capital of California, and alleviating traffic congestion. Taken together, the entire freeway system had the unfortunate effect of cutting off the original city from the outlying neighborhoods. It also cut the city off from the Sacramento River, which along with the railroad was a major part of the economy. (Courtesy *Sacramento Bee* Collection.)

Five

COMMUNITY LIFE

ADAPTIVE AND CULTURALLY DIVERSE

BY *LISA C. PRINCE*

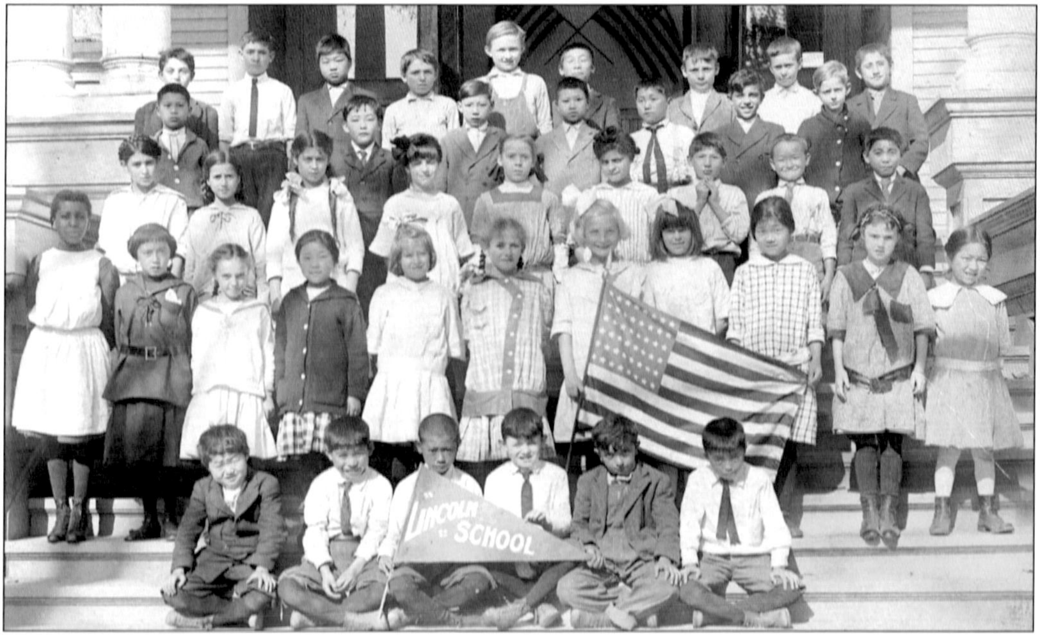

The heterogeneous nature of the Sacramento community goes back to the 1849 founding of the city and its gold-rush roots, when people from around the world came to seek their fortune and a more promising life. The diversity of its residents is represented by 19 nationalities in this 1917 photograph of a class at the Lincoln Grammar School, originally built in 1867 at Second and P Streets and moved to Fourth and Q Streets in 1872. The Sacramento community remains an ethnic and cultural mix. According to the 2000 United States Census, Sacramento was found to be the most diverse city in the nation. Coming to an unfamiliar, and at times hostile, land meant the different groups carved out their own communities within the larger one. Churches were a welcoming center and offered a social core for many immigrants and settlers. They provided a place to share common interests, find helpful guidance and support in their own language, and were important aspects of a familiar cultural heritage that could be retained and celebrated. (Courtesy *Sacramento Bee* Collection.)

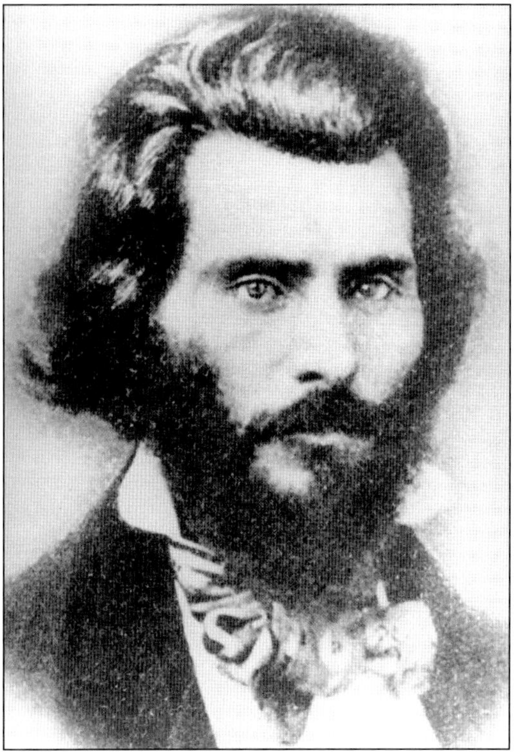

John Rollin Ridge (1827–1867), a Cherokee born in Georgia and educated in New England, came to California in 1850. He wrote for periodicals and newspapers in San Francisco and Marysville after having failed at mining and trading. In 1857, Ridge was the first editor of the *Daily Bee* (later *Sacramento Bee*). He later wrote about concerns regarding the treatment and fate of American Indians. (Courtesy Sacramento Ethnic Survey Collection.)

A crowd watches as children and members of the Federated Indians of California, dressed in traditional tribal clothes, headdresses, and adornments, participate in a downtown parade, *c.* 1950s. The float is decorated with Native American symbols, banners, and basketry. (Courtesy Sacramento Ethnic Survey Collection.)

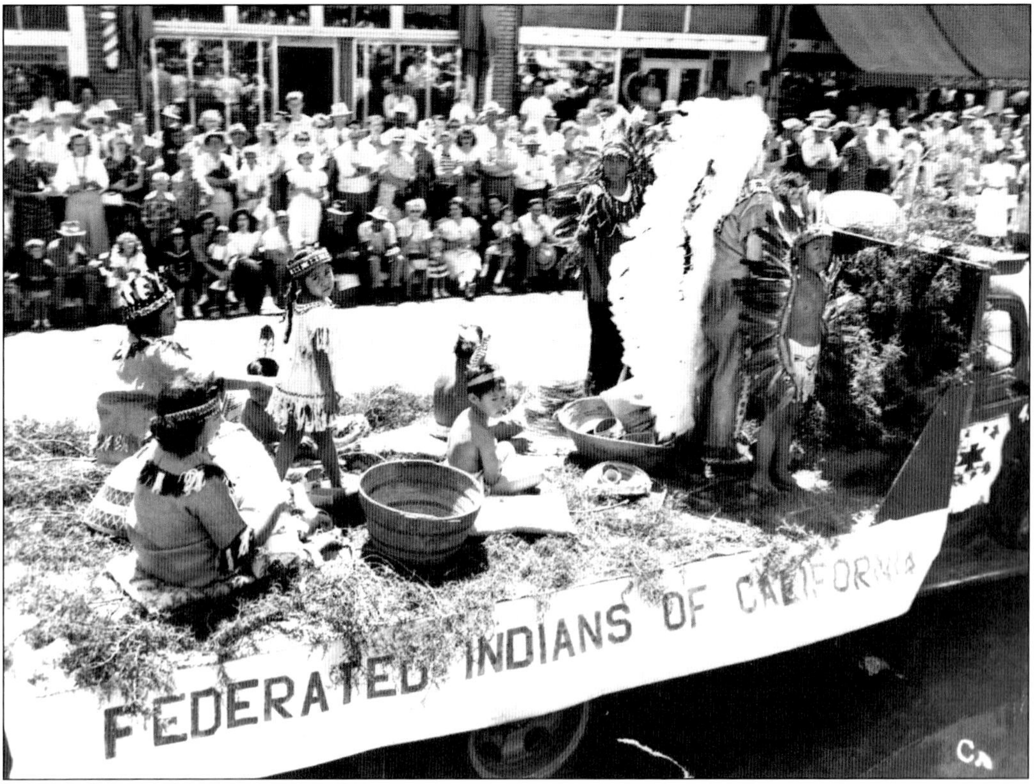

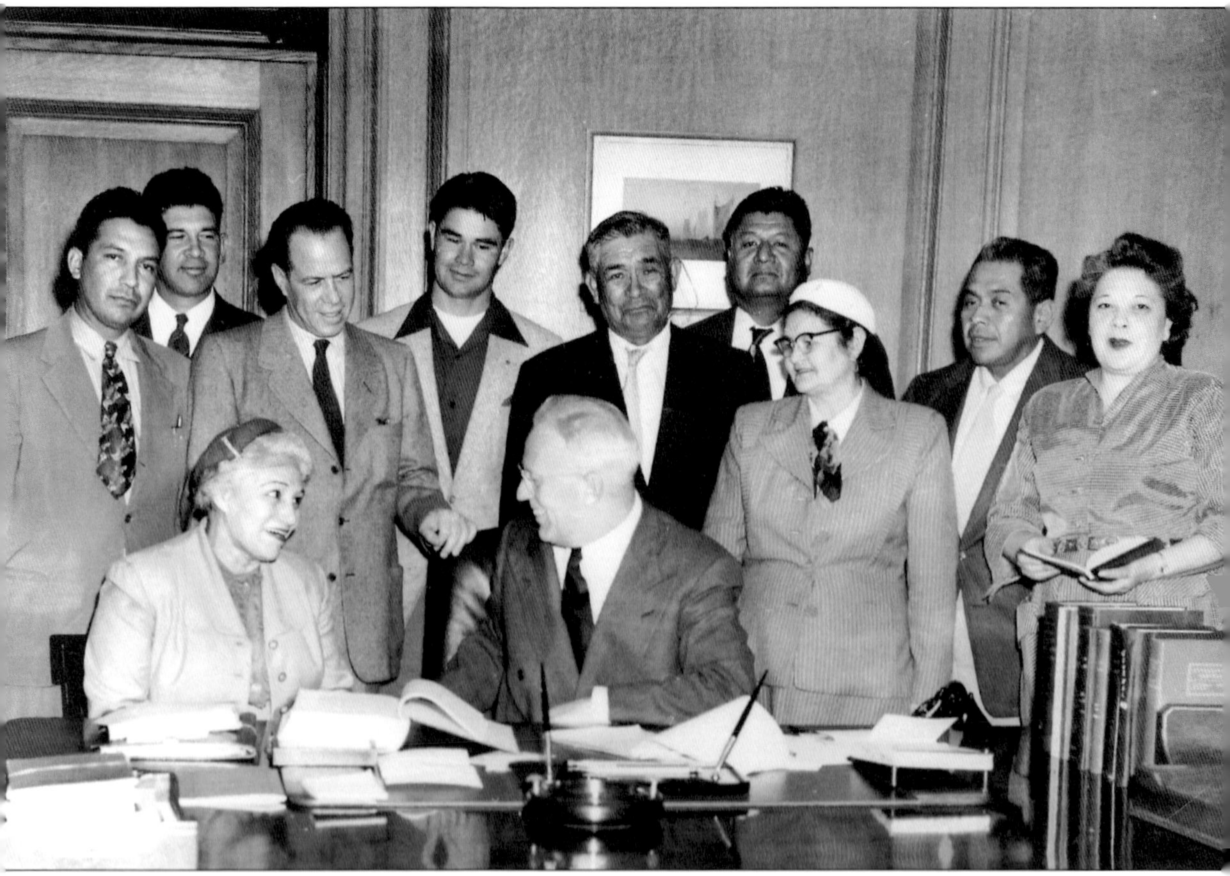

In this 1964 photograph, the California Indian Delegation visits U.S. Supreme Court Chief Justice Earl Warren (seated) in his Washington, D.C. office. In the 1920s, politicized California Native Americans sought a united front to address the legal and financial issues of Indians. Groups such as the Indians of California Incorporated and the Indian Board of Cooperation led attempts to integrate the public schools and to finally settle the 18 unratified treaties of 1851 and 1852. Indian leaders founded the Federated Indians of California (FIC) in 1946 in order to press their land claims case against the federal government before the Indian Claims Commission. The woman seated to Warren's right is founding officer and president Bertha Stewart. The woman standing to his left is Marie Mason Potts, a Sacramento resident, Native American historian, FIC activist, and editor of its newspaper, *The Smoke Signal,* which was published from 1948 through 1977. Potts was an active organizer in the FIC, the California Indian Education Association, the Intertribal Council of California, and was a regular visitor to many Sacramento schools. (Courtesy Sacramento Ethnic Survey Collection.)

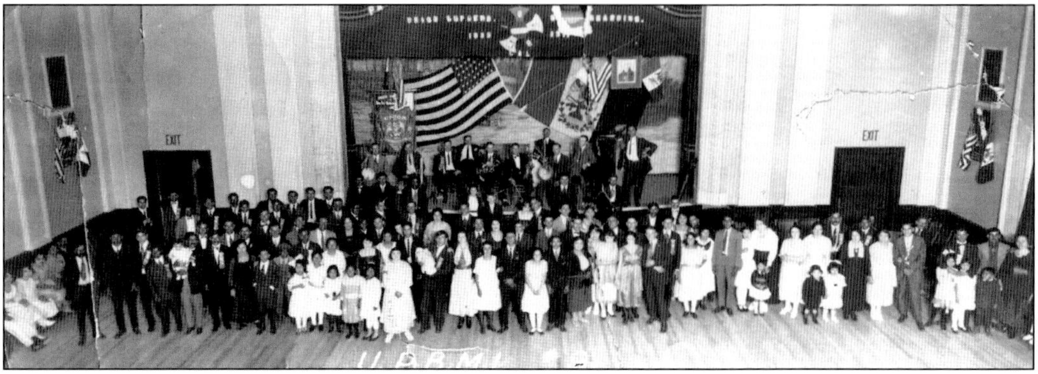

Shown in 1921 is the Union Patriotica Benefica Mexicana Independencia (Patriotic Union to Benefit Mexican Independence). Many in the photograph are from original Mexican families of Sacramento, such as Bias, Cesneros, Martinez, Ramirez, Alejo, Garcia, Guzman, Sota, and Macias. The group is celebrating the centennial of Mexico's independence at the Native Sons' Hall, 924 Eleventh Street. Mexicans and Mexican Americans in Sacramento have retained a traditional sense of community and shared values. (Courtesy Andaloza/Falgado/Zuniga Collection.)

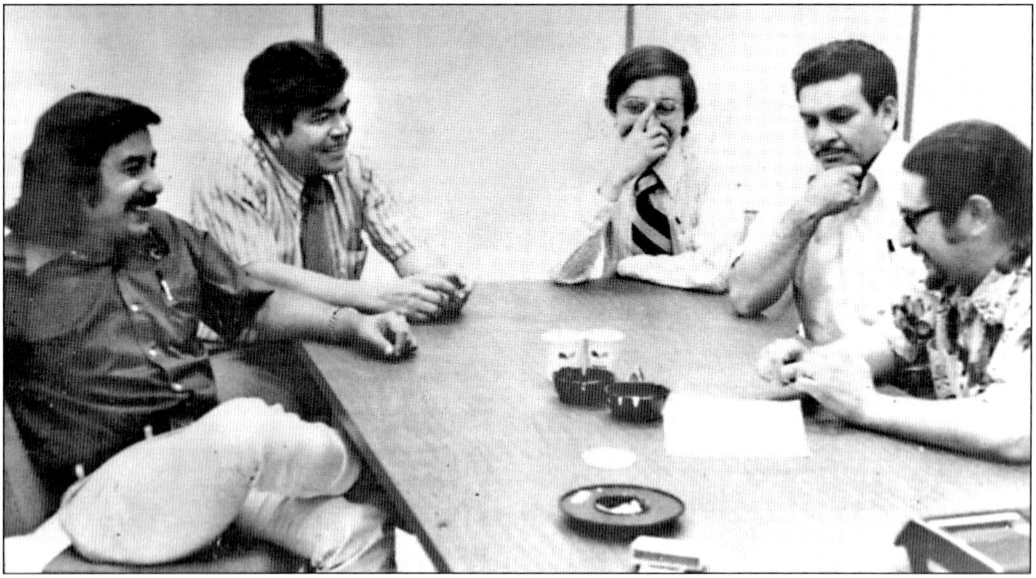

Hispanic Sacramento politicians, artists, and activists meet in 1976. Pictured, from left to right, are Joe Serna, Manuel Ferrales, John Valencia, Rudolfo Cuellar, and Jose Montoya, a poet and member of the artist/activist group known as the Royal Chicano Air Force. Serna, born to farm-working parents, taught government at California State University, Sacramento, was a city councilman, and served as mayor of Sacramento from 1992 until his death in 1999. (Courtesy Sacramento Ethnic Survey Collection.)

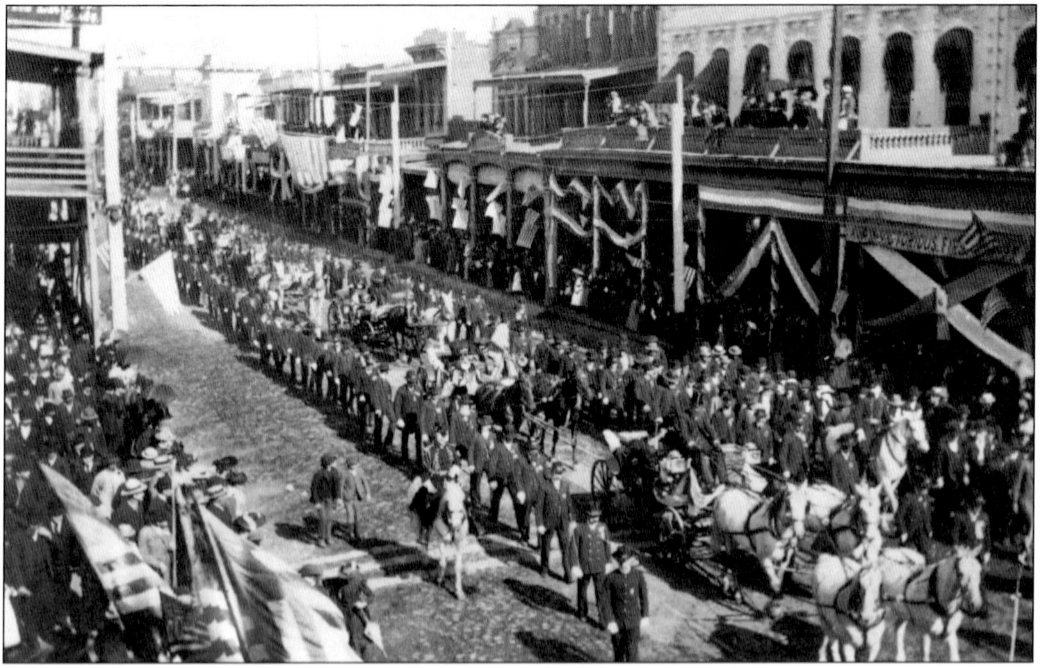

Many Sacramentans joined the festivities to celebrate former Pres. Ulysses S. Grant's visit to Sacramento on October 22, 1879. The procession on K Street featured Grant, along with Gov. William Irwin, Sen. Newton Booth, and Mayor Jabez Turner in the lead carriage, escorted by numerous military units. Grant, the first president to visit the city, stayed at the Golden Eagle Hotel at Seventh and K Streets. (Courtesy Noel LaDue Collection.)

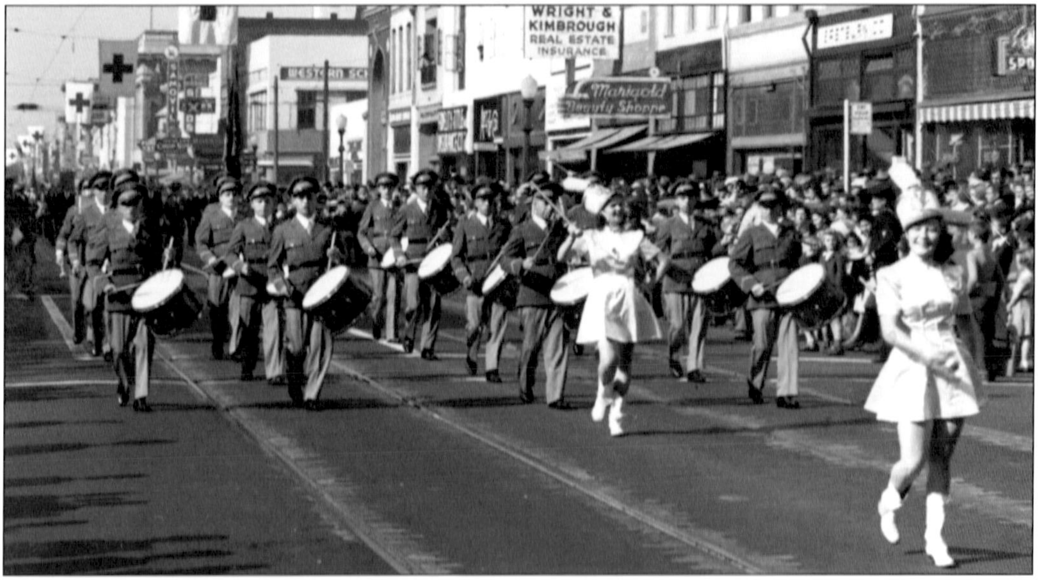

The Native Sons of the Golden West Drum Corp celebrate Armistice Day 1941 in downtown Sacramento on J Street between Eighth and Ninth Streets. In 1875, Gen. Albert M. Winn, a Virginian, organized the Native Sons as a way to immortalize the fortitude of the pioneer men and women of the gold-rush period. The organization actively promotes the study and celebration of California history. (Courtesy Frank Christy Collection.)

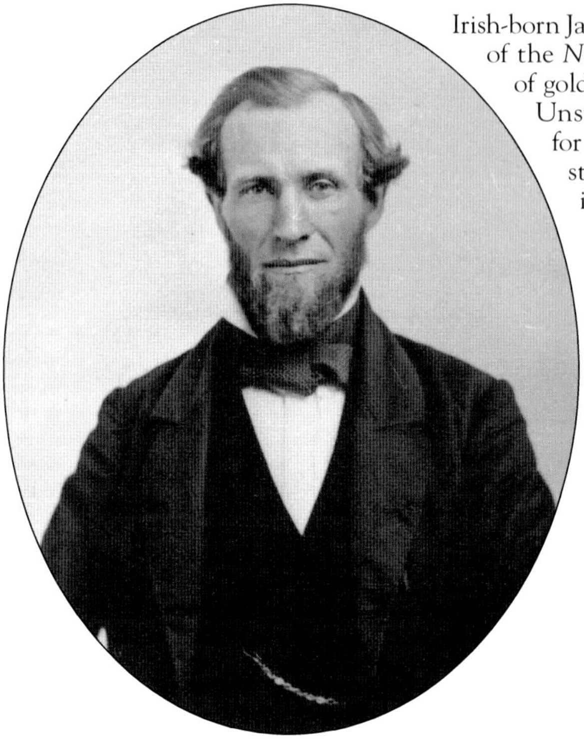

Irish-born James McClatchy (1824–1883) was an editor of the *New York Tribune* in 1848 when the news of gold in California prompted him to go west. Unsuccessful at mining and seeing a need for civil order in the new city, he thought a strong newspaper could benefit the public interest. Not long after its founding in 1857, McClatchy became editor of the *Sacramento Bee.* (Courtesy Eleanor McClatchy Collection.)

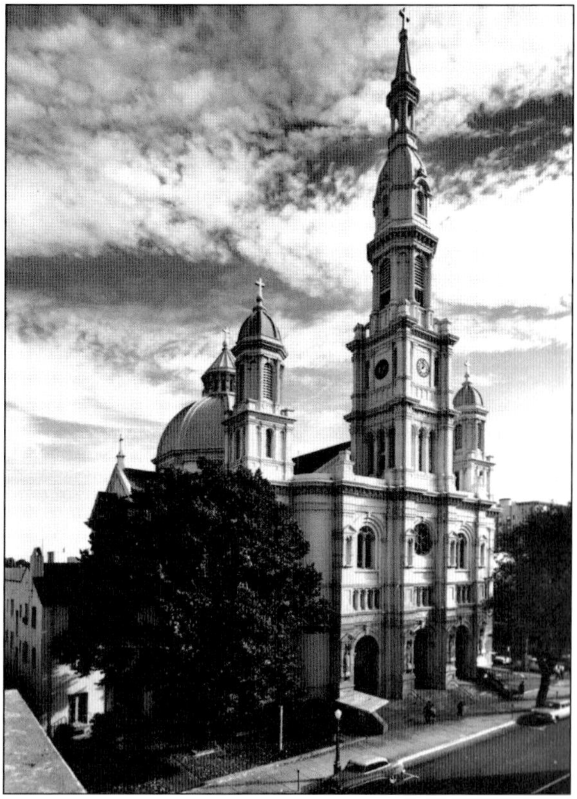

The recently renovated Cathedral of the Blessed Sacrament was dedicated on July 1, 1889, at Eleventh and K Streets, where it still stands. Irish-born Rev. Patrick Manogue (1832–1895) was named bishop of the newly created Diocese of Sacramento in 1886. He soon began planning for a grand cathedral. A symbol of non-sectarian civic pride, the building of the cathedral drew many contributors. (Courtesy Sacramento Ethnic Survey Collection.)

Located at Twelfth and K Streets, St. John's German Lutheran Church was built in 1873. German-speaking churches were one of the major social organizations that Germans brought with them when they came to Sacramento. St. John's was the central Protestant church in the Sacramento area where many influential members of the German community, and of the city, worshipped together. (Courtesy Frank Christy Collection.)

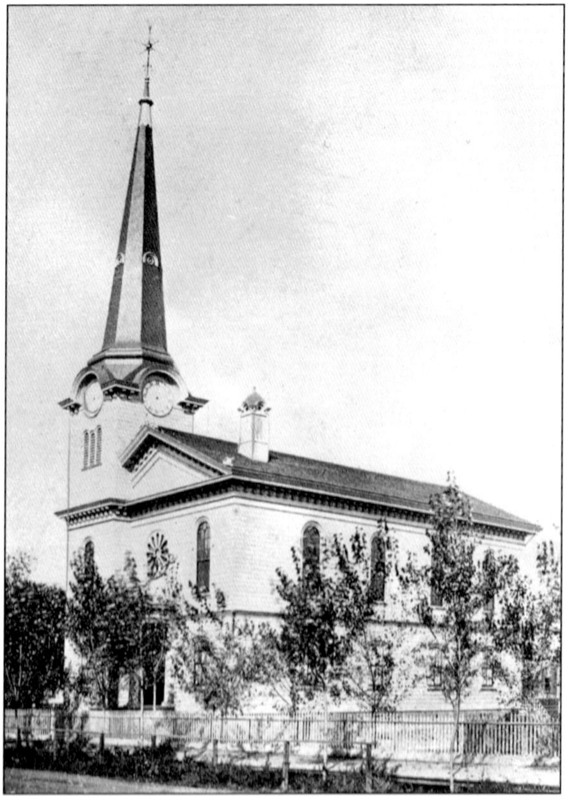

Photographed in 1880, from left to right, are local brewer Frank Ruhstaller and merchants August Heilbron, Adolph Heilbron, and Joseph F. W. Maier. They are members of the Sacramento Hussars, the only cavalry unit in Sacramento County. It was almost exclusively made up of native-born and ethnic Germans. Their uniforms and equipment were modeled after the units in most European armies of the time. The Sacramento Hussars was established in 1859. (Courtesy Eleanor McClatchy Collection.)

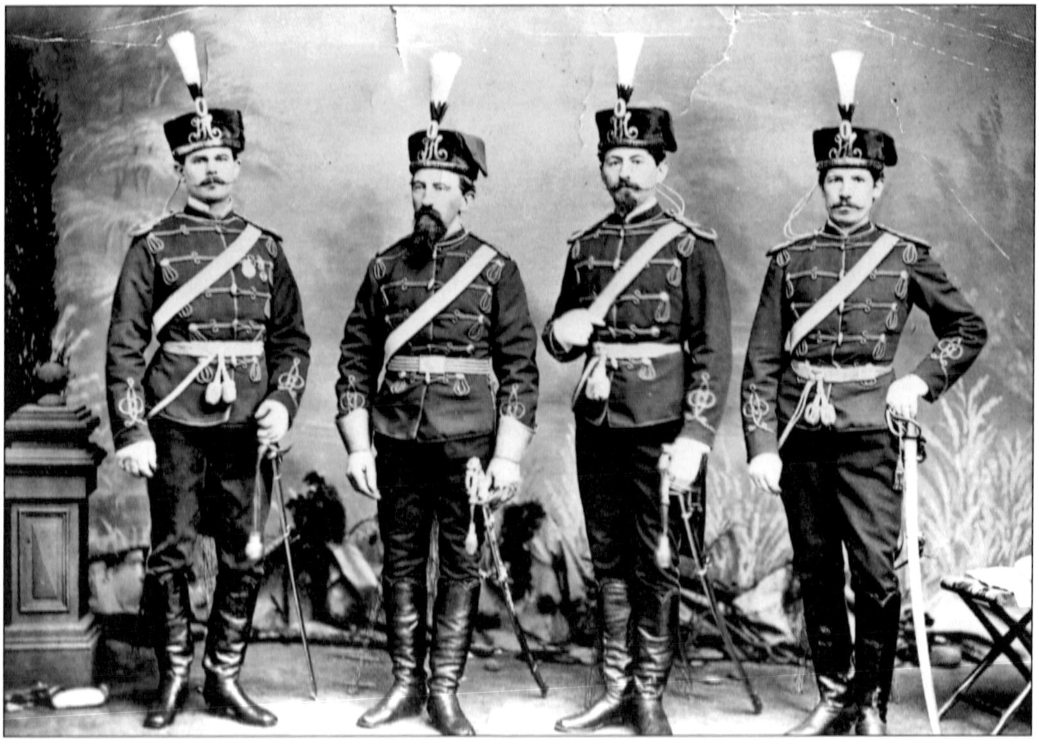

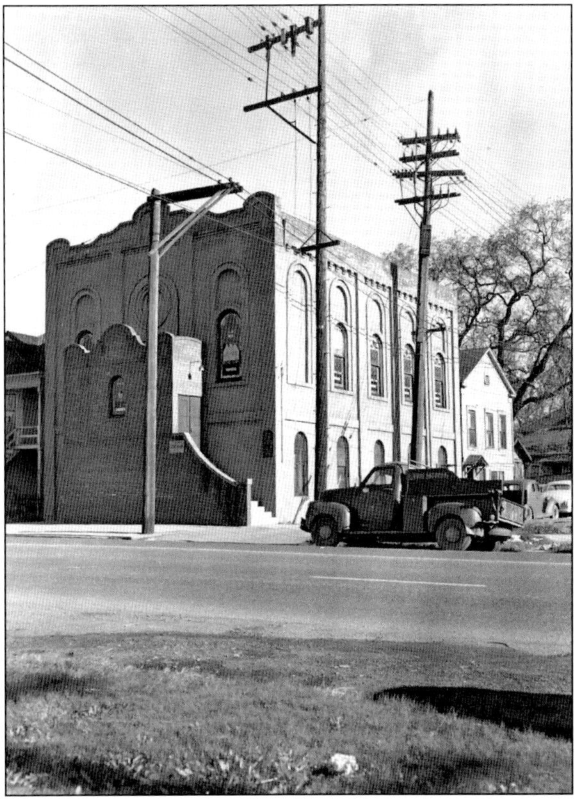

This is a 1950 photograph of the St. Andrews African Methodist Episcopal Church, located at Seventh and G Streets. St. Andrews was organized in 1850 and was the first visible black institution in Sacramento. The church was a center for black social and political activity in the early years of the city. In 1854, Elizabeth Thorne Scott opened the first public school for minority children in the church's basement. (Courtesy Ralph Shaw Collection.)

The Zanzibar Club, located at 530½ Capital Avenue (M Street), was opened in 1943 by owners Louis and Issac Anderson and W. C. "Nitz" Jackson. In the 1940s and 1950s, it became one of Sacramento's hottest nightclubs, along with the MoMo Club that was owned by brothers Alex and Hovey Moore. Pictured are Vincent "Ted" Thompson on saxophone and Walter Robinson on piano. (Courtesy Sacramento Ethnic Survey Collection.)

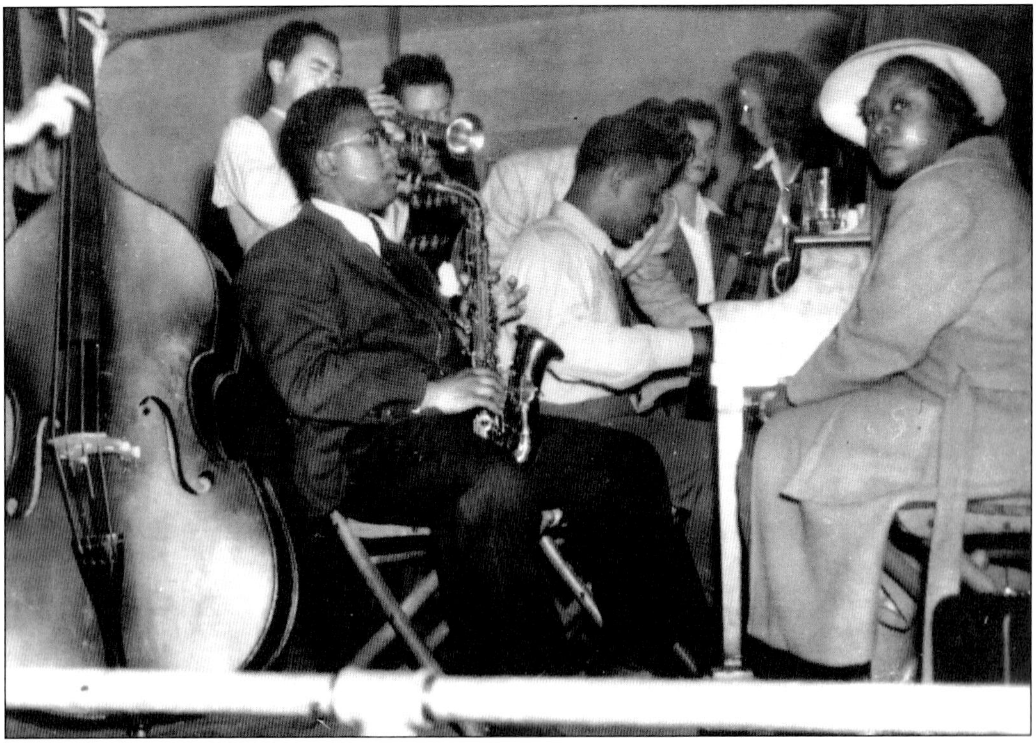

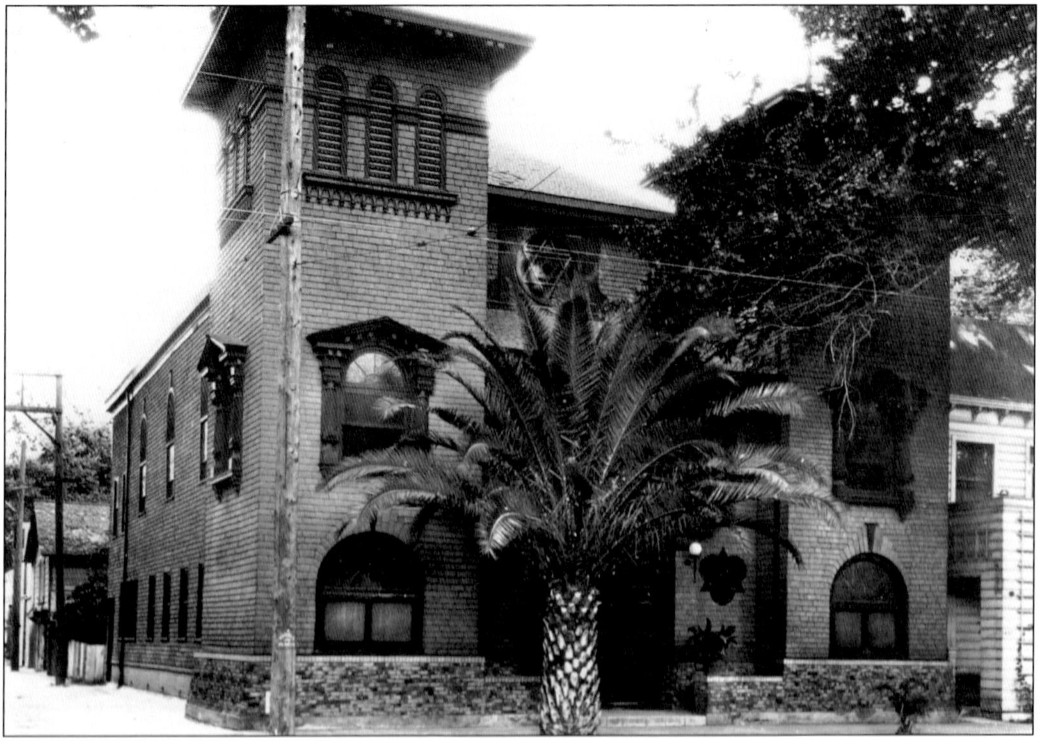

The synagogue located on Fifteenth Street is pictured here around 1920. The Jewish community in Sacramento had, by 1849, a Jewish cemetery and a Hebrew Benevolent Society. The Temple B'nai Israel at 1212 Seventh Street was dedicated on September 3, 1852, and was the first congregationally owned synagogue on the West Coast. (Courtesy Ralph Shaw Collection.)

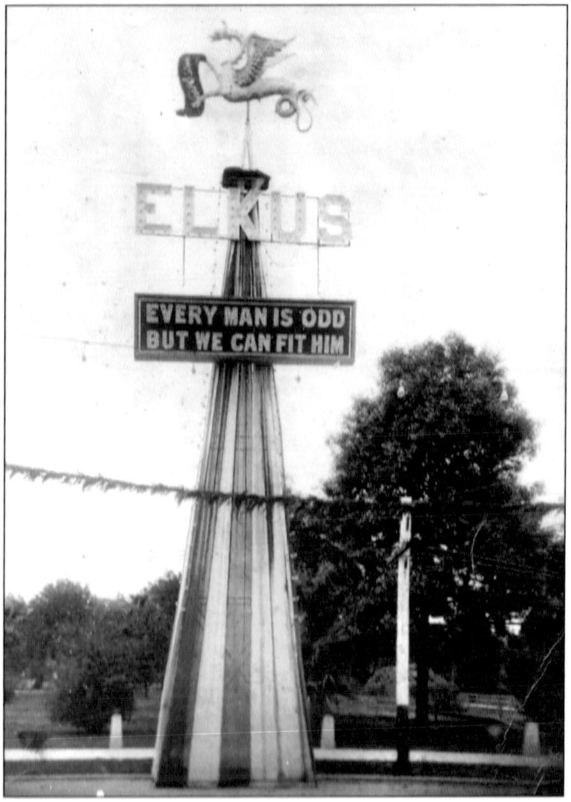

This was the first electrical advertising sign, erected in 1901 by George Borne, and was located on the south side of L Street, between Twelfth and Thirteenth Streets. Albert Elkus was a member of the Jewish community and owner of Elkus Clothiers. He was also the mayor of Sacramento from 1921 to 1925. (Courtesy Frank Christy Collection.)

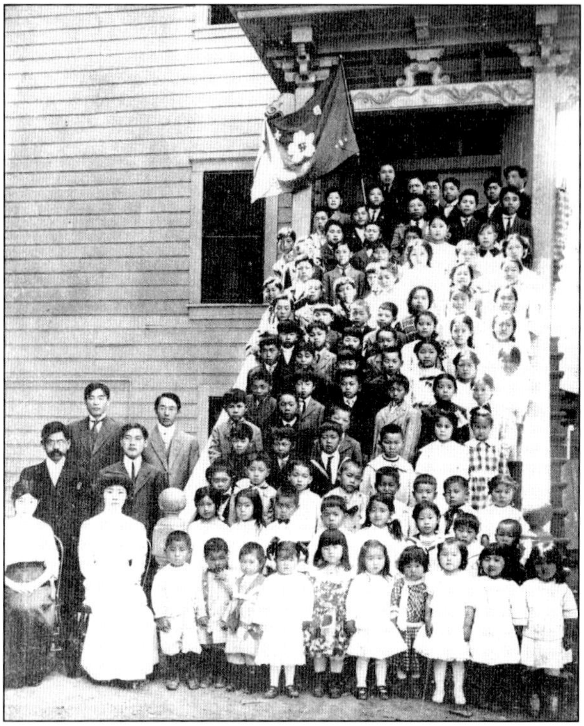

This is the Buddhist Mission at 418 O Street where many Nisei (second-generation Japanese) children were taught Japanese language, history, geography, and given ethical training. The children attended the American school (most went to Lincoln Grammar School) during regular hours and then attended classes here from 3:00 p.m. to 5:00 p.m. There were also several Christian churches that provided this training. (Courtesy Sacramento Ethnic Survey Collection.)

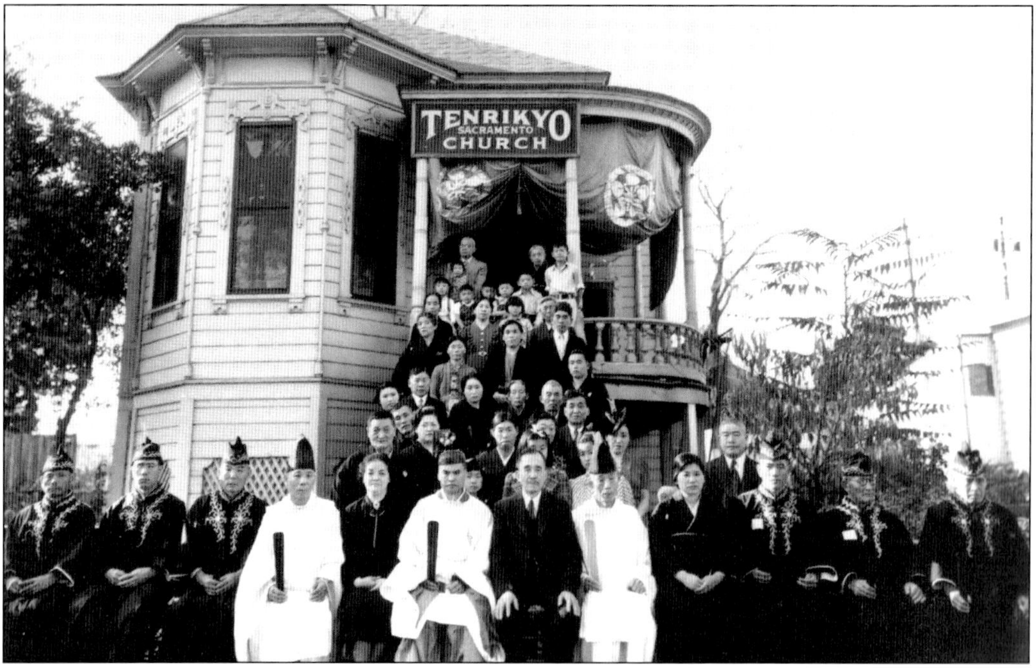

The Tenrikyo Sacramento Church, located at 1420 Second Street, pictured in 1939, had the largest congregation of any Japanese church in Sacramento. The churches were the community's cultural and social center where residents could find moral and spiritual guidance and support, as well as advice and assistance on employment, language training, and sponsors for team sports. (Courtesy Sacramento Ethnic Survey Collection.)

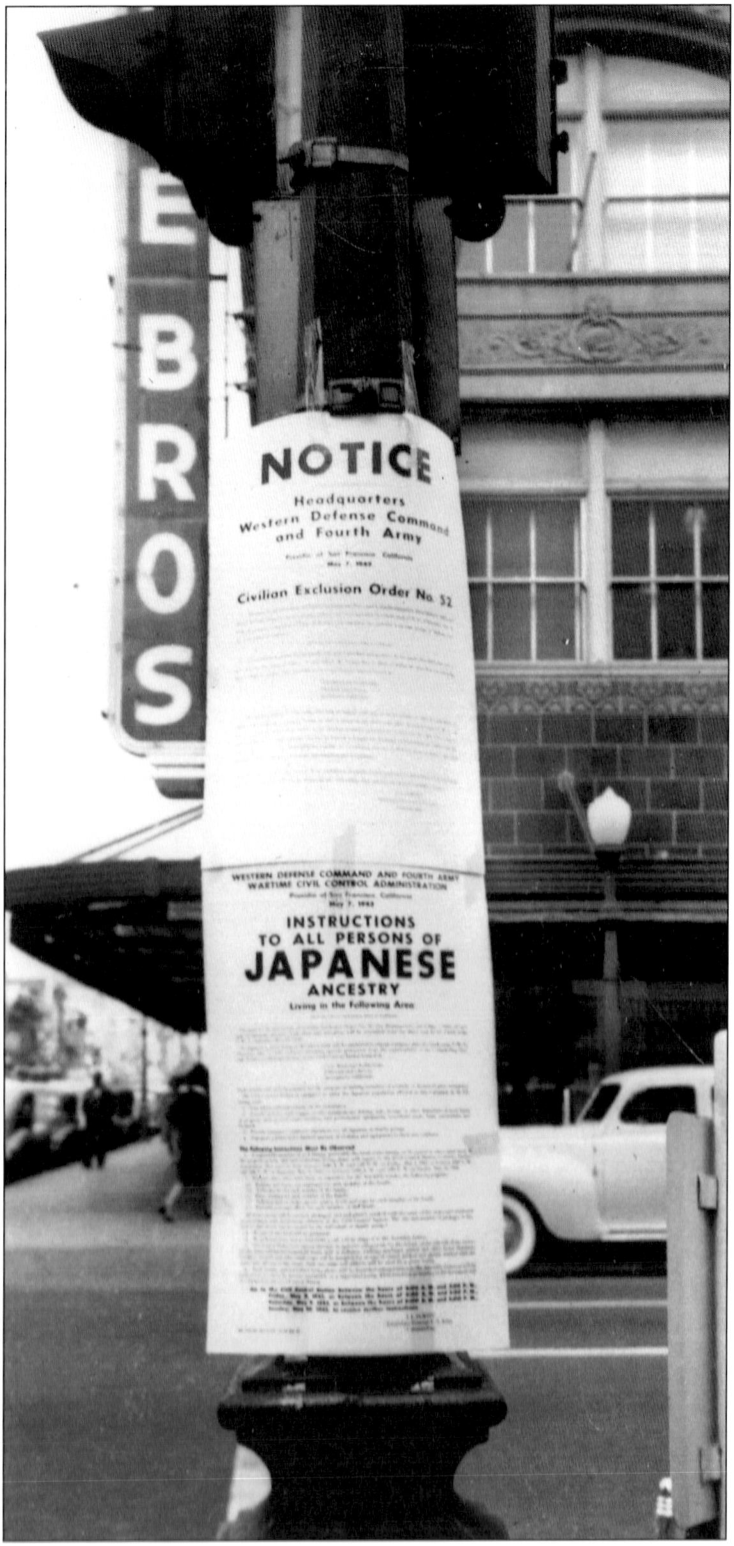

Anti-Japanese sentiment in California and Sacramento resulted in the segregation of the business and residential community, as well as many schools and health services. This led to the establishment of Japanese schools, banks, hospitals, and churches in the downtown area bounded by Second, Fifth, L, and O Streets, known as "Japantown." After the December 7, 1941, attack on Pearl Harbor, hatred and hysteria were inflamed by unsubstantiated rumors and fears of sabotage and threats to national security. By May 1942, all West Coast residents of Japanese descent, two-thirds of whom were American citizens, were ordered to evacuate and were sent to relocation centers for the duration of the war. Sacramento's 3,000 members of the Japanese community were sent to Walerga Assembly Center, about 10 miles northeast of downtown, while they waited to be shipped to camps. Here the "Evacuation Notice to those of Japanese Ancestry" is posted at the corner of Ninth and K Streets on May 8, 1942. (Courtesy Eugene Hepting Collection.)

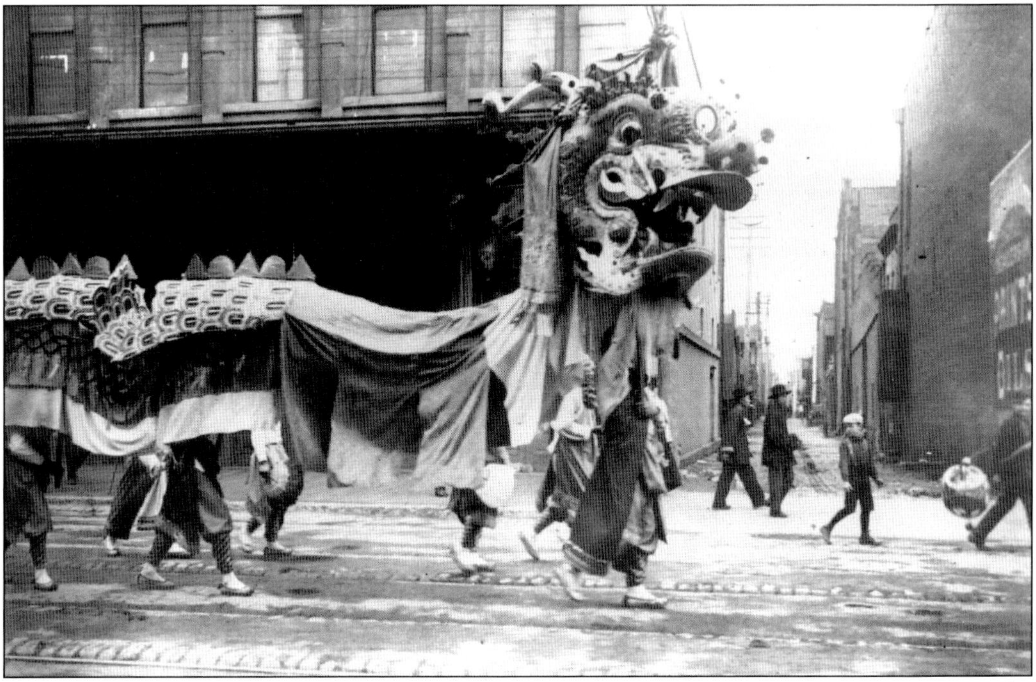

Pictured is a Chinese dragon in a parade at Second Street between I and J Streets during the "Grand Electric Carnival" on Admission Day, September 9, 1895. The celebration heralded the transmission of hydroelectric power from the new Folsom Power House to Sacramento. Many of Sacramento's Chinese community worked on the dam, canal, and the powerhouse of the completed electrical system. (Courtesy Eugene Hepting Collection.)

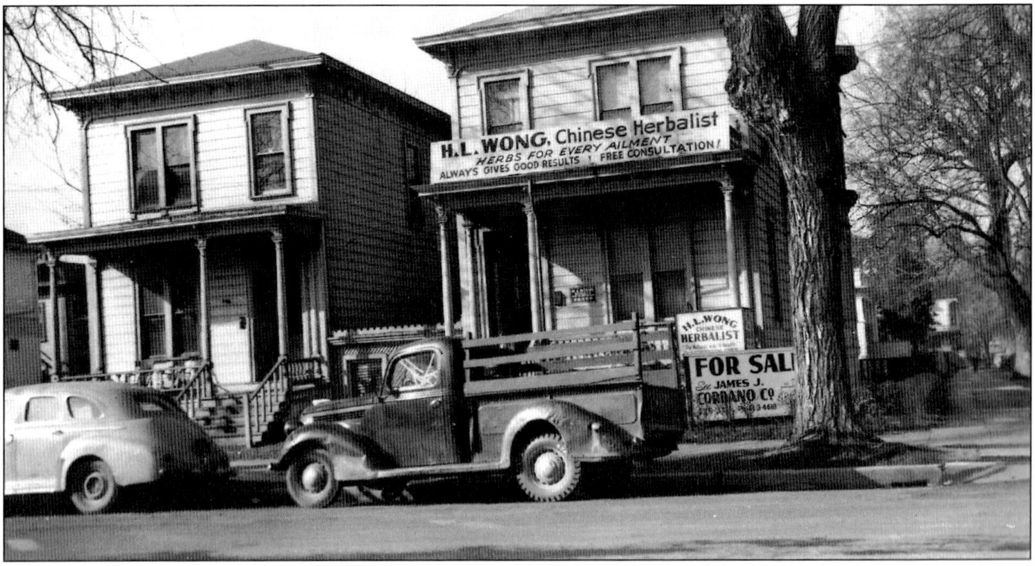

This 1950 photograph shows the home and herb shop of H. L. Wong at the southwest corner of Seventh and N Streets. Traditional Chinese medicine, which included the use of herbs for many diverse ailments, was an intrinsic and important aspect of the Chinese community. However, licensing for this practice was not available to Wong, who consequently put the building up for sale. (Courtesy Eugene Hepting Collection.)

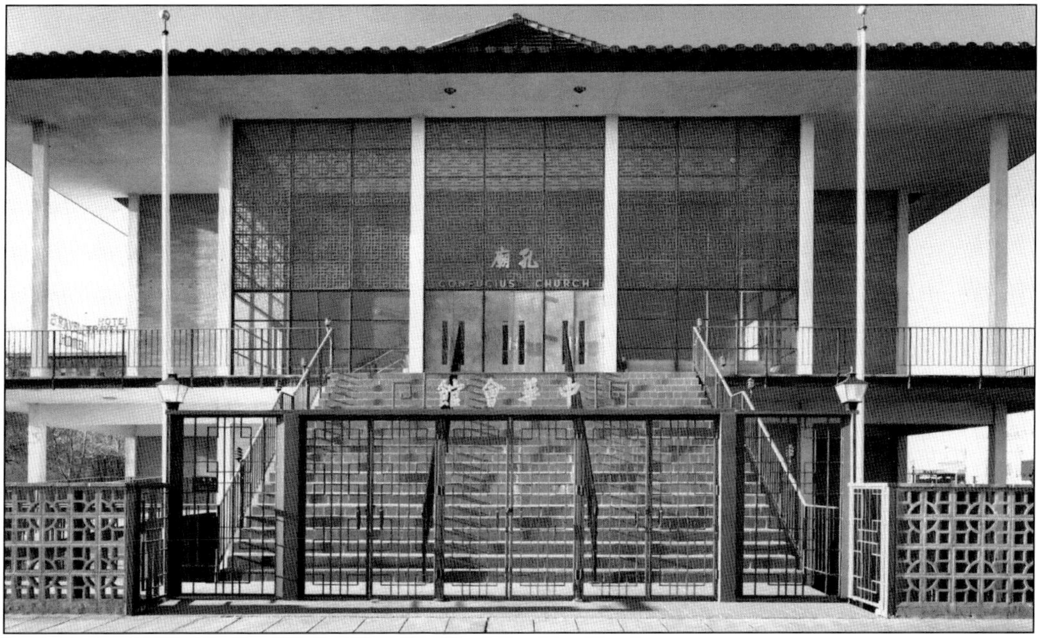

The Confucius Church was built in 1959 and located in Sacramento's Chinatown at the southeast corner of Fourth and I Streets. A project of the Chinese Benevolent Association, the three-story church and community center contained a 700-seat auditorium, seven classrooms, and a gym. While most of the Chinese community's children attended the Lincoln School at Fourth and Q Streets, they also attended Chinese language classes at this site. (Courtesy James E. Henley Collection.)

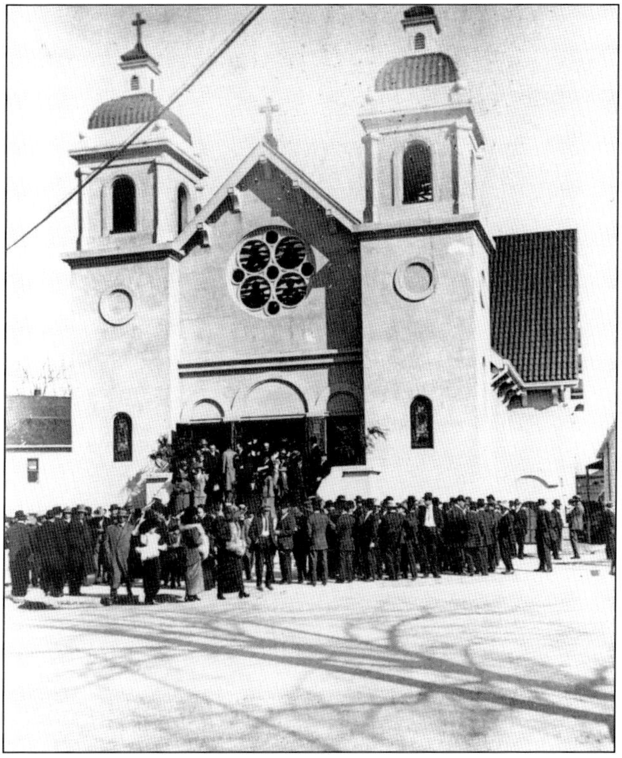

St. Elizabeth's Portuguese National Church, the oldest Portuguese National church in the West, was organized in 1909. The Portuguese community attended other local Catholic churches, but they wanted their own church with services in Portuguese and appealed to Bishop Grace to appoint Joao V. Azevedo as its pastor. Consequently, St. Elizabeth's was built on donated land on Twelfth and S Streets. (Courtesy Sacramento Portuguese Historical and Cultural Society Collection.)

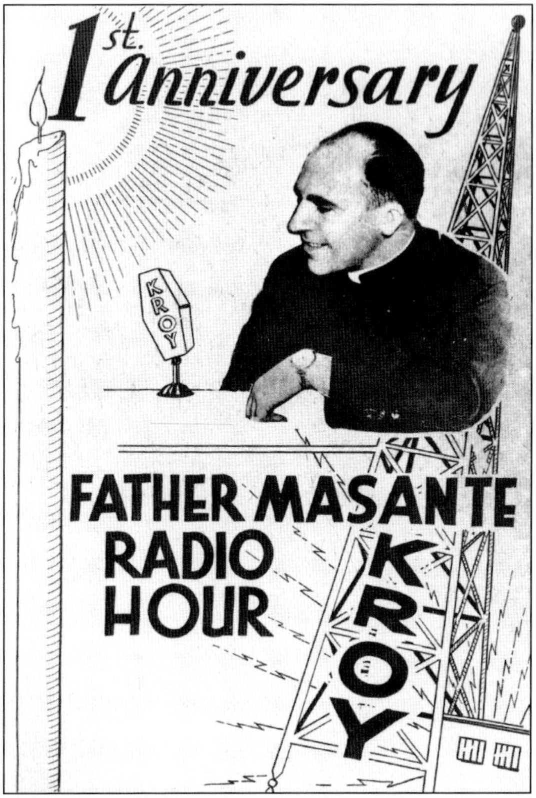

Fr. Silvio Masante came to Sacramento in 1934 as the Pacific Coast correspondent for *L'osservatore Romano,* the Vatican City daily newspaper. Masante was very active at St. Mary's in the 1930s. Among numerous projects that ministered to the parishioners was a weekly hour-long radio show on local station KROY. (Courtesy Sacramento Ethnic Survey Collection.)

Established in 1907, St. Mary's was a welcoming social and cultural center for non-English speaking immigrants from Italy and Portugal. This photograph shows participants of a first communion at the church located at 1915 Seventh Street in the 1920s. The church was originally located at 818 N Street and moved in 1946 to Fifty-eighth and M Streets. (Courtesy Sacramento Ethnic Survey Collection.)

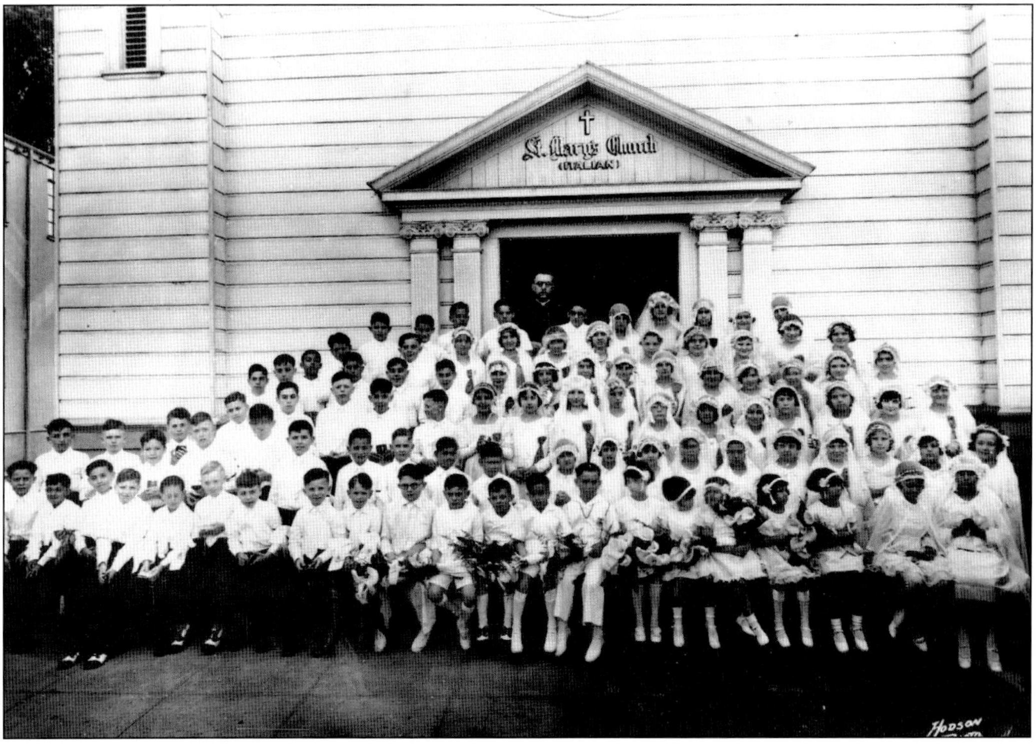

Six

COMMERCE

TRADING FOR A FUTURE

BY DYLAN MCDONALD

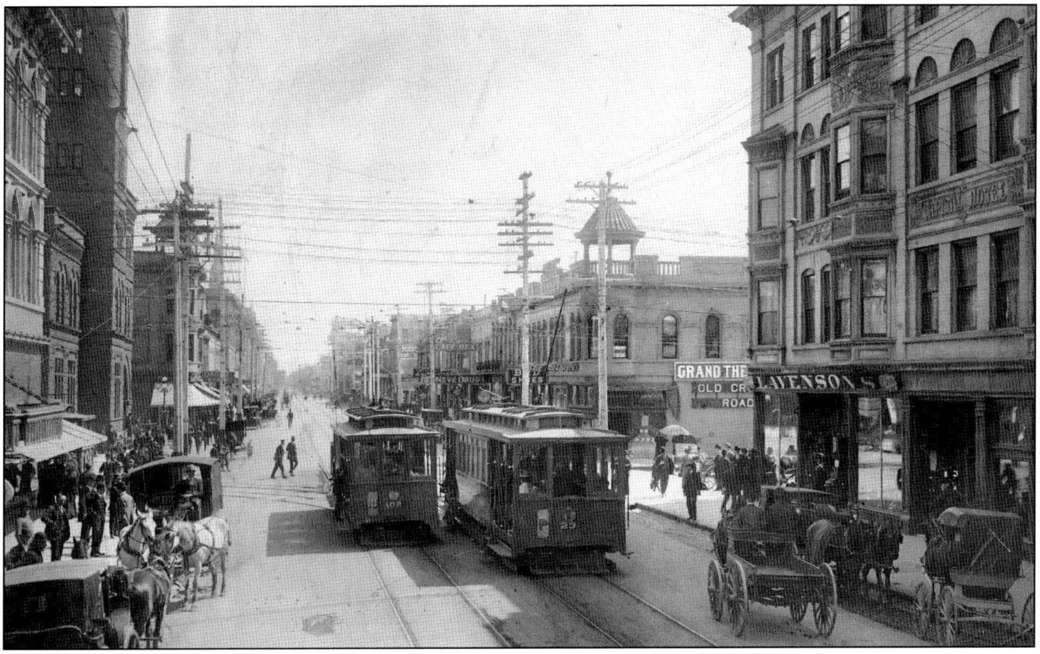

The birthplace to many highly successful business ventures, Sacramento offered a unique set of circumstances to those who decided to open shop after a grueling trip west. Often hindered by the elements, early Sacramentans willed their city to live after fire and water threatened—after all, too much money was to be made. Sam Brannan, Collis Huntington, and Leland Stanford are names well known because of the opportunities they seized in the emerging city. Sacramento's entrepreneurs were ever pushing for innovation, and while most failed, many were frequently rewarded for their risk-taking. The Sacramento River's course ensured the city would be a major supply point for the forty-niners. The completion of the railroad over the Sierra Nevada Mountains made certain Sacramento would remain an important transportation hub. Communication flowed through the city, as did agricultural goods. Secure as the seat of government, Sacramento drew on another source to drive its economic engine. This scene looking east along Sacramento's K Street corridor near the intersection of Seventh Street, *c.* 1910, is indicative of a vibrant business district. (Courtesy Eleanor McClatchy Collection.)

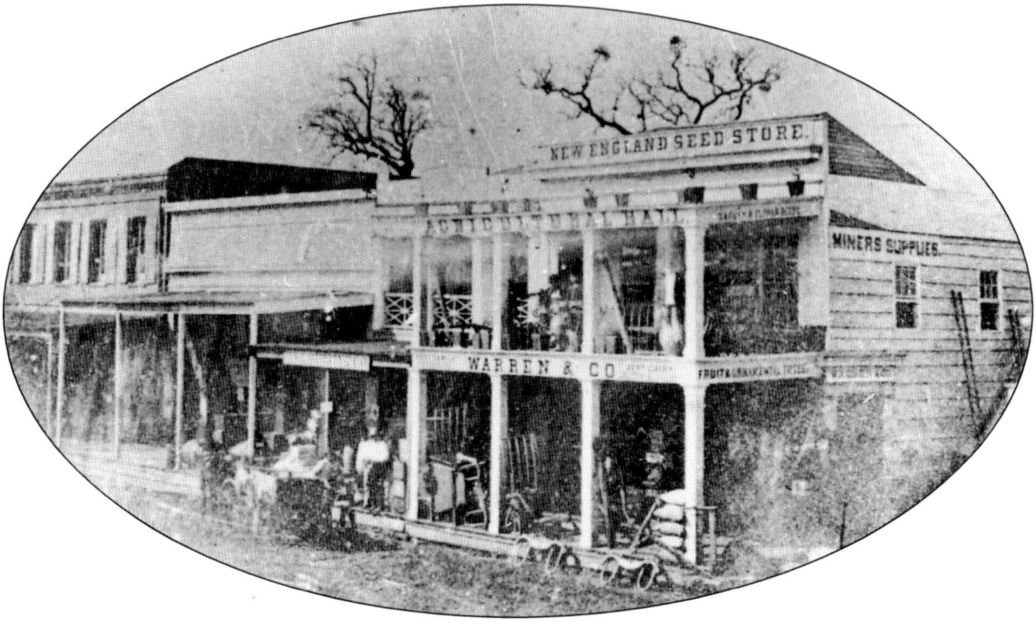

Leaving the mining at Mormon Bar behind him, James Lloyd Lafayette Franklin Warren opened the New England Feed Store on J Street between Front and Second Streets. The store fell victim to the 1852 fire, but was quickly rebuilt and operating several weeks later. Warren is credited with bringing the camellia flower to Sacramento and being the founder of the annual state fair. (Courtesy Tiera B. Franz Collection.)

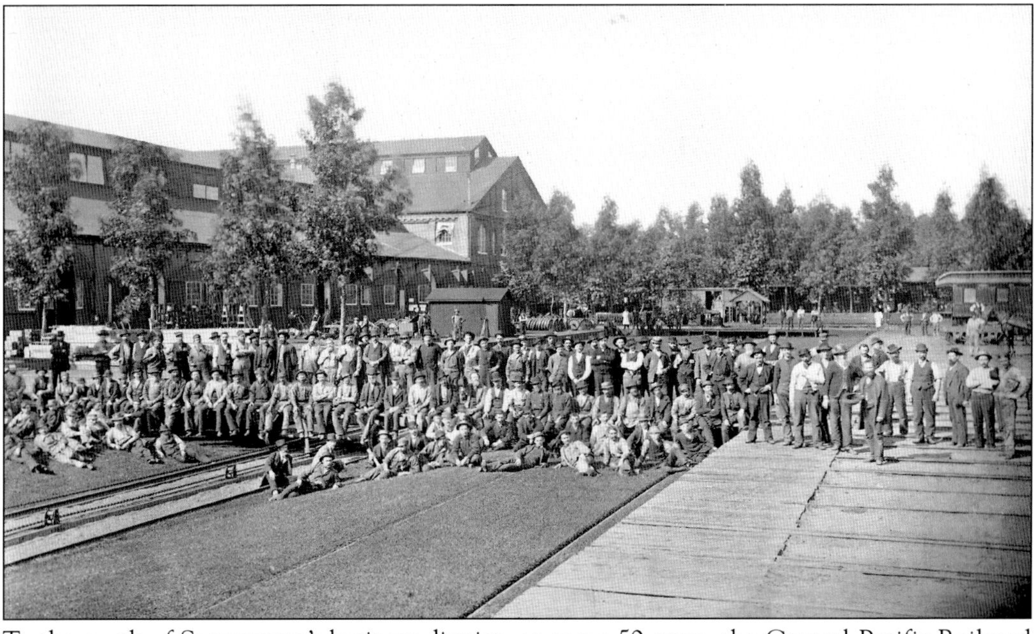

To the north of Sacramento's business district, on some 50 acres, the Central Pacific Railroad (CPRR), conquerors of the Sierra Nevada Mountains, built a large railroad works near its depot. Employing over 1,200 men with a payroll of $1.5 million in 1883, the shops built locomotives and all types of railcars. This photograph by O.V. Lange, from October 1882, is of employees of the CPRR car works. (Courtesy Julius Frieseke Collection.)

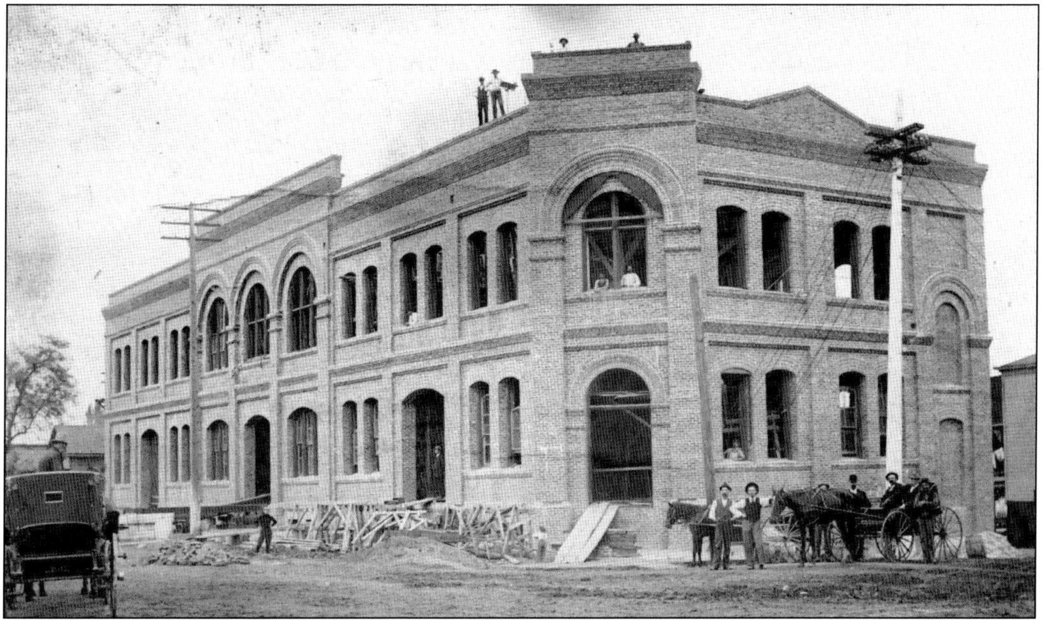

Work stops for this photograph of the Sacramento Electric Power and Light Company station at Sixth and H Streets around 1894. The building, later known as Station A, cost $10,500 and served as the distribution point for the electrical current flowing 22 miles from the Folsom Power House along the American River. As the electricity began to flow on July 13, 1895, city leaders hoped it would attract new manufacturing businesses. (Courtesy Audrey Shore Collection.)

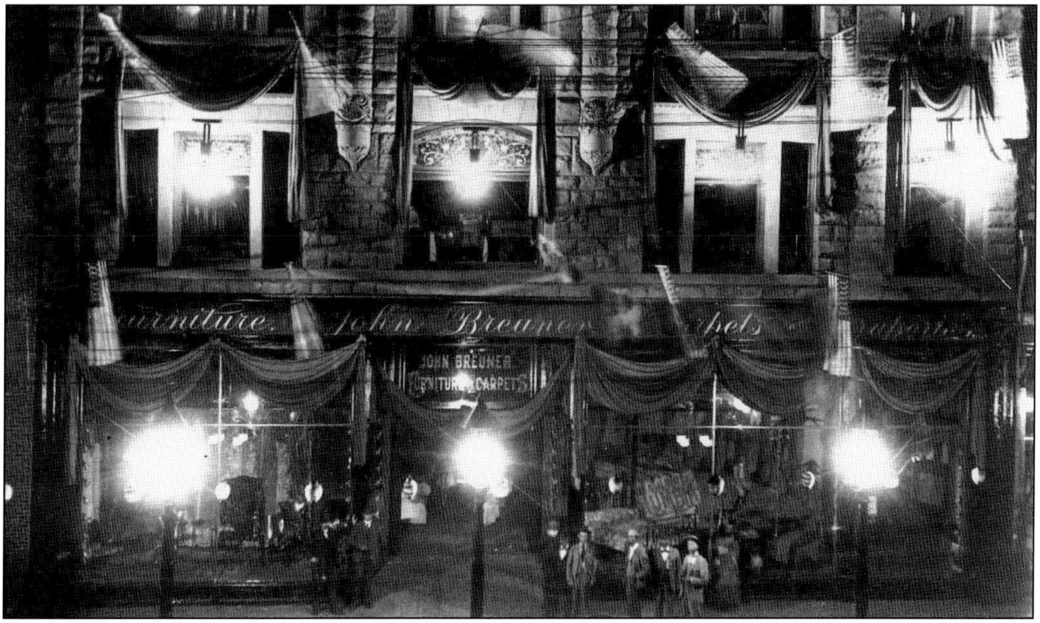

Decorations adorn the John Breuner Building at 604 K Street during the "Grand Electric Carnival" on September 9, 1895, a citywide commemoration of the transmission of electric power from Folsom. A landmark department store, Breuner's would delight shoppers with its holiday window displays for some 40 years. The once prosperous Northern California chain closed in 2004 after nearly 148 years in operation. (Courtesy Sacramento Public Library Collection.)

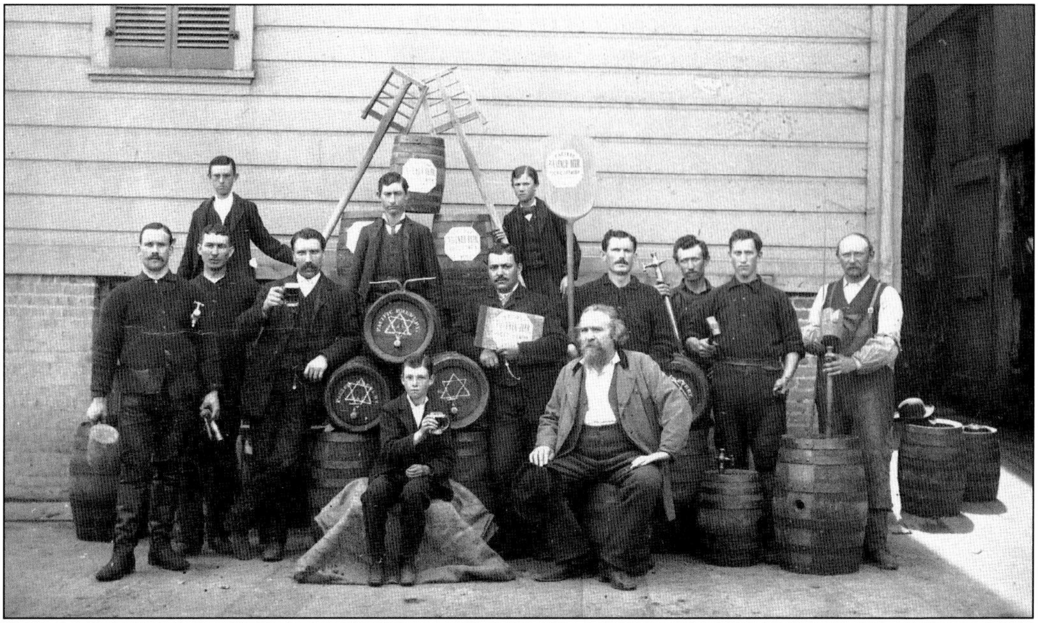

Employees of the Pacific Brewery Company pose with their beer-making paraphernalia and product, *c.* 1890s. Established in 1858 by Fred Knauer, it operated until the turn of the century at the southwest corner of Ninth and P Streets. The Sacramento Brewery, the city's first brewer, was founded in 1849 and produced its first beer the next year. By 1878, eight breweries in the area were producing some 530,000 gallons annually. (Courtesy John Queirolo Collection.)

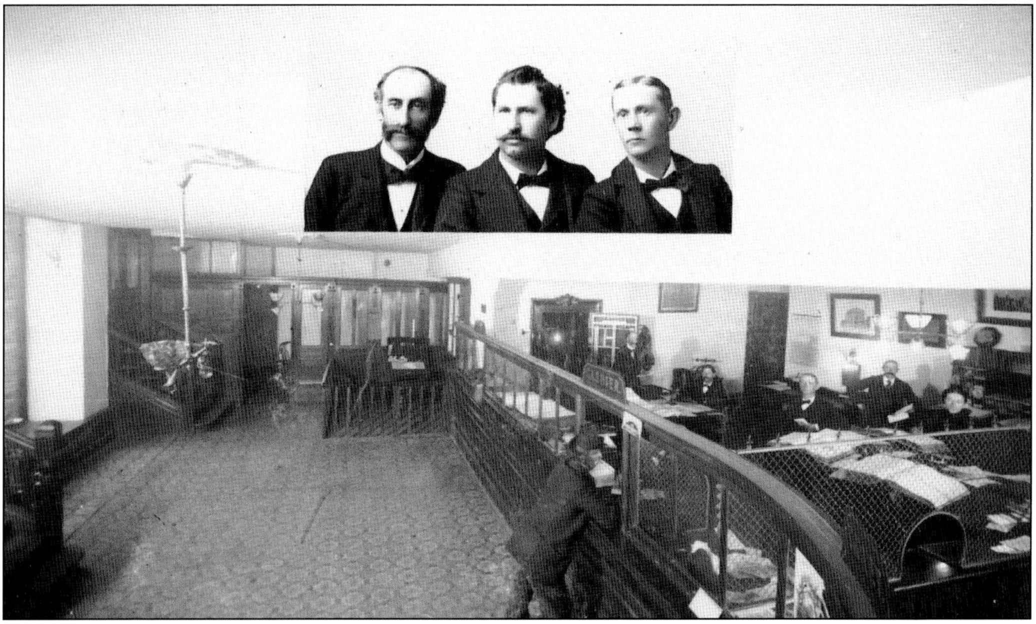

Advertised as the "leading real estate and insurance firm of Sacramento," Curtis, Carmichael and Brand occupied the first floor of the California State Bank Building at Fourth and J Streets. This 1896 photograph of the firm's office includes an inset of the three partners, M. John Curtis, Daniel W. Carmichael, and George Samuel Brand. Carmichael later served as Sacramento mayor in 1917 and developed the nearby area of Carmichael. (Courtesy Frank Christy Collection.)

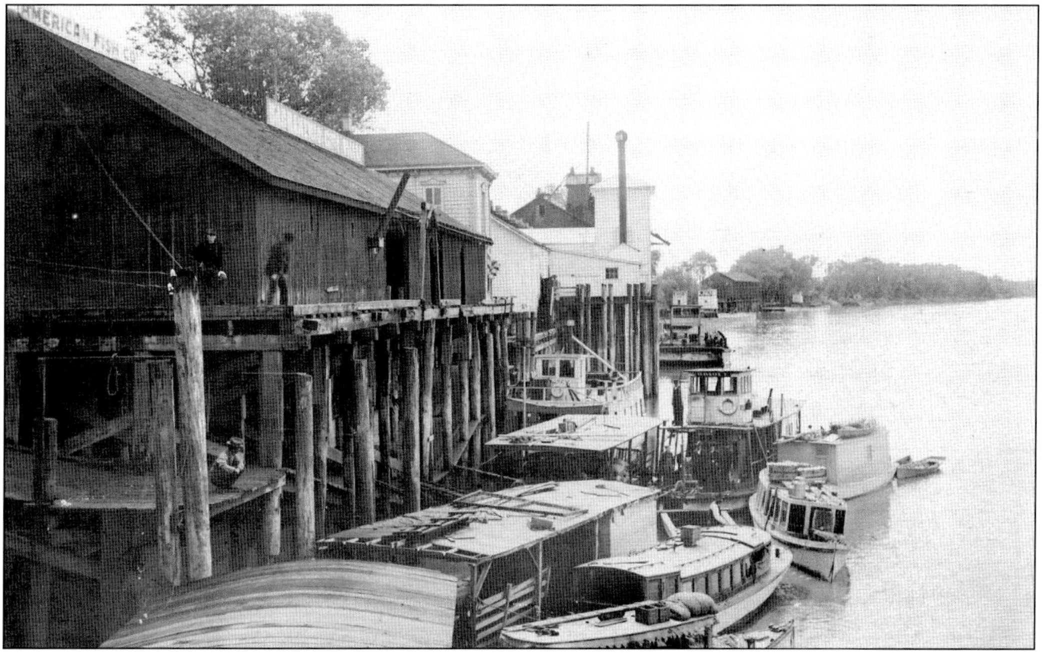

The Sacramento River provided a natural transportation corridor for goods, and the numerous wharves and warehouses along its banks are a testament to role the river played in developing the city. This c. 1902 photograph shows the industrial look of the area. Numerous boats are moored below the City Wharf and Warehouse, with the American Fish Company leasing space in the block-long structure on Front Street between M and N Streets. (Courtesy Eleanor McClatchy Collection.)

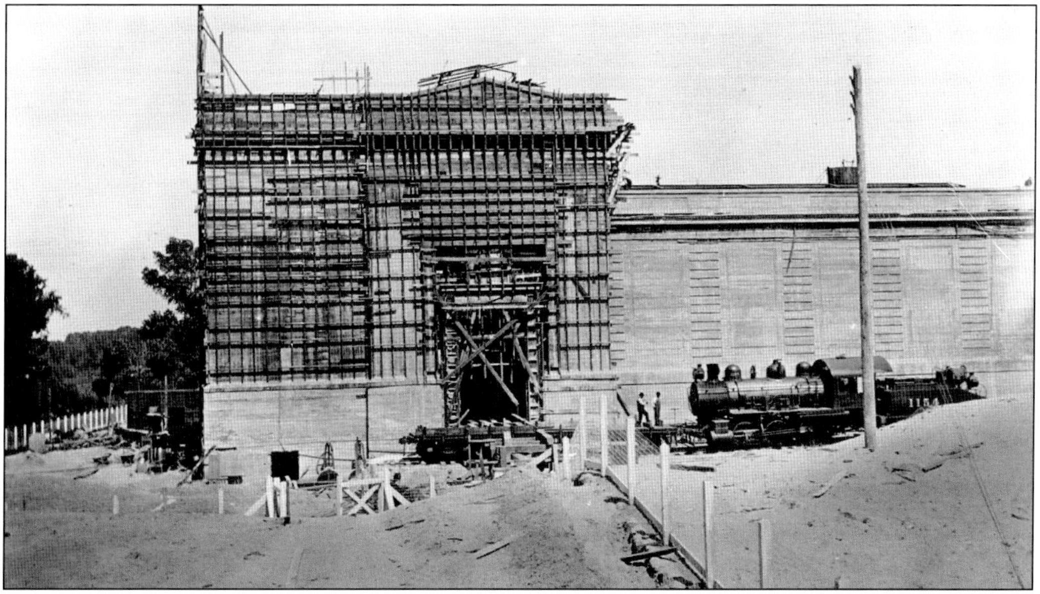
With the growing demand for electricity, Pacific Gas and Electric built a large steam-generated power plant along the riverfront just south of the confluence. Work progresses in this June 1912 photograph on the walls of the generator wing, while the first indications of a smokestack above the boiler room are visible. The plant was retired in November 1954, and the empty building awaits redevelopment today. (Courtesy Bob McCabe Collection.)

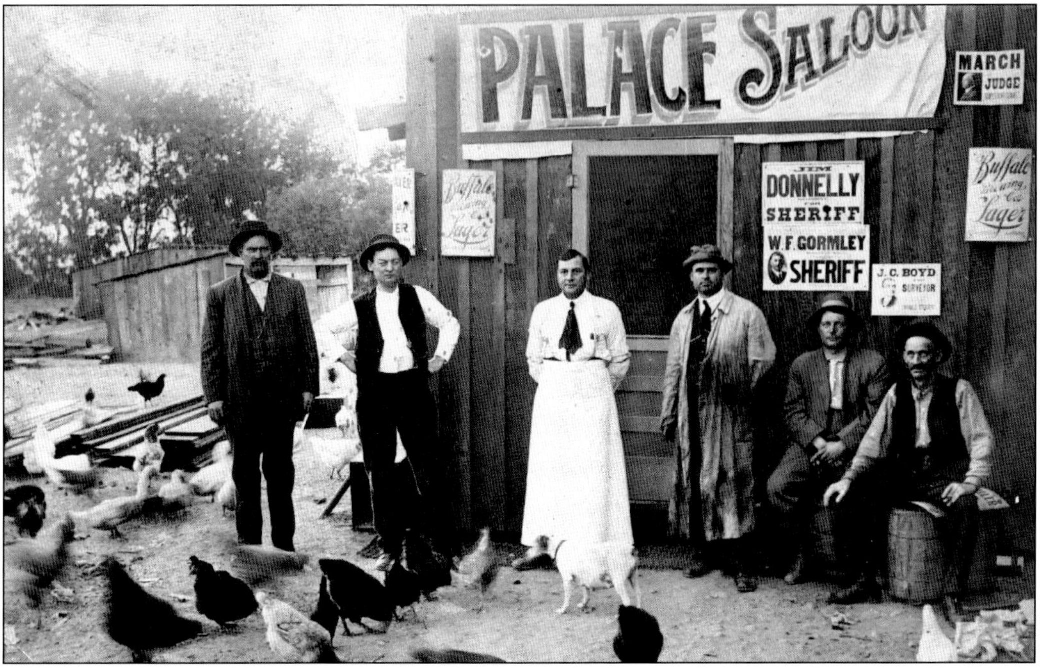

Due to high water along the American River, the primitive Palace Saloon was forced to relocate to higher ground near today's North Twelfth Street and Richards Boulevard. Taken in 1914, the photograph captures the peculiar scene in front of the watering hole, including several campaign posters for the upcoming local election. The November election would eventually see W. F. Gormley elected sheriff. Will Hayden, second from the left, was the saloon's proprietor. (Courtesy Barry Wackford Collection.)

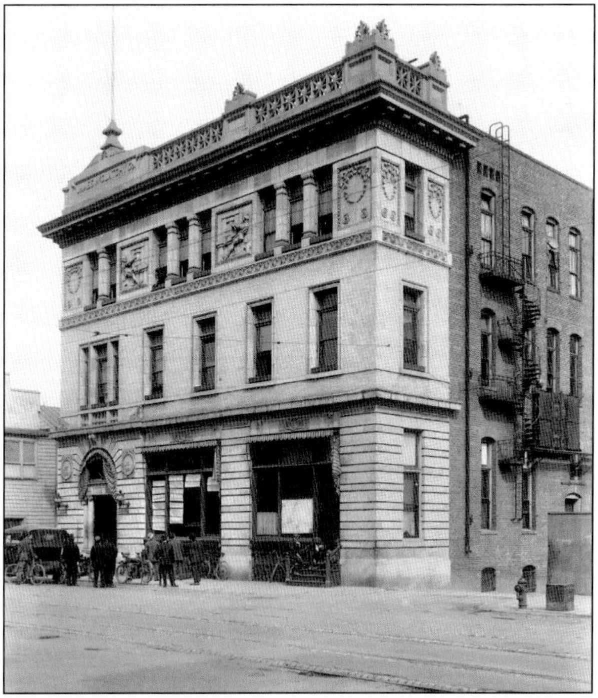

A group gathers outside the *Sacramento Bee* building at 911 Seventh Street to read the posted headlines in this March 1915 photograph. The first edition of the newspaper, then the *Daily Bee*, came off the press on February 3, 1857. Still publishing daily, the paper has played an active fourth-estate role throughout its history, often siding with progressive causes in the city and region. (Courtesy Eleanor McClatchy Collection.)

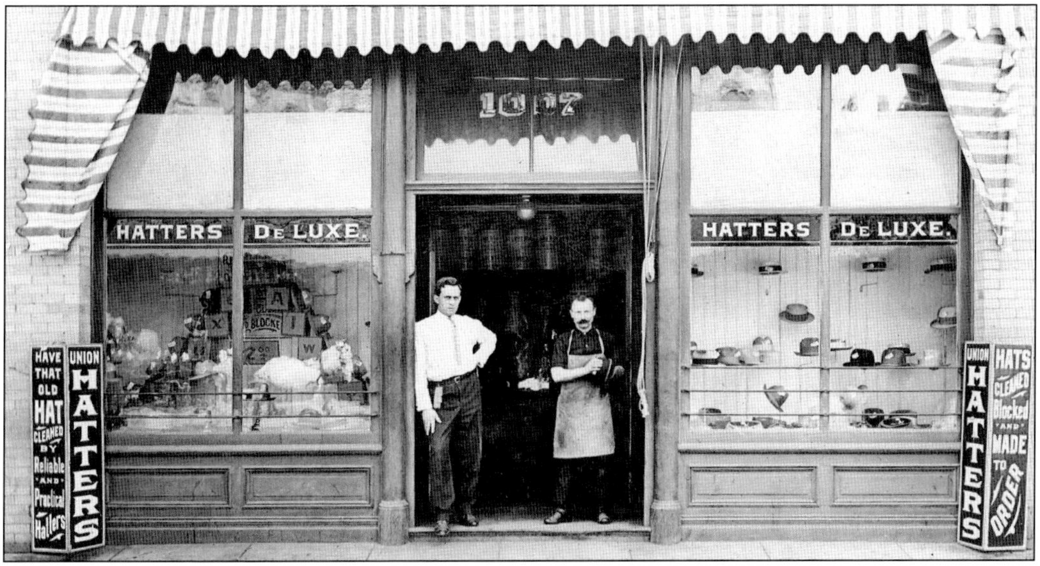

From an era when hats were an integral part of men's attire, Hatters De Luxe for a time had two locations in Sacramento; one on Seventh Street and another was this storefront at 1007 Third Street. With an advertising slogan of "Always $2" for a hat, this c. 1912 photograph is likely of the two business partners, John Wegesser and H. W. Thompson. (Courtesy Phyllis Hill Azevedo Gemar Collection.)

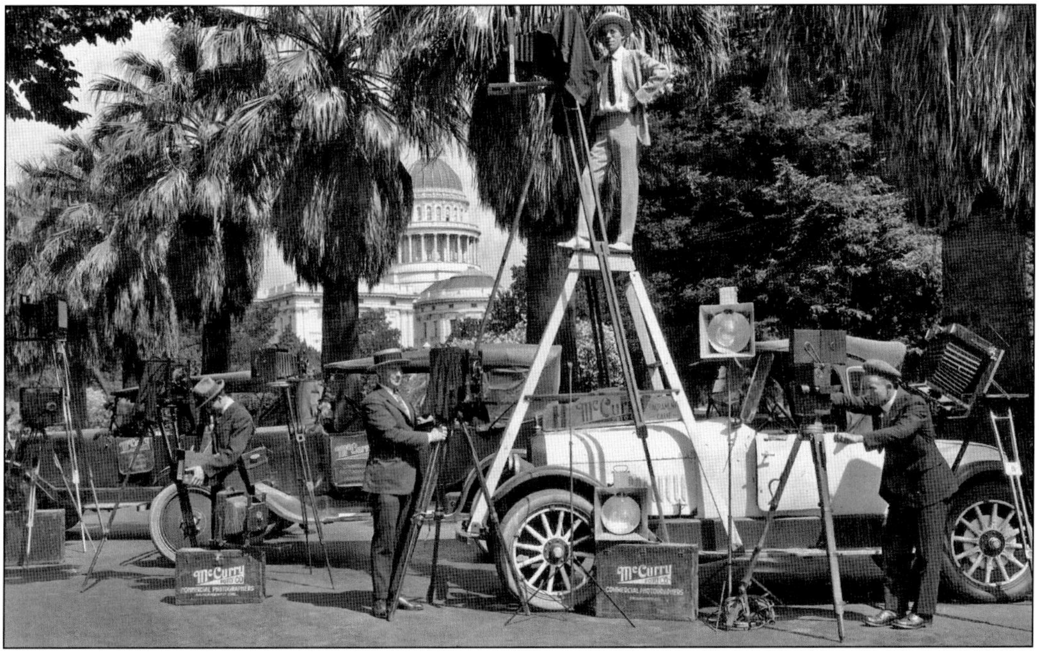

Harold J. McCurry founded the McCurry Foto Company in 1908. The native Pennsylvanian learned photography in San Francisco before coming to Sacramento in 1906. Prominent in business and political circles, McCurry served as the city's postmaster for 12 years. Here McCurry photographers pose with their equipment on the capitol grounds for a company promotional in 1924. At its height, the company had 10 stores between San Francisco and Reno. (Courtesy McCurry Company Collection.)

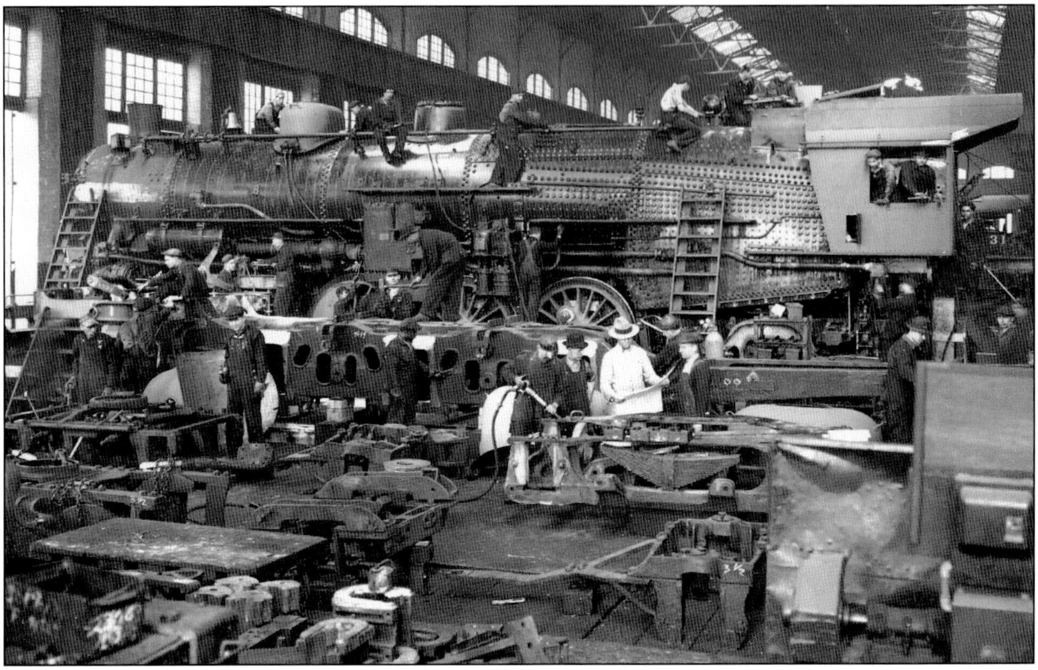

The Southern Pacific Shops at the company's rail yard was one of the largest employers in the city. This *c.* 1925 photograph, taken in the Southern Pacific erecting shop, shows some 30 employees building one of the company's 4-8-2 locomotives, likely No. 4357. The last locomotive came off the lines in 1937, and the shop's focus shifted to maintaining the larger diesel engines. By 1999, after the merger with Union Pacific, the shops closed. (Courtesy Sacramento Metropolitan Chamber of Commerce Collection.)

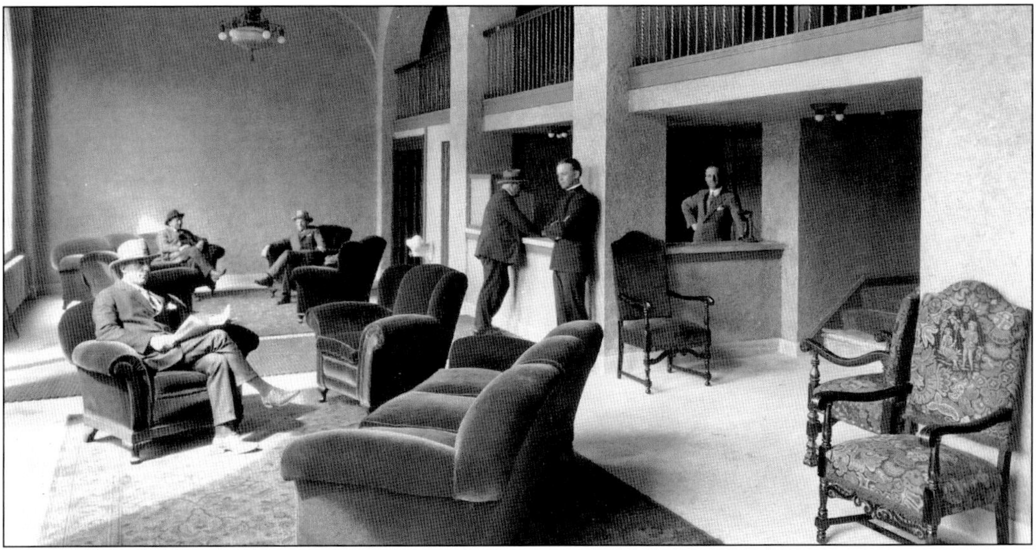

The Hotel Berry, seen here in 1926 with its early mission-style lobby, was advertised as a "class-A type" building. The six-story structure cost around $300,000 to build and had 117 rooms and a garage annex. Located at the northwest corner of Eighth and L Streets, it was once part of the Berry Hotels System owned by B. S. and Harry Berry of San Francisco. (Courtesy Sacramento Metropolitan Chamber of Commerce Collection.)

The California State Life Insurance Building (also known as the Cal West building), pictured here around the late 1920s, ushered Sacramento into the era of skyscrapers. Opening in 1924, the insurance company had already paid the $1 million price tag before moving into its new headquarters. Built at the corner of Tenth and J Streets, the high-rise is still one of the city's architectural gems with its mixed classical and Renaissance style. (Courtesy Norwood Silsbee Collection.)

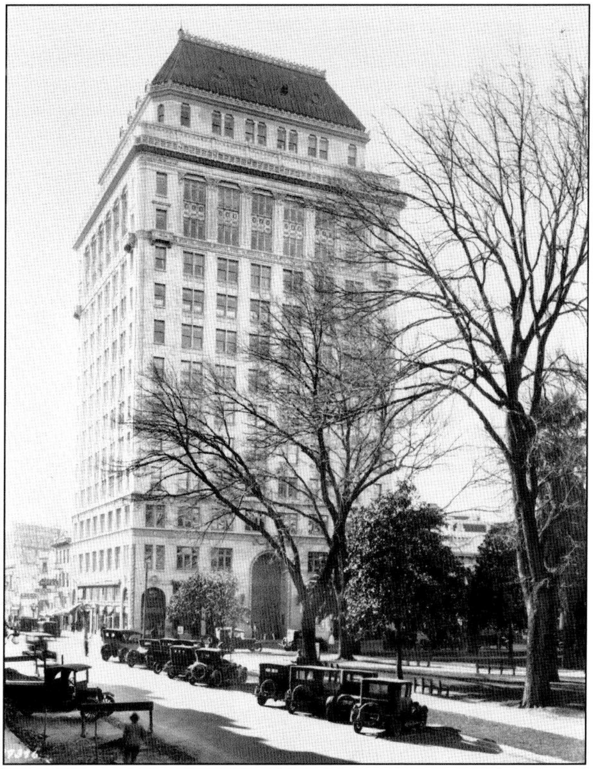

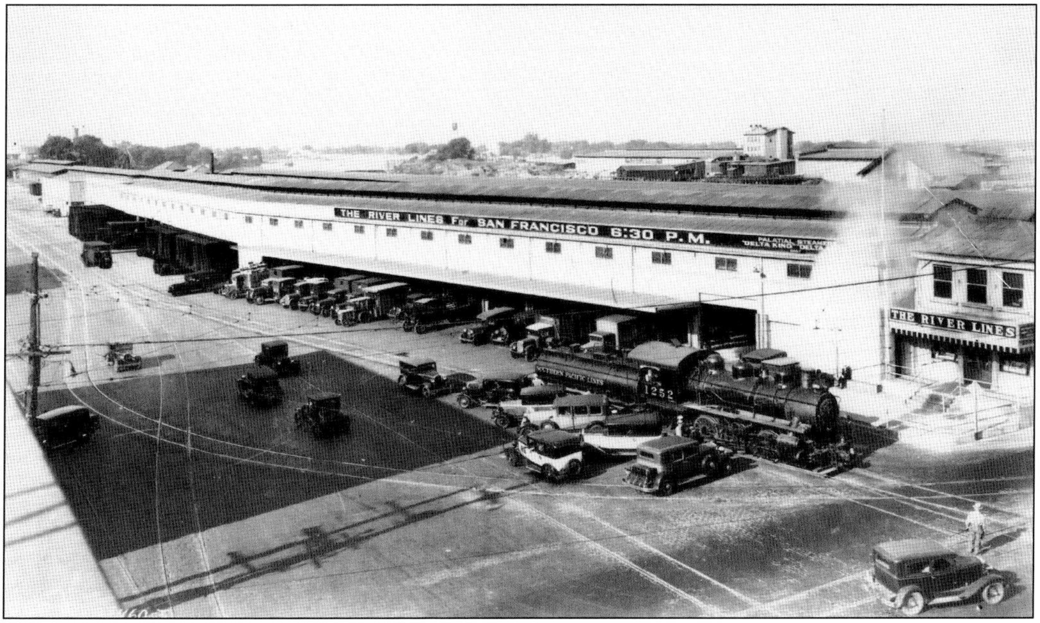

A busy waterfront is evident in this c. 1934, southwesterly-looking photograph from Front and M Streets that show the River Lines dockage point. This city-owned wharf was rebuilt in the 1920s to increase storage space and the movement of goods. At least 17 freight vehicles and a Southern Pacific engine are visible in the image, along with several taxis waiting near the passenger terminal. (Courtesy City of Sacramento Collection.)

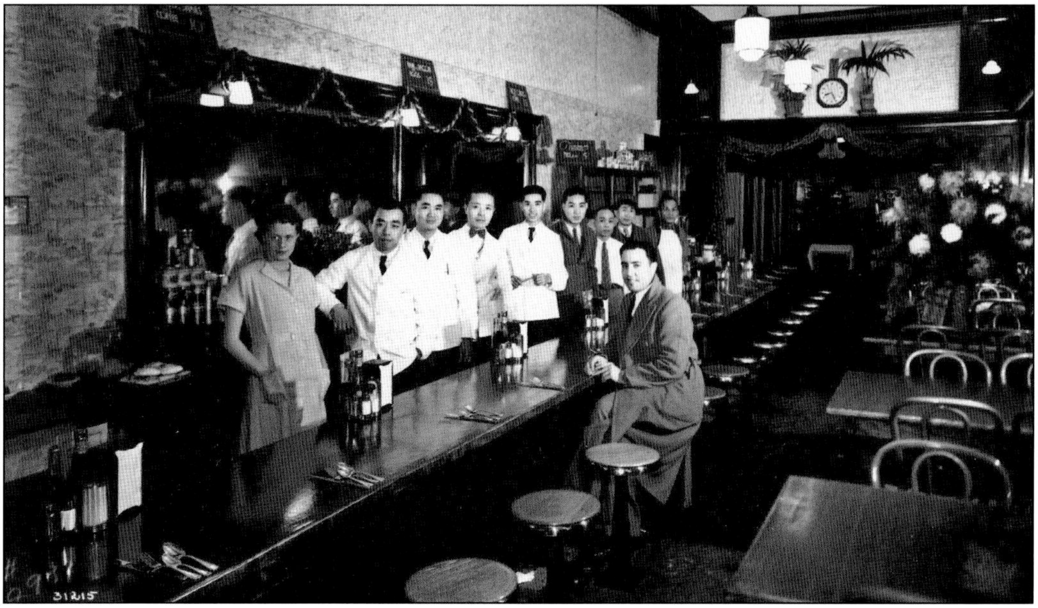

This c. 1936 photograph captures the staff and interior of the Sincere Café, once located at 315 K Street. The café's menu included a slice of pie for 5¢, donuts and coffee for 10¢, and hotcakes and coffee for 15¢. As redevelopment projects reshaped downtown in the 1950s, the café closed and the building fell victim to the wrecking ball. (Courtesy Sacramento Valley Photographic Survey Collection.)

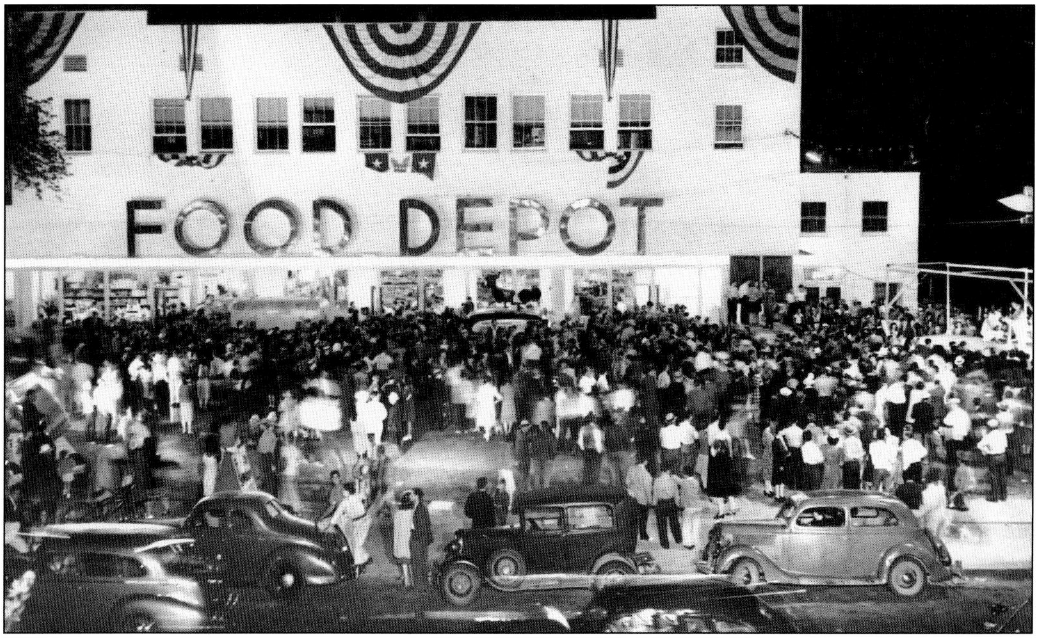

Opening day of business for the Food Depot on June 13, 1941, brought out many Sacramentans to visit what was advertised as a "sparkling market" with "thrilling displays." Customers were also told of the parking space for over 150 cars, an indication of the growing place of the automobile in American social life. Located at 1120 H Street, the building formerly housed an interurban electric railroad station. (Courtesy Frank Christy Collection.)

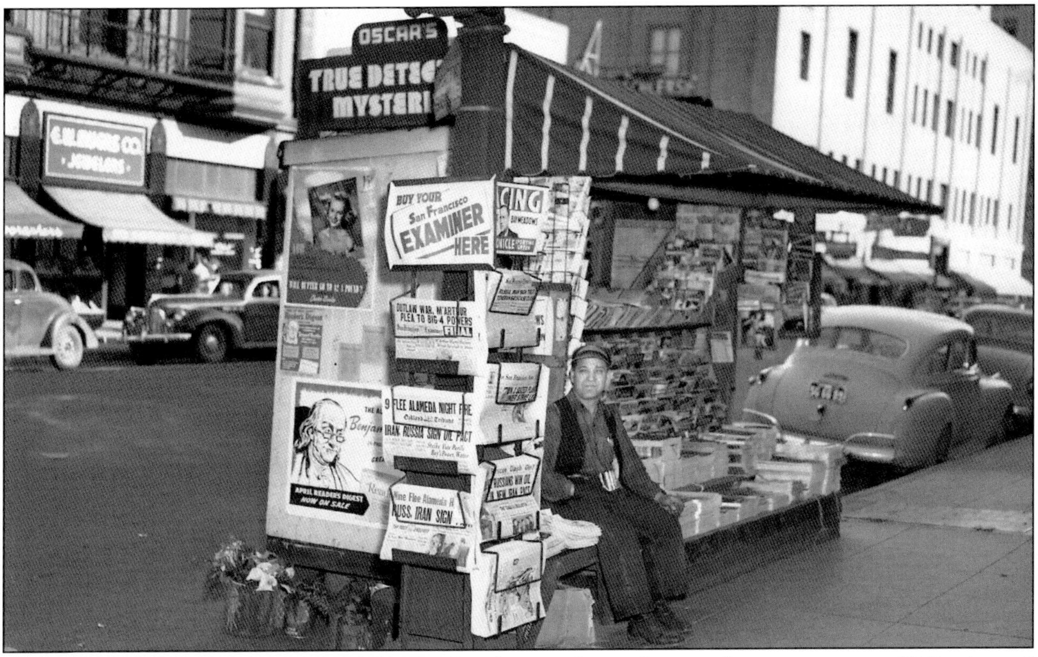

News dealer Oscar Parisi sits at his curbside stand on the southwest corner of Ninth and J Streets in April 1946. Offering a full complement of magazines, paperbacks, Northern California newspapers, and even flowers, Oscar's kept customers up to date with the latest post–World War II news. (Courtesy Eleanor McClatchy Collection.)

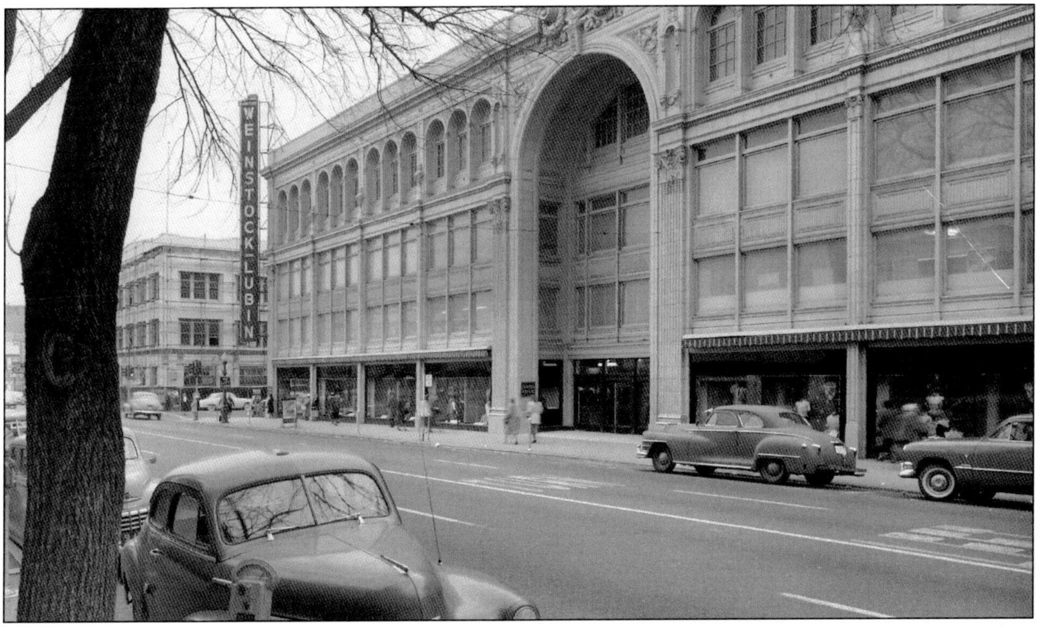

Opening in 1874, Weinstock-Lubin founders Harris Weinstock and brother-in-law David Lubin set prices on all their merchandise, thereby avoiding the haggling that was the common practice of the time. As Weinstock's grew, the business changed downtown locations several times; this early 1950s photograph shows their Twelfth and K Streets department store. The larger Macy's Corporation bought out the company in 1996. (Courtesy Weinstock's Collection.)

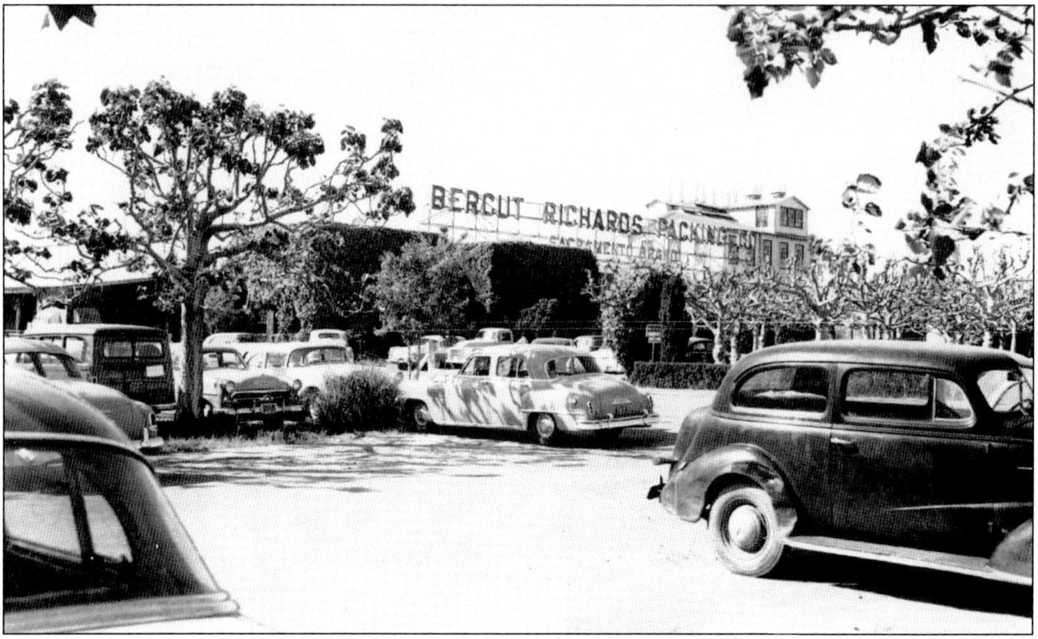

The Bercut Richards Packing Company, along with other large canneries like Del Monte and Libby, McNeil, and Libby, were once a vital part of the city's economy. Located at North Seventh and Richards Boulevard, Bercut Richards canned and froze California fruits and vegetables for distribution across the country. By the early 1980s, each of these businesses had folded due to changing technology and the nation's eating habits. (Courtesy Franz Dionne Collection.)

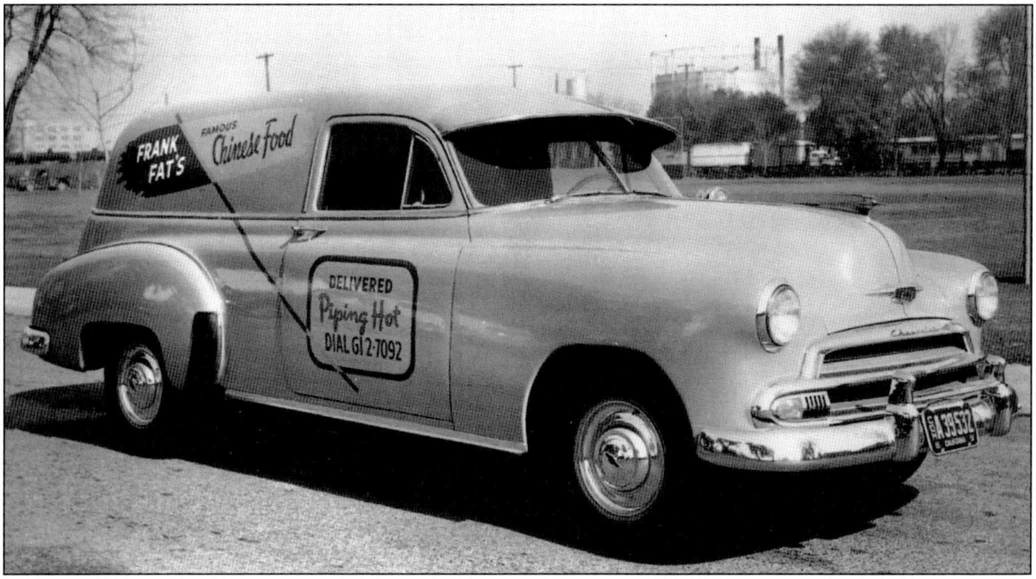

A once penniless immigrant from Canton, China, Frank Fat opened his first restaurant in 1939 at Eighth and L Streets. It soon established itself as a favorite of legislators and became legendary as California's "third house," where bills were drafted over meals. Having since expanded to multiple locations and offering delivery, the family-run business is prominent in community affairs with its foundation and annual Pacific Rim Street Festival in Old Sacramento. (Courtesy City of Sacramento Collection.)

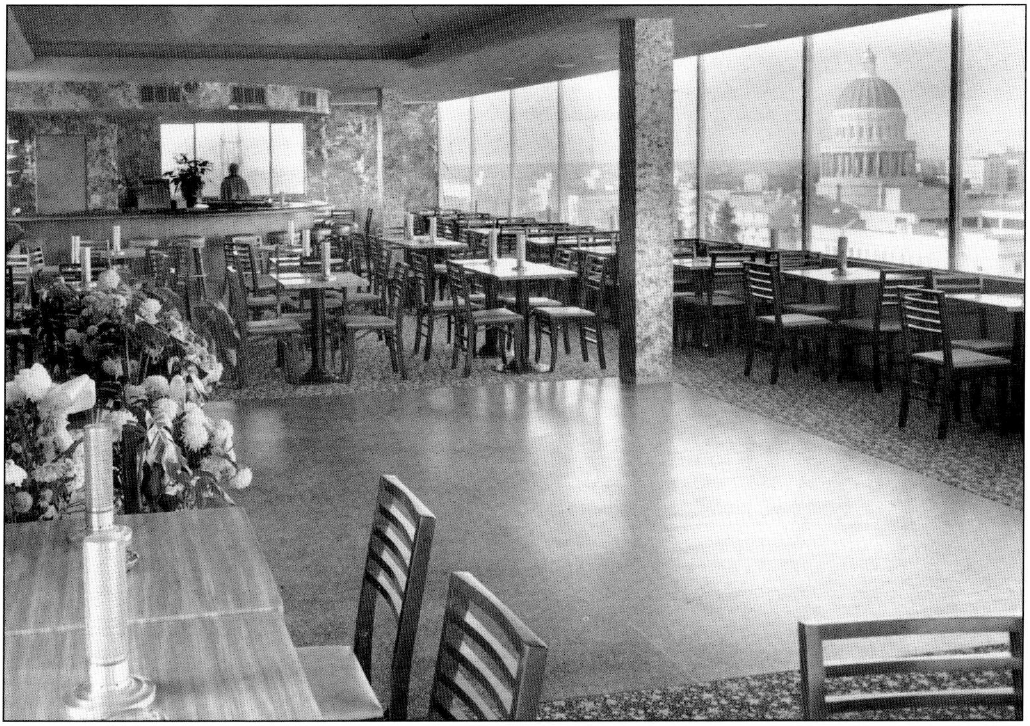

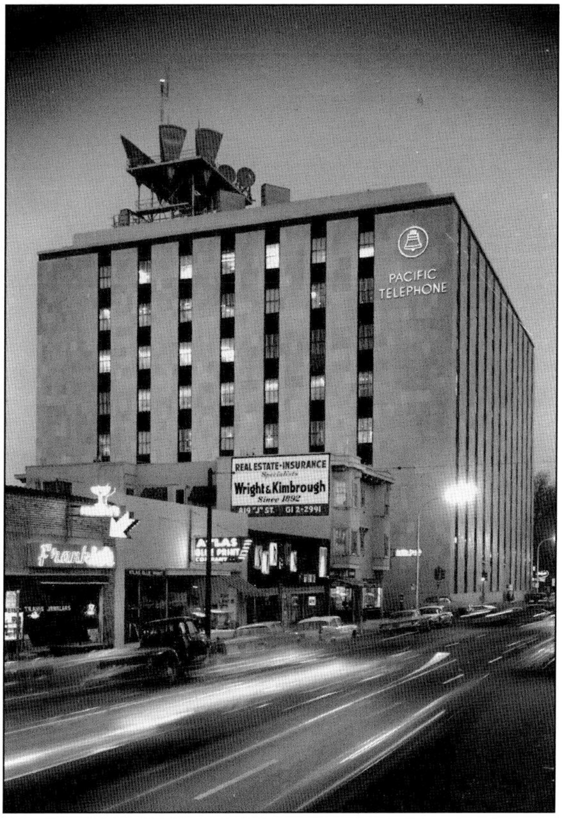

The modern Hotel El Mirador offered spectacular views of Sacramento from its fourteenth-floor Sky Room. Opening in late 1957 at Thirteenth and N Streets, the $1.8 million, 15-story hotel had 160 rooms, all facing Capitol Park. Calling itself the hotel of tomorrow, the establishment offered a television and recorded music in every room, air conditioning, two pools, and underwater ballet performances twice a week. (Courtesy Frank Christy Collection.)

Dusk enshrouds the Pacific Telephone Company's building at 1407 J Street in 1962. The development of communications has helped bridge Sacramento's remoteness—first with the telegraph on October 19, 1853, then the Pony Express's arrival on April 13, 1860, and finally the first telephone in 1878. The Sacramento Telephonic Exchange, founded in 1880, would merge with another company, changing its name in 1906 to Pacific Telephone and Telegraph Company. (Courtesy McCurry Company Collection.)

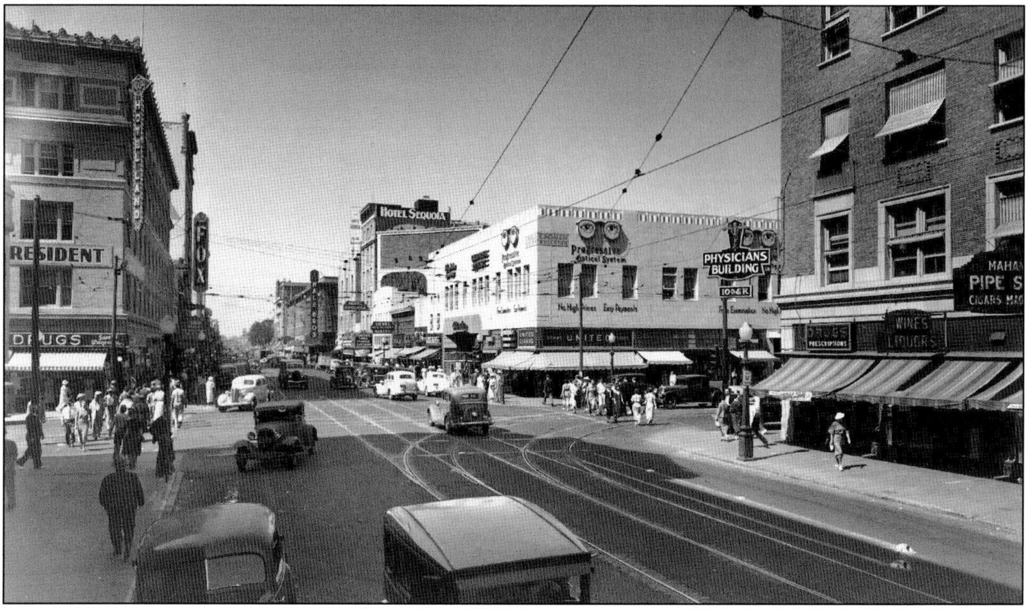

Since the city's founding in 1849, K Street quickly emerged as the heart of Sacramento's business district. In this September 1936 photograph looking west from just before the intersection of Tenth and K Streets, numerous businesses are identifiable, including the Hotel Land, the Fox Senator Theater, Hale Brothers Department Store, and United Cigars. Two-way automobile traffic then shared the road with electric streetcars. (Courtesy Eleanor McClatchy Collection.)

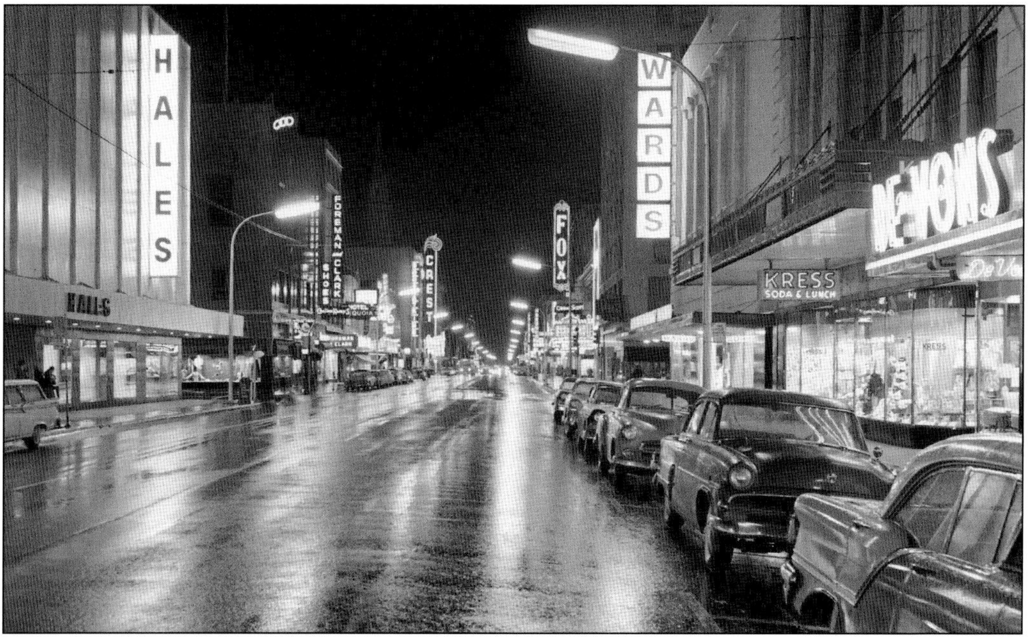

Automobiles now rule K Street in this 1950s photograph. At this time, as a one-way street without any tracks, the neon signs and new fluorescent streetlights reflect off of the damp pavement. Some 20 years later than the previous photograph, many of the businesses remain, including Hales, Hotel Sequoia, the Crest and Fox Senator Theaters, Wards, and the five-and-dime Kress. (Courtesy City of Sacramento Collection.)

Seven

Amusements

Sacramento's Pastimes

by Patricia J. Johnson

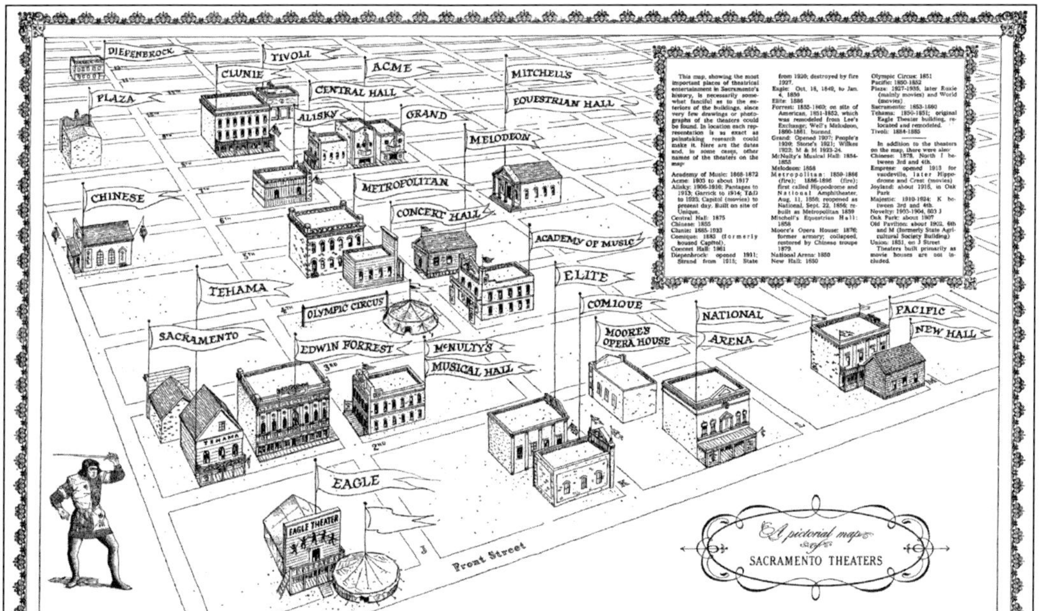

Entertainment in Sacramento was an important aspect of life from the very beginning. Whether it was live theater, museums, libraries, sports activities, or neighborhood parks, Sacramentans had a variety of amusements to keep them entertained. From theaters that ranged from high drama to opera to vaudeville, there was something for everyone in the 19th century. This pictorial map (1850–1900) of the most important Sacramento theaters shows the location and dates these houses operated in Sacramento. Stars like Edwin Booth, Lotta Crabtree, and Lola Montez performed on their stages. People found respite in the Crocker Art Museum, the public library, the YMCA, a new convention and community center, and area parks. As the 20th century dawned, lavish movie houses replaced the old vaudeville venues. By the 21st century, some of those movie palaces had been restored and are again flourishing. (Courtesy Eleanor McClatchy Collection.)

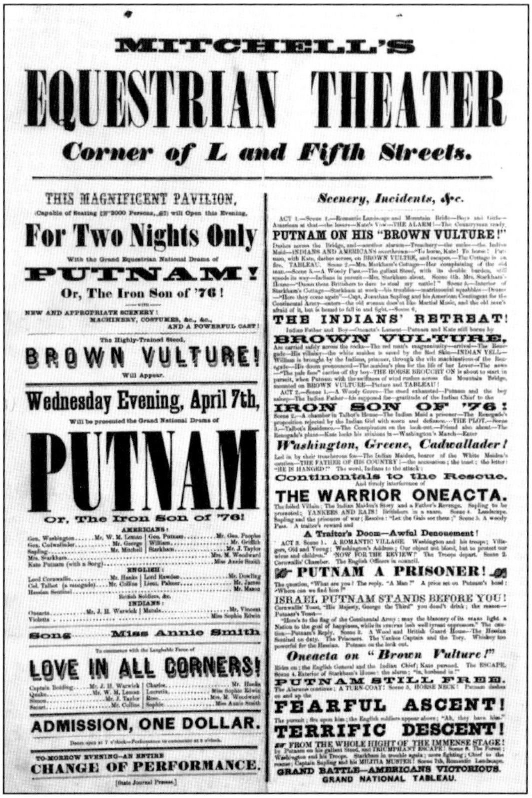

MITCHELL'S

EQUESTRIAN THEATER

Corner of L and Fifth Streets.

THIS MAGNIFICENT PAVILION,

(Capable of Seating 2000 Persons,) will Open this Evening,

For Two Nights Only

With the Grand Equestrian National Drama of

PUTNAM!

Or, The Iron Son of '76!

—WITH—

NEW AND APPROPRIATE SCENERY! MACHINERY, COSTUMES, &c., &c., AND A POWERFUL CAST!

The Highly-Trained Steed,

BROWN VULTURE!

Will Appear.

Wednesday Evening, April 7th,

Will be presented the Grand National Drama of

PUTNAM

Or, The Iron Son of '76!

AMERICANS:

Gen. Washington....Mr. W. M. Leman | Gen. Putnam....Mr. Geo. Peoples
Gen. Cadwallader....Mr. George | William....Mr. Griffith
Sapling....Mr. Mitchell | Starkham....Mr. J. Taylor
Mrs. Starkham....Mrs. M. Woodward
Kate Putnam (with a Song)....Miss Annie Smith

ENGLISH:

Lord Cornwallis....Mr. Hanks | Lord Rawdon....Mr. Dowling
Col. Talbot (a renegade)....Mr. Collins | Lieut. Palmer....Mr. James
Hessian Sentinel....Mr. Mason

British Soldiers, &c.

INDIANS:

Oneacta....Mr. J. H. Warwick | Matula....Mr. Vincent
Violetta....Miss Sophia Edwin

Song....Miss Annie Smith

To commence with the Laughable Farce of

LOVE IN ALL CORNERS!

Captain Bolding....Mr. J. H. Warwick | Charles....Mr. Hanks
Quake....Mr. W. M. Leman | Lucretia....Miss Sophia Edwin
Simon....Mr. J. Taylor | Rose....Mrs. M. Woodward
Smart....Mr. Collins | Sophie....Miss Annie Smith

ADMISSION, ONE DOLLAR.

Doors open at 7 o'clock—Performance to commence at 8 o'clock.

TO-MORROW EVENING—AN ENTIRE

CHANGE OF PERFORMANCE.

[State Journal Presses.]

Scenery, Incidents, &c.

ACT 1.—Scene 1.—Romantic Landscape and Mountain Bridge—Boys and Girls—American at that—the lovers—Kate's Vow—THE ALARM!—The Countryman ready.

PUTNAM ON HIS "BROWN VULTURE!"

THE INDIANS' RETREAT!

BROWN VULTURE,

IRON SON OF '76!

Washington, Greene, Cadwallader!

Continentals to the Rescue.

And timely interference of

THE WARRIOR ONEACTA.

A Traitor's Doom—Awful Denouement!

PUTNAM A PRISONER!

ISRAEL PUTNAM STANDS BEFORE YOU!

Oneacta on "Brown Vulture!"

PUTNAM STILL FREE.

FEARFUL ASCENT!

TERRIFIC DESCENT!

FROM THE WHOLE HIGHT OF THE IMMENSE STAGE!

GRAND BATTLE—AMERICANS VICTORIOUS.

GRAND NATIONAL TABLEAU.

A handbill for "Mitchell's Equestrian Theater—Corner of L and Fifth Streets" published the coming attractions that would entice patrons to the establishment. This announcement was typical of the 19th-century advertisements for stage presentations at a variety of theaters. Mitchell's was capable of seating 2,000 people and opened April 7, 1858, with a grand equestrian drama. (Courtesy Eleanor McClatchy Collection.)

The Primrose Minstrels pose for a 1906 photograph in front of the Clunie Theater, which operated from 1885 to 1923 at the northeast corner of Eighth and K Streets. Minstrel groups often had their own orchestras accompany their performance. With the closing of the Clunie in 1923, Marshall Hale of Hale's Department Store remodeled the theater to make room for the expansion of his store. (Courtesy Eleanor McClatchy Collection.)

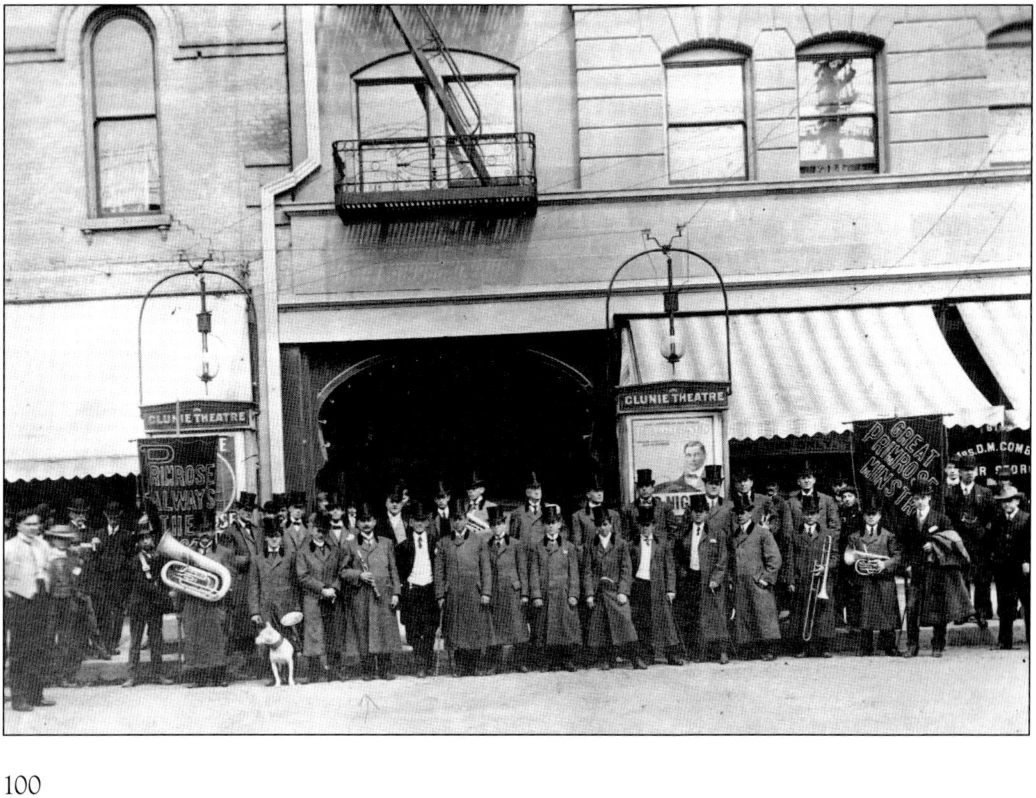

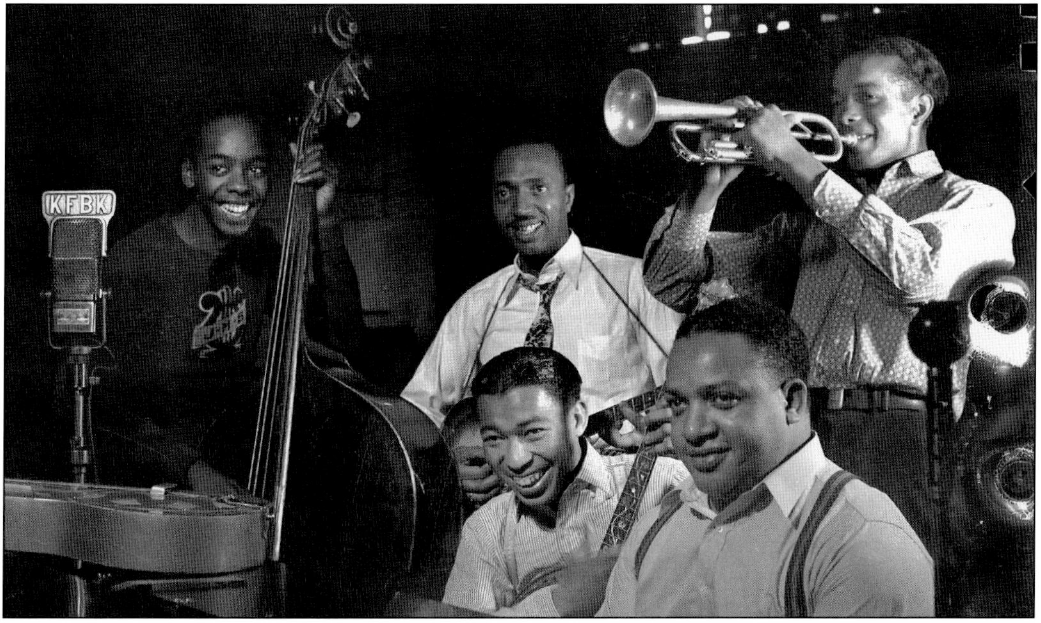

KFBK Radio broadcast live performances during the 1930s and 1940s from its studios in the *Sacramento Bee* building at 708 I Street. The studio had space for a large audience, a control booth, and several stages for the musicians. Often performing at Sacramento's Zanzibar Club, Ray Jenkins, at right with the trumpet, and Ted Thompson, seated at front right, performed at the KFBK studio. (Courtesy *Sacramento Bee* Collection.)

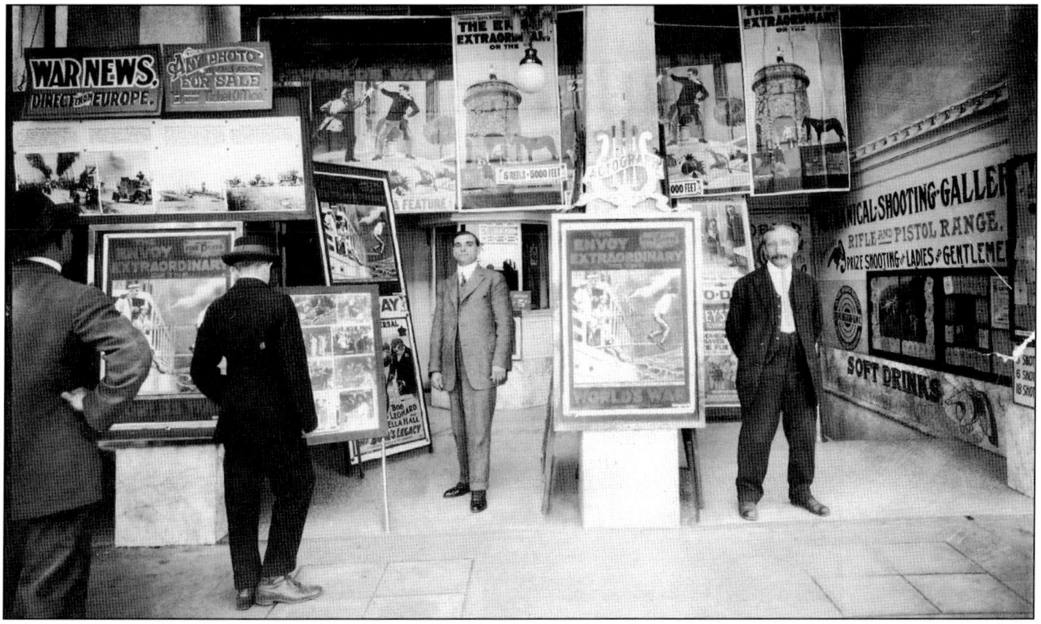

The Lyric Theater operated for a short period during World War I. Opened by Vincent DiStasio in 1910 at 1114 Sixth Street in the Masonic Building, DiStasio is pictured here in 1917 with three other unidentified men reading posters about war news in Europe. Before radio or television, most people got their news from papers or by attending these types of theaters. (Courtesy Verna Whybark Collection.)

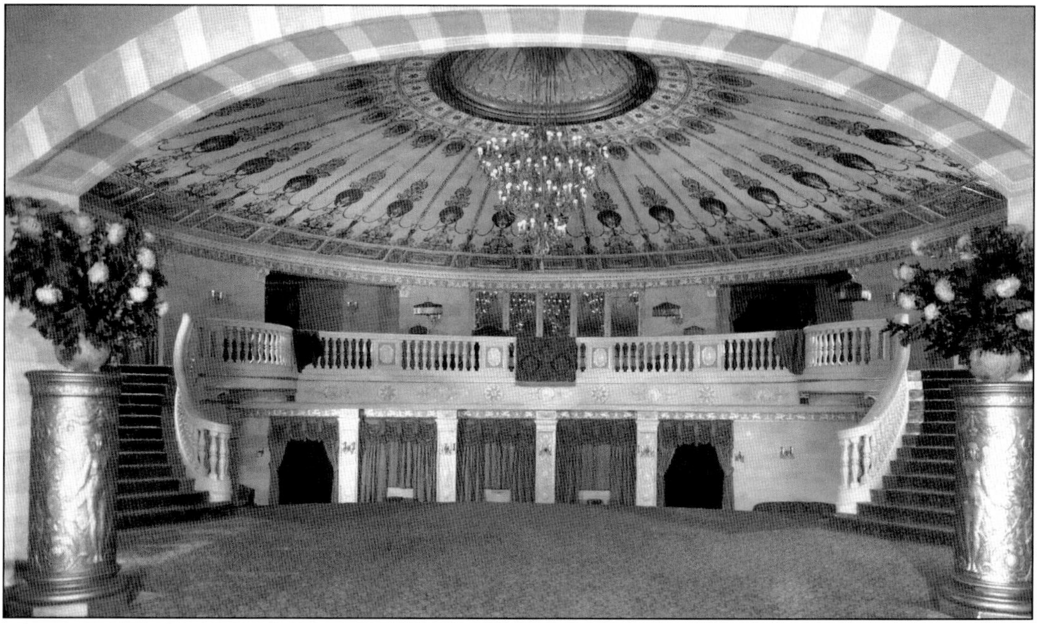

The Senator Theater was among the most lavish of the picture palaces in Sacramento. A sister to the now gone Alhambra Theater, Leonard Stark and Edward Flanders designed both. This photograph is of the Senator's entrance from K Street in 1924 before it opened. Note the elaborate sculpture work in plaster. Thomas Scollan, a local plastering contractor and former mayor of Sacramento, did this work. (Courtesy Thomas Scollan Collection.)

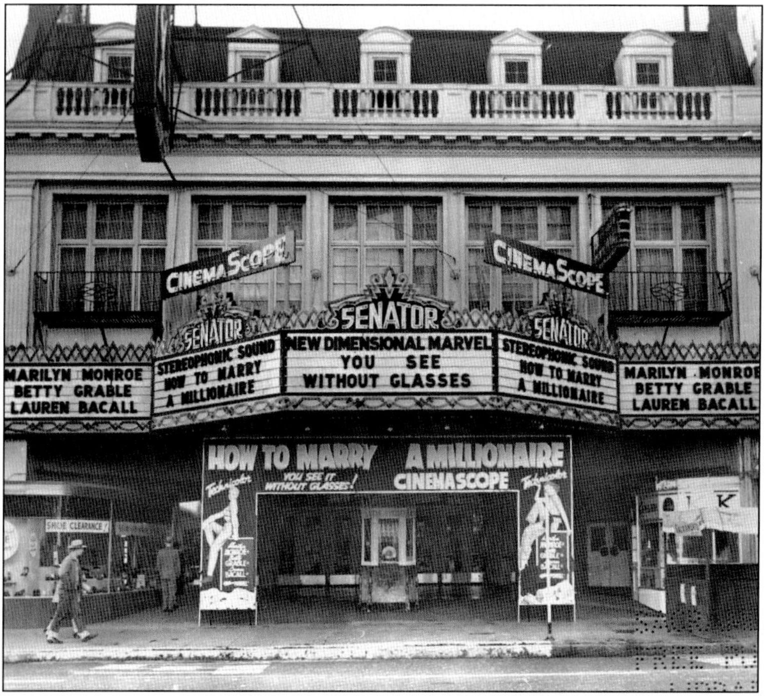

Located on the south side of K Street between Ninth and Tenth Streets, the Senator Theater was a very popular venue for Sacramentans in the 1950s. By the 1970s, these old theaters were closing. The Fox Senator, as it was then known, shut down nearly 48 years to the date of its opening on September 24, 1972. Its sister theater, the Alhambra, closed the next year. (Courtesy Sacramento Public Library Collection.)

Over 5,000 people attended the gala opening in October 1949 of the premier at the new Crest Theater, including movie stars and politicians. Previously known as the Hippodrome at 1013 K Street, it was the site where on September 14, 1946, the outside marquee collapsed, killing one person. The theater closed for renovations and reopened as the Crest three years later. (Courtesy Joseph Benetti Collection.)

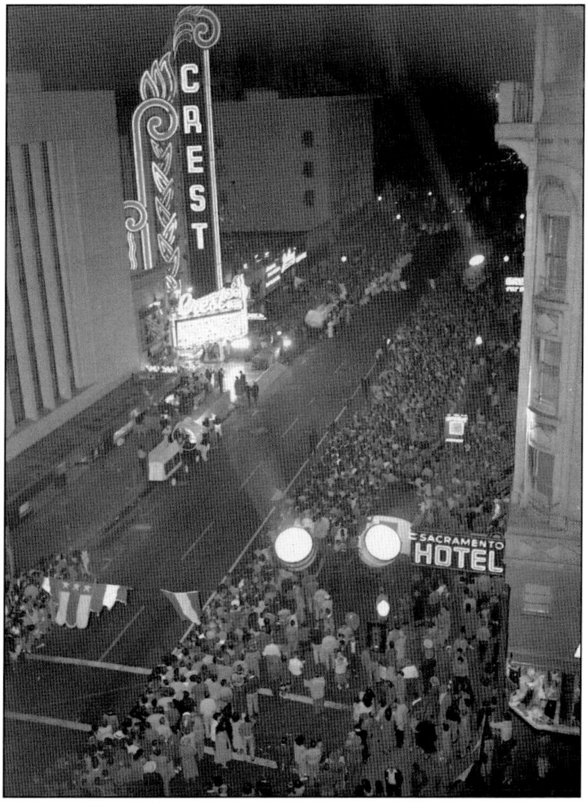

The newly renovated Crest welcomed moviegoers in 1949. This theater and others on K Street, such as the Esquire, the Times, and the State, competed in lavishness with the other suburban theaters that were opening as Sacramento expanded in population and development. These theaters provided air conditioning, a new creature comfort, which most Sacramentans did not have in their homes. (Courtesy Sacramento Valley Photographic Survey Collection.)

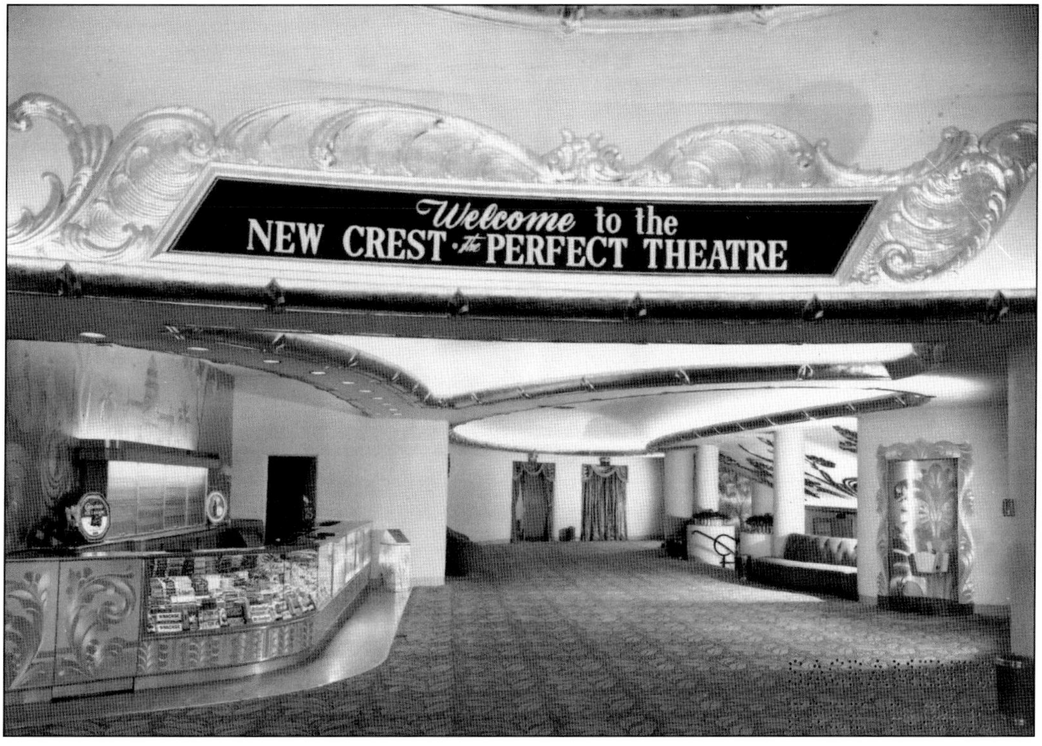

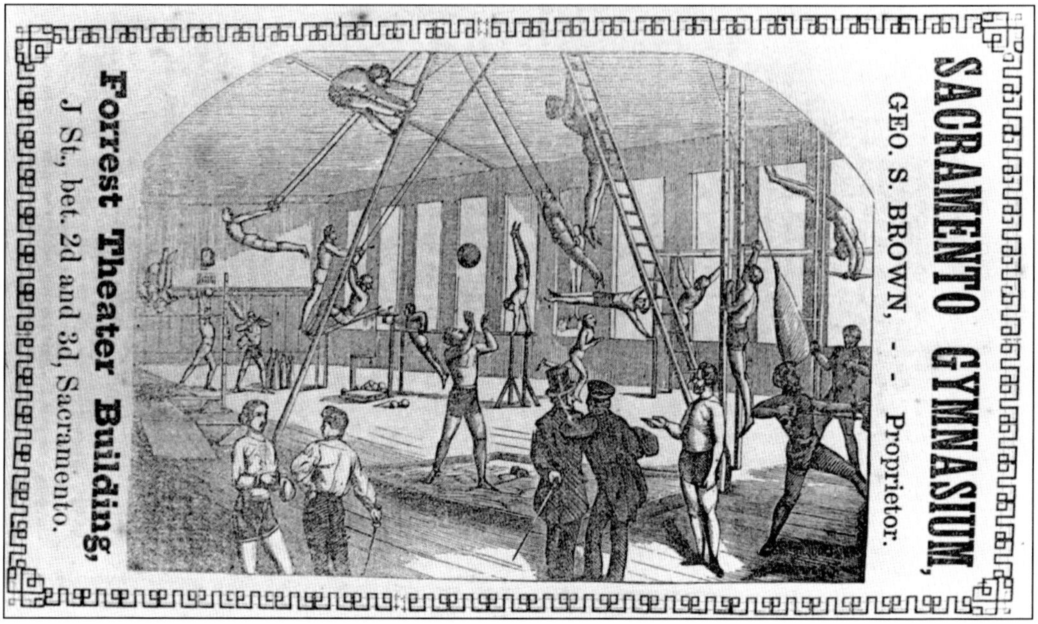

In the Forrest Theater Building on J Street between Second and Third Streets, owner George S. Brown operated the Sacramento Gymnasium on the floors above it, from 1857 to 1861, as an early exercise facility in Sacramento. Treadwell and Company, a hardware business, tore down the building after a fire in 1866 to build the largest storehouse in Sacramento for hardware and farm implements. (Courtesy Eleanor McClatchy Collection.)

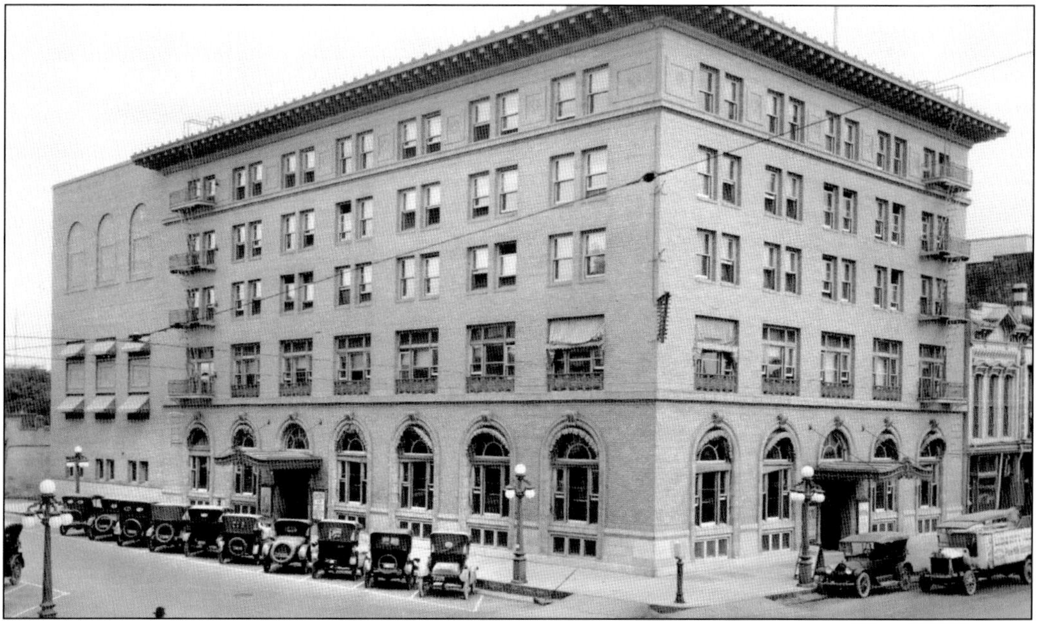

The YMCA, or "Y" as it is commonly called, opened in 1899 at the corner of Fifth and J Streets. The structure in this *c.*1920 photograph remained until 1913, when a new five-story building opened on the same site that served Sacramento until 1951. The YMCA provides all people with a place to develop the body through health and fitness programs, including swimming. (Courtesy Sacramento Metropolitan Chamber of Commerce Collection.)

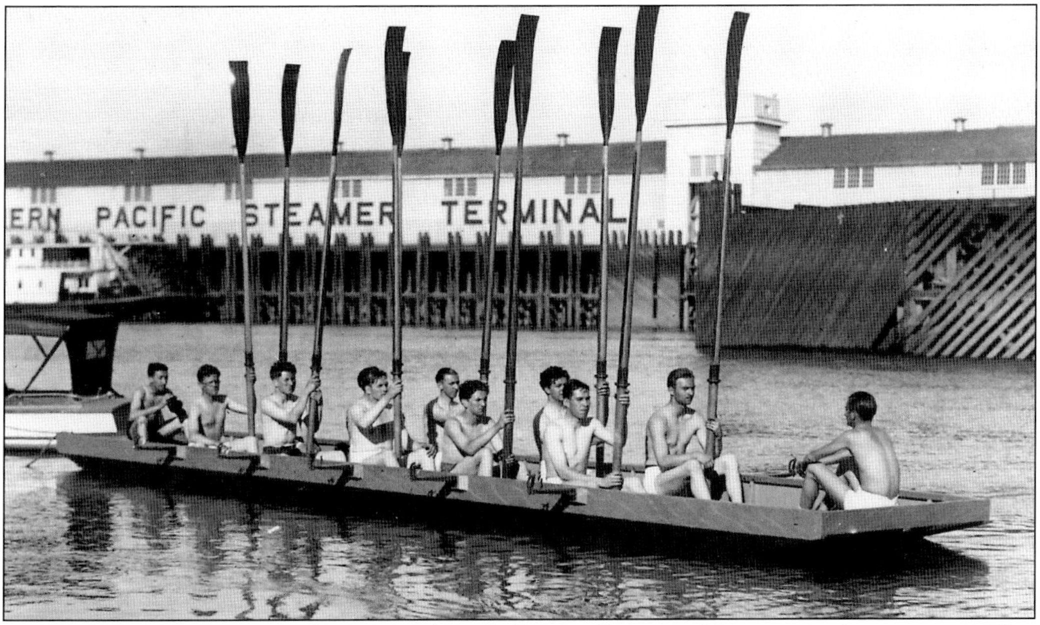

Water sports activities found many outlets at the confluence of Sacramento's two rivers. This c. 1935 photograph of an unidentified crew of young oarsmen is on the Sacramento River near the Southern Pacific Steamer Terminal north of the Tower Bridge. These Sacramentans appear ready for a workout as they prepare for an outing on the river. (Courtesy Sacramento Valley Photographic Survey Collection.)

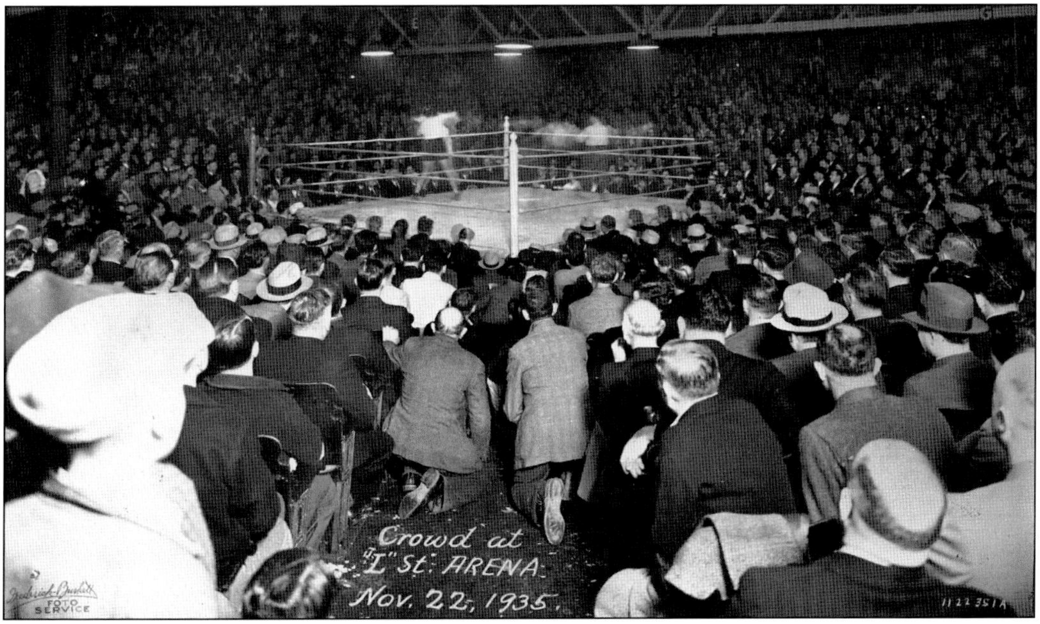

The "L" Street Boxing Auditorium was at 223 L Street. This photograph from November 22, 1935, shows James Braddock, the world's heavyweight champion fighting a three-round exhibition with his sparring partner, John McCarthy. Attending the match was Sacramento boxer Max Baer, who lost earlier that year to Braddock. The arena occupied the L Street site from 1925 through the end of World War II. (Courtesy Joseph Benetti Collection.)

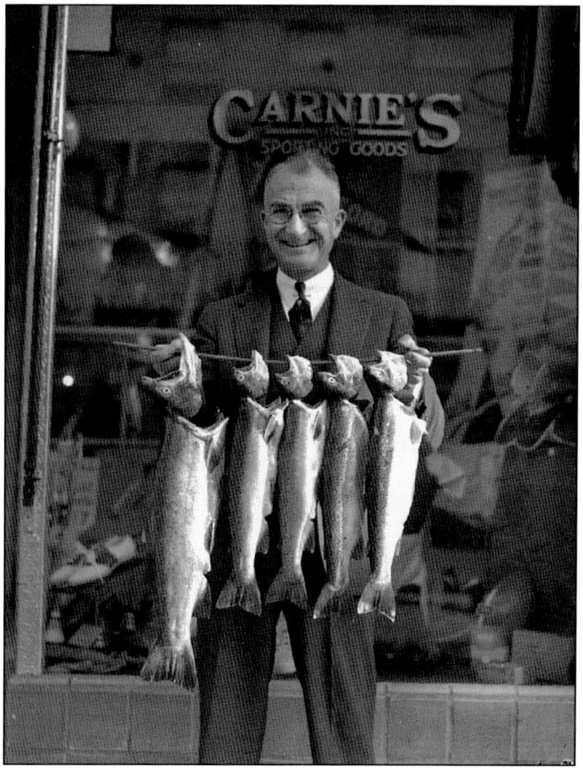

Carnie's Sporting Goods Store was at 1023 K Street in the 1930s. The unidentified man in the suit holding the stringer of fish was promoting just one type of sporting goods available at Carnie's. In addition, the store was the official representative for A. G. Spalding and Brothers sporting and athletic goods. (Courtesy Ernest Myers Collection.)

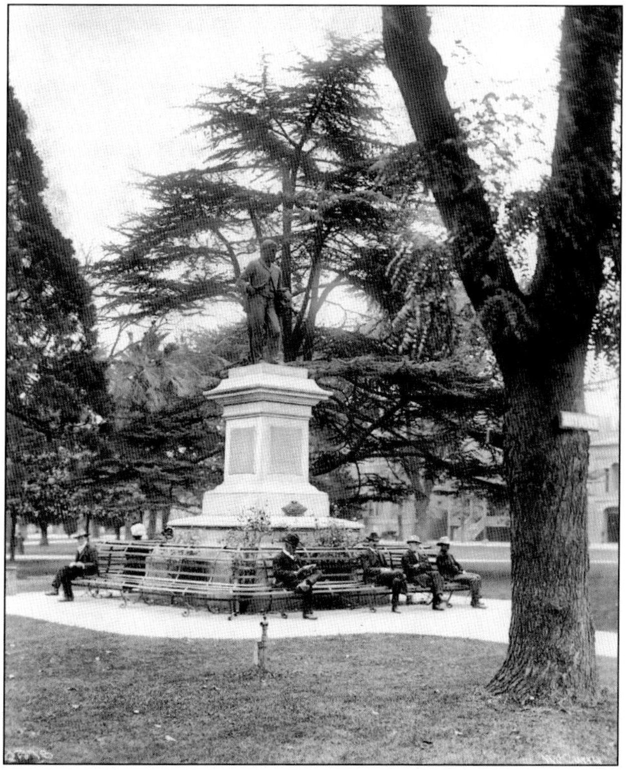

When John Sutter Jr. laid out Sacramento City, he set aside various blocks for public squares. Plaza Park, as it was originally known, bounded by Ninth, Tenth, I, and J Streets, was just such a square. In this 1900 photograph, people are lounging at the base of the A. J. Stevens' statue, a memorial to the locomotive designer and inventor. (Courtesy Sacramento Metropolitan Chamber of Commerce Collection.)

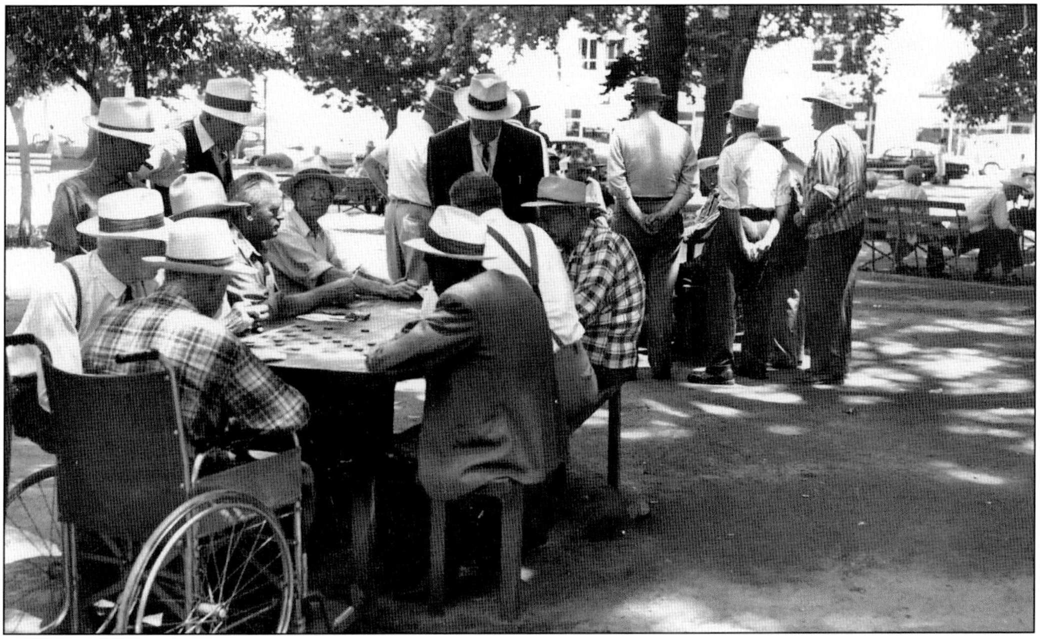

Plaza Park, now known as Cesar Chavez Park in honor of the California farm labor leader, was a gathering place for gentlemen checker and chess players in the 1940s and 1950s. Located across from city hall, the park is still a gathering place for Sacramentans who enjoy festivals, concerts, political rallies, and farmers' markets. (Courtesy Sacramento Parks and Recreation Collection.)

Providing a place for youngsters to go after school, the Sacramento Parks and Recreation Department operated a number of recreation centers in many of the parks around the city. In this 1950s image taken inside the Southside Youth Center, a group of young people has gathered around a jukebox. Southside Center was in Southside Park at Seventh and T Streets. (Courtesy Sacramento Parks and Recreation Collection.)

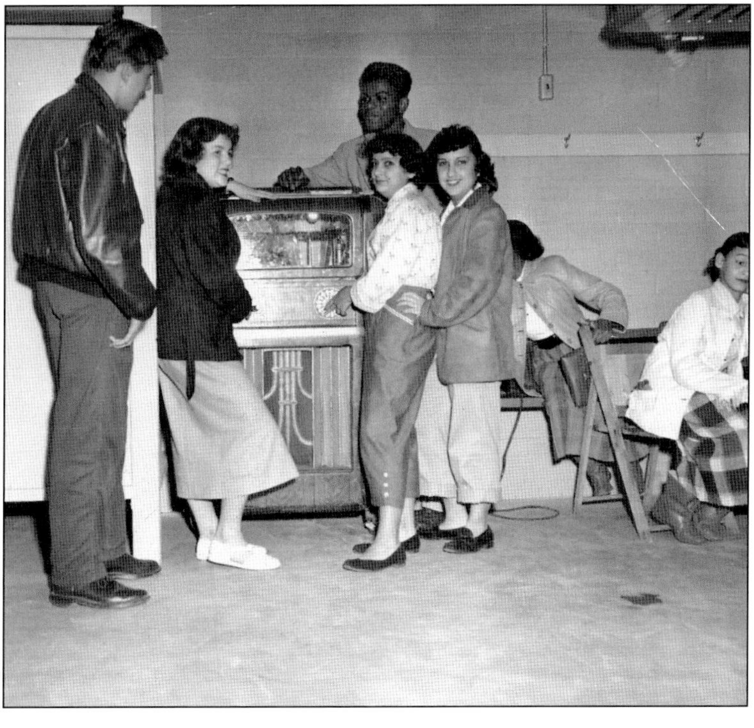

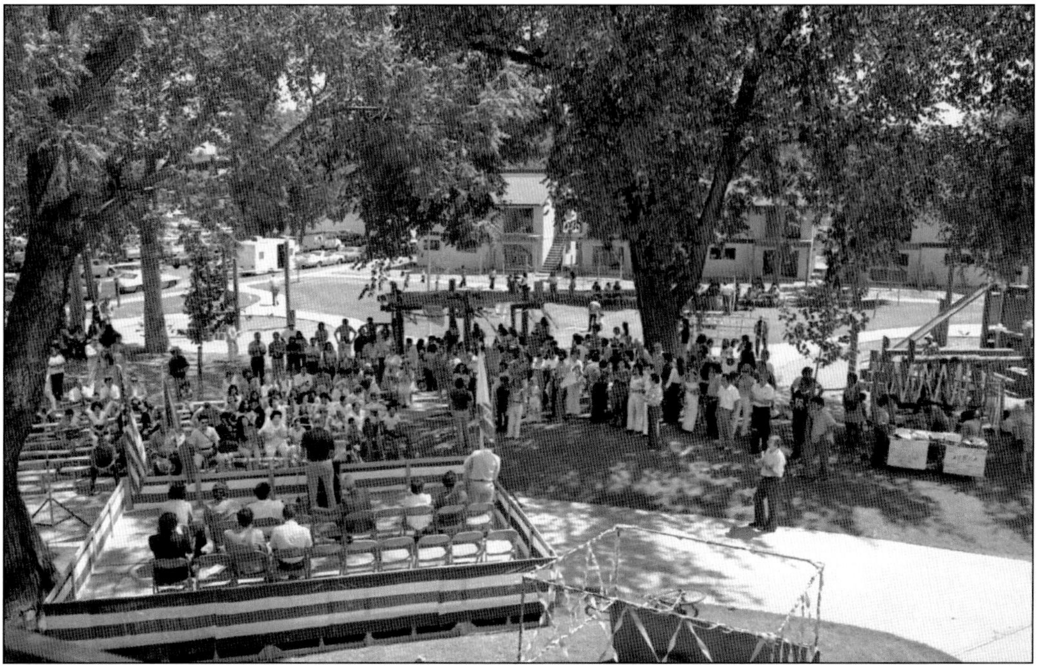

Dedication ceremonies at Emiliano Zapata Park in the Alkali Flat neighborhood drew a large crowd August 11, 1975. Located at Ninth and E Streets, the park was cosponsored by the Alkali Flat Project Area Committee and the Sacramento Housing and Redevelopment Agency. The people of Alkali Flat named the park for the hero of the Mexican Revolution. The park also has a playground and picnic area. (Courtesy *Sacramento Bee* Collection.)

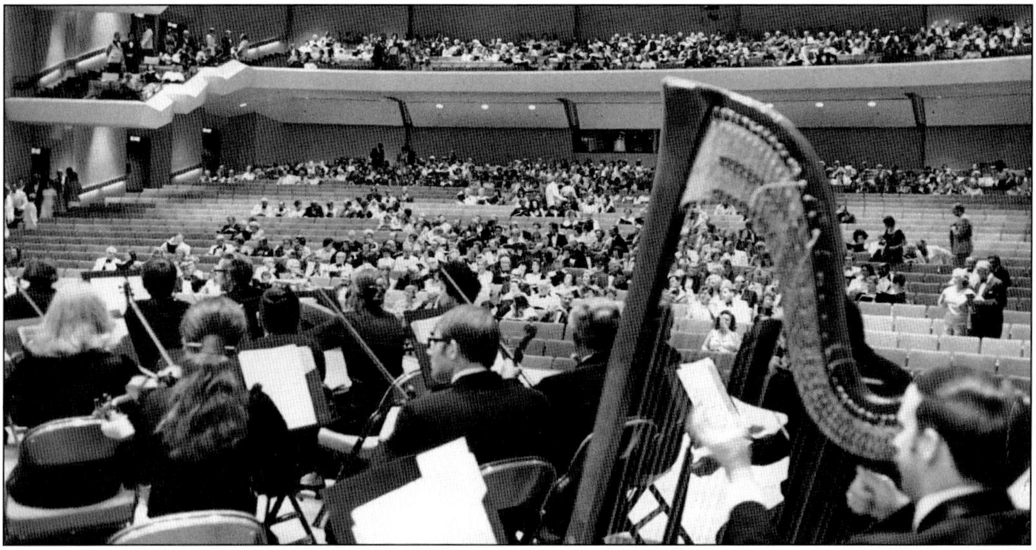

The Sacramento Convention Center opened in June 1974 with a performance by the Sacramento Symphony in the 2,400-seat auditorium. Also opening that year was the 50,000-square-foot exhibit hall adjacent to the theater. Located at the upper end of the K Street Mall, the theater and exhibit hall provide an anchor to the mall and continue to attract first-rate productions and conventions to Sacramento. (Courtesy *Sacramento Bee* Collection.)

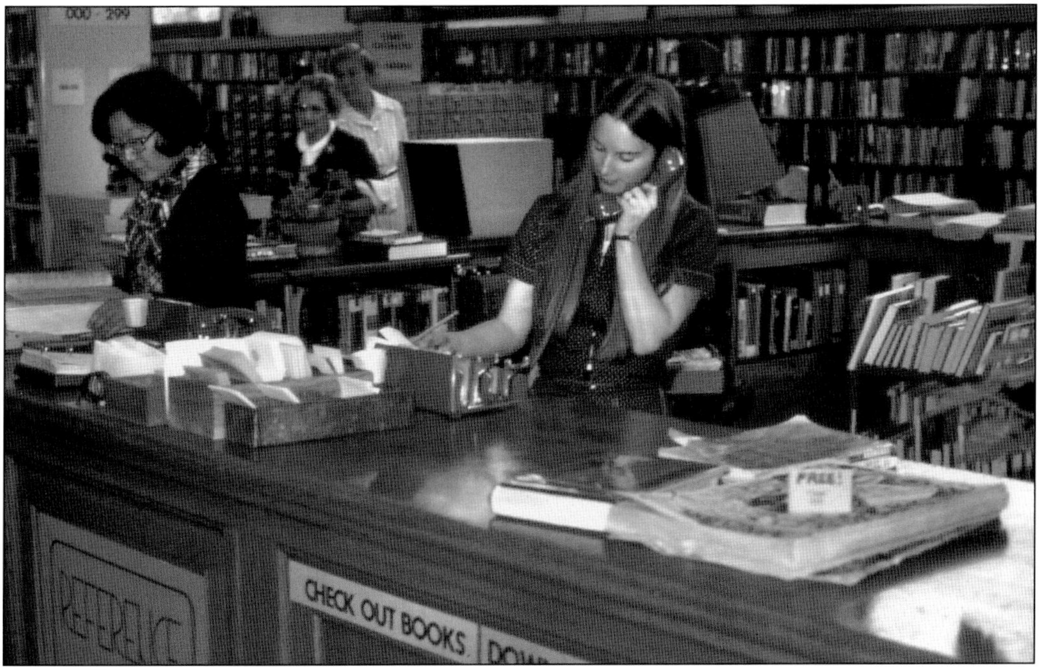

Sacramentans formed a library association in 1857. By 1872, citizens built a library at Eighth and I Streets. In 1879, the property was donated to the city, making it Sacramento's first free library. The present library was built at the same location in 1918. At left, at the reference desk, is librarian Janice Abe, and to her right, on the telephone, is Ann Cousineau. (Courtesy City of Sacramento Collection.)

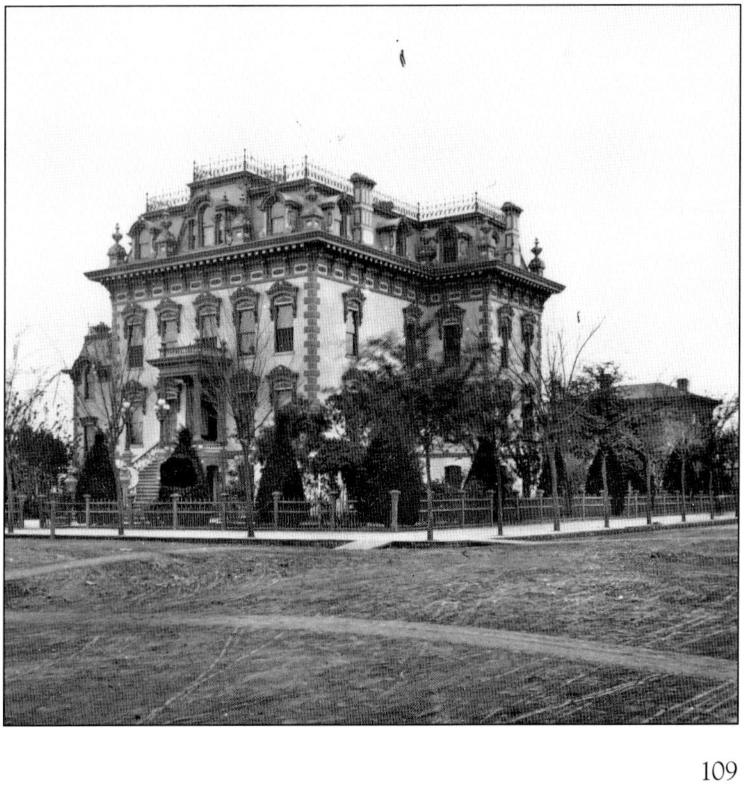

In 1872, Leland and Jane Stanford commissioned photographer Eadweard Muybridge to document their family home in Sacramento after its remodeling. This photograph shows the north and west side of the home at Eighth and N Streets. Now part of the California State Parks system, the Stanford Mansion Museum underwent a major restoration and is the official site for protocol activities for the State of California. (Courtesy Eleanor McClatchy Collection.)

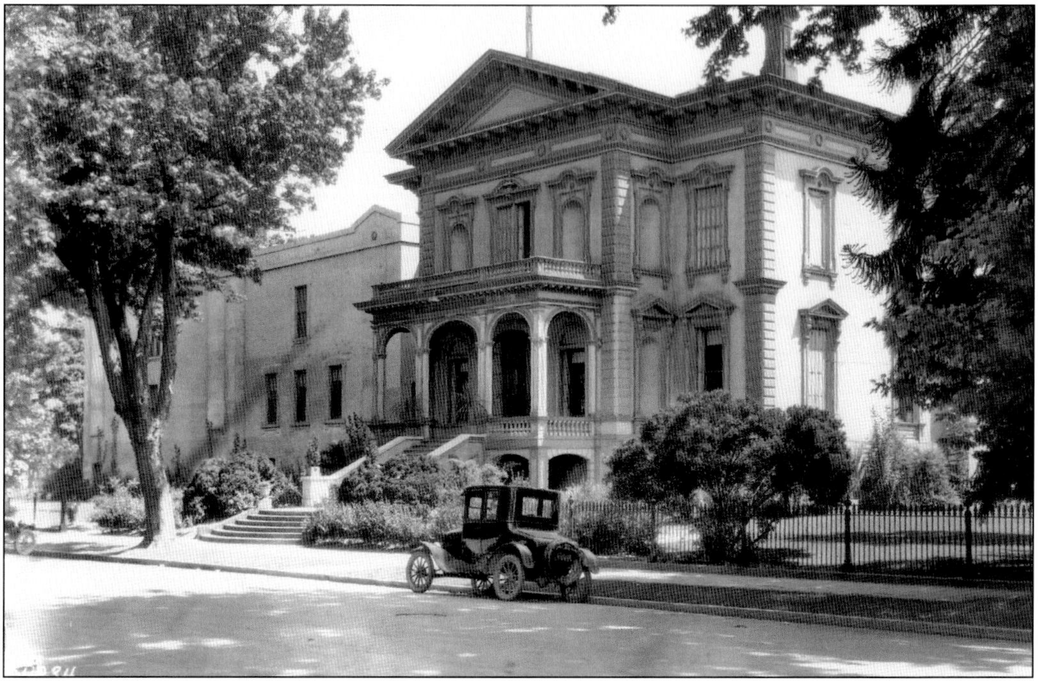

Considered one of the finest art galleries in the United States and the "first in the west," the E. B. Crocker Art Gallery was envisioned by Edwin and Margaret Crocker in the 1870s. Located at Third and O Streets, this 1934 photograph shows the original house and gallery. Margaret gave the gallery to the City of Sacramento in 1885. (Courtesy McCurry Company Collection.)

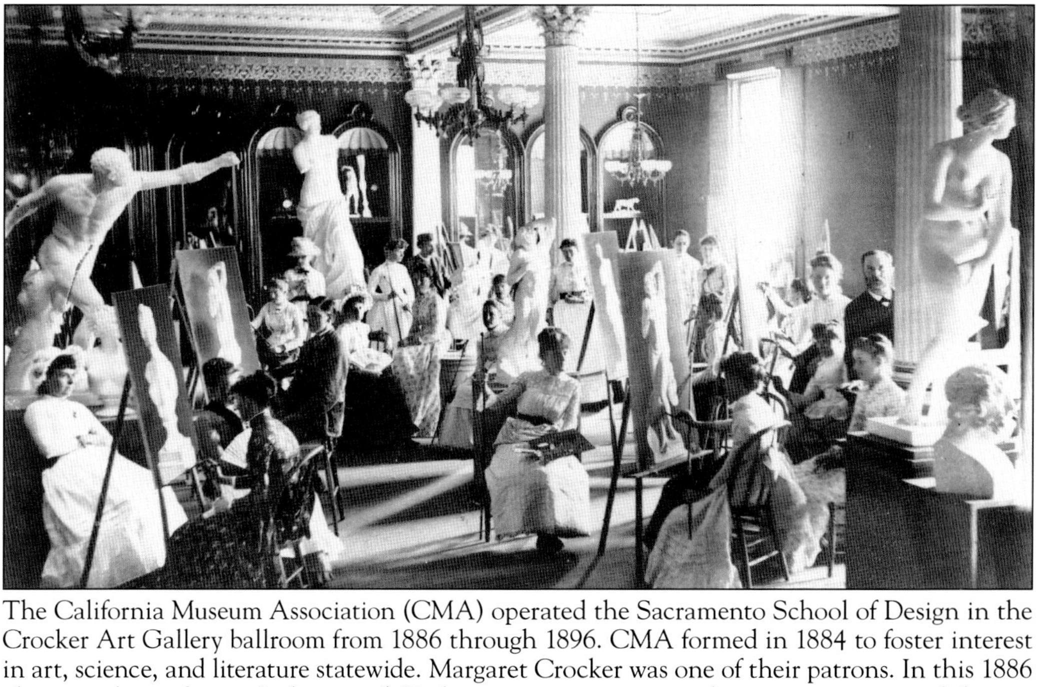

The California Museum Association (CMA) operated the Sacramento School of Design in the Crocker Art Gallery ballroom from 1886 through 1896. CMA formed in 1884 to foster interest in art, science, and literature statewide. Margaret Crocker was one of their patrons. In this 1886 photograph, professors Jackson and Carlson are instructing students in painting and design. (Courtesy Sacramento Valley Photographic Survey Collection.)

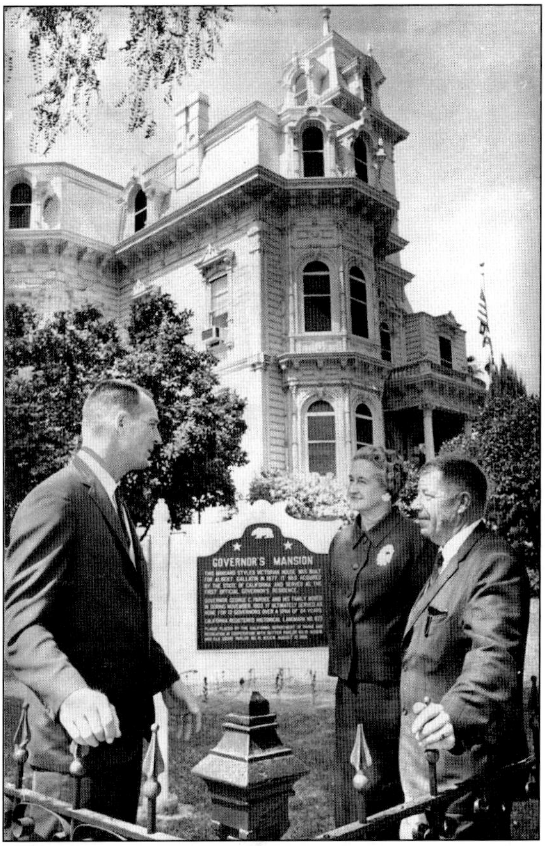

Originally built in 1877 by Albert Gallatin as his home at Fifteenth and H Streets, the State of California purchased the home in 1903 as the residence for its governors. Pictured here, from left to right, at the mansion's dedication as a landmark in 1968, are Deputy Director of State Parks Ray Hunter, former grand president of the Native Daughters of the Golden West Audrey Brown, and Native Son of the Golden West Henry Lynch. (Courtesy Frank Christy Collection.)

The Sacramento History Center opened August 3, 1985. The museum, a replica of the old 1854 City Hall and Waterworks Building is on the exact site of that building in Old Sacramento. Pictured at the dedication, joining Jim Henley at the podium at his left in the front row, from left to right, are Tom Hammer, Illa Collin, and Joe Serna, all city and county dignitaries. (Courtesy City of Sacramento Collection.)

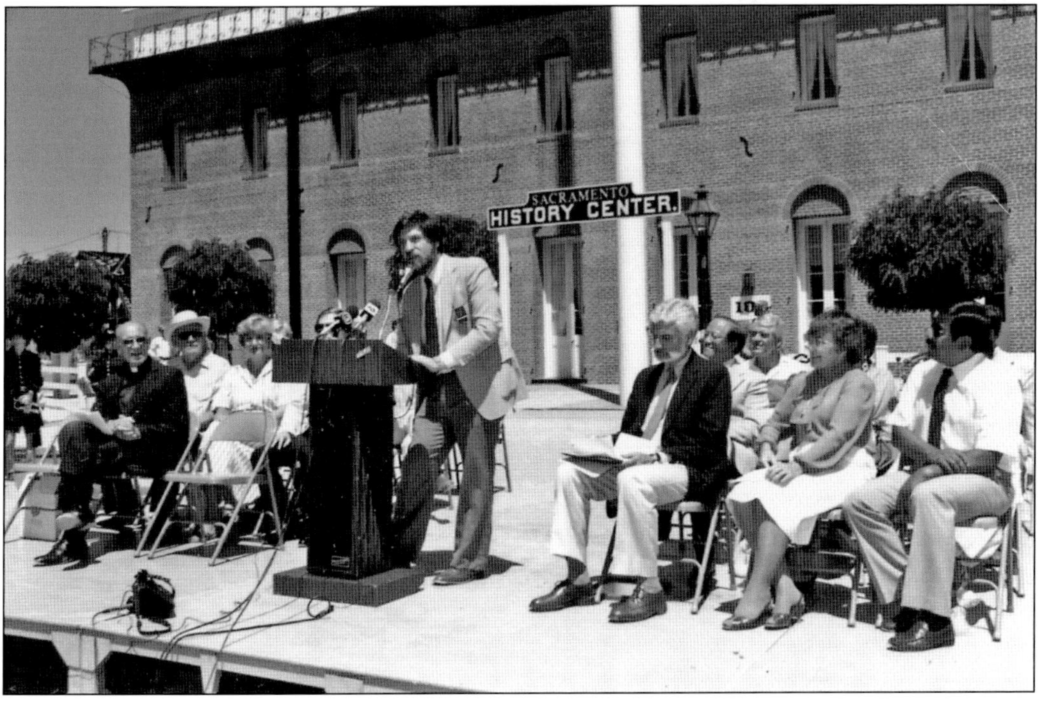

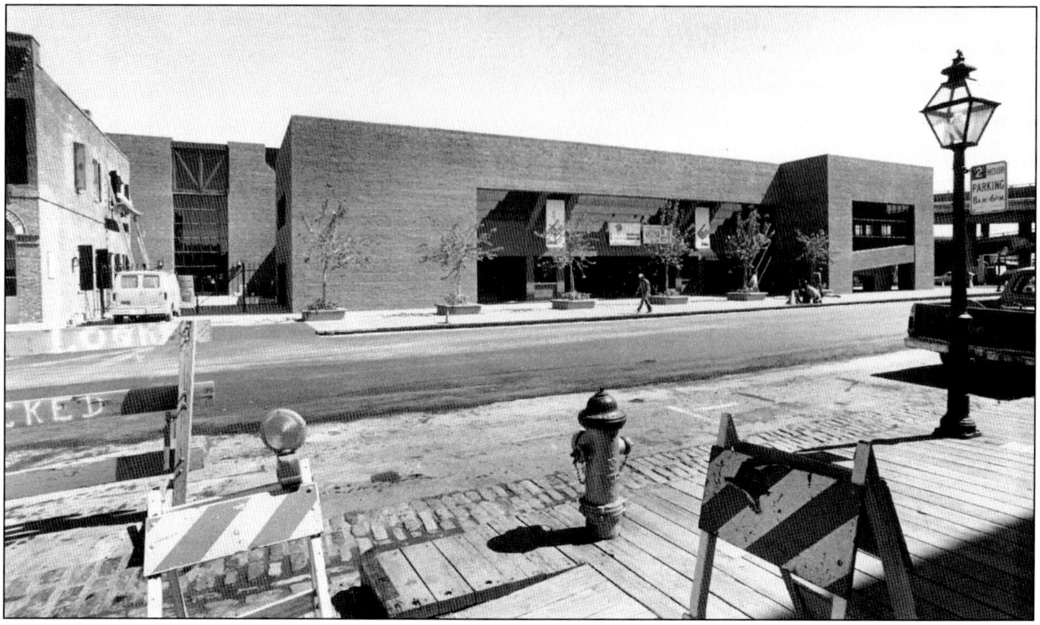

Being the western terminus of the transcontinental railroad, it is appropriate that a museum dedicated to its history in California be in Sacramento. Opened in 1981, the California State Railroad Museum is one of California's most popular attractions. The museum boasts 500,000 visitors a year. Located in historic Old Sacramento, this photograph of its exterior on I Street was taken just before the grand opening. (Courtesy *Sacramento Bee* Collection.)

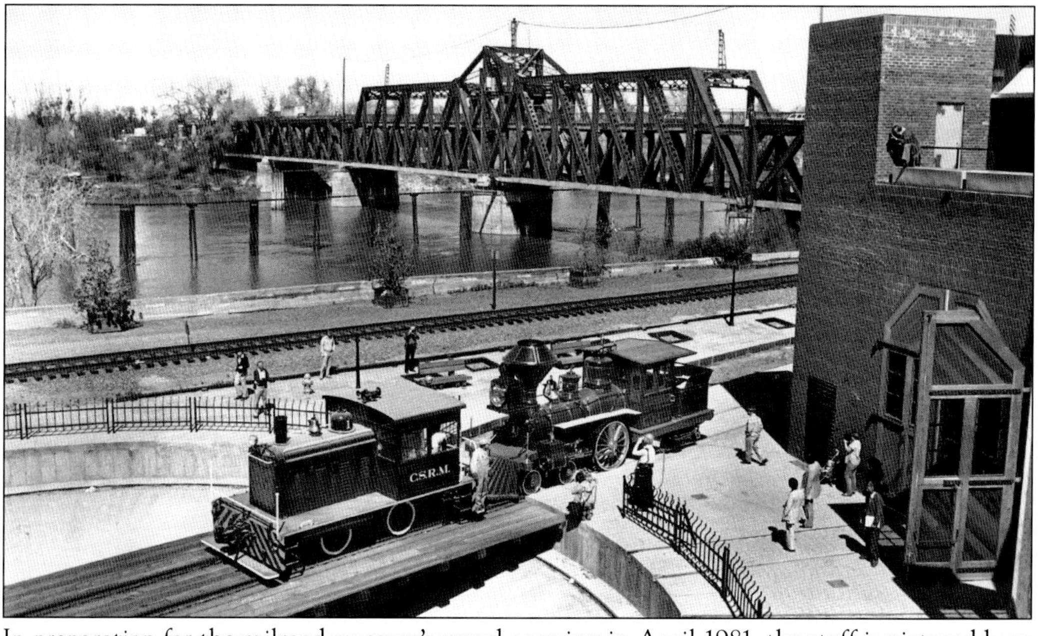

In preparation for the railroad museum's grand opening in April 1981, the staff is pictured here moving engines. The museum's Whitcomb Switch Engine pulls the *C. P. Huntington* onto the turntable. The *Huntington* was the Southern Pacific Railroad's first locomotive. The museum is one of the anchors for the Old Sacramento Historic District. The I Street Bridge and the Sacramento River are visible in the background. (Courtesy *Sacramento Bee* Collection.)

Eight

Redevelopment

Everything New Is Old Again

by Carson Hendricks

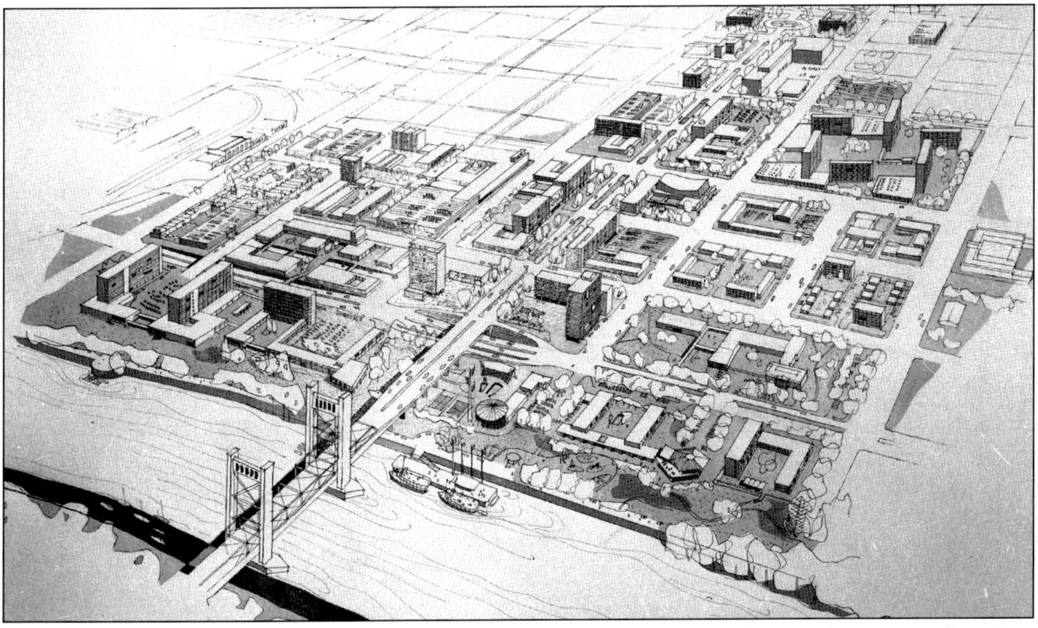

In 1950, the city council designated as blighted a 60-block area of the city known as the West End. The concept shown here was put forth in 1954 by the Sacramento Redevelopment Agency and showed what planners envisioned for the Capitol Mall Project in Redevelopment Area No. 1. It is important to note what is not shown—the interstate that would later divide the area from the river, a lack of buildings over 10 stories, and the Employment Development Department Building then under construction at Eighth and N Streets. A pedestrian mall along K Street is also mentioned and was eventually realized. The various projects were undertaken partly because the West End was considered by many a slum and akin to a "skid row." The many redevelopment projects drastically changed the face of Sacramento by eliminating large parts of the area's housing and businesses and replacing them with state offices and wide boulevards. This was but one of many ideas to rebuild Sacramento's image. (Courtesy *Sacramento Bee* Collection.)

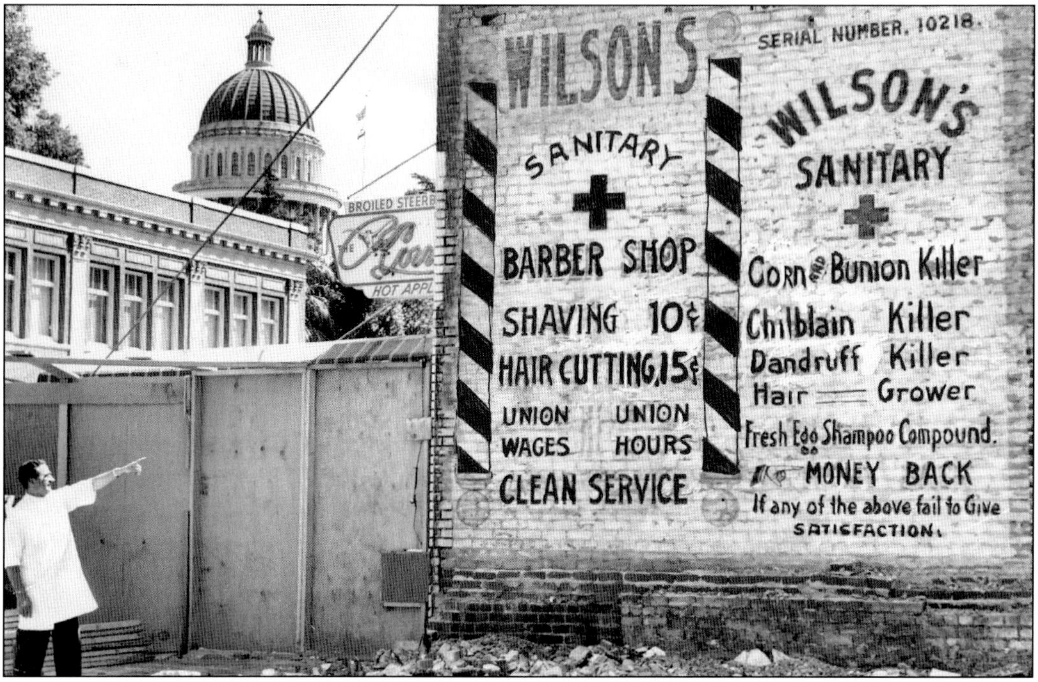

When the building at 1116 Tenth Street was torn down in May 1950, it revealed an advertisement painted on the adjacent building for Wilson's Sanitary Barber, once located at 904 K Street. The man in the photograph is George Likes, who in 1950 was the proprietor of the barbershop in the Land Hotel. He was able to give a detailed history of barbers in Sacramento. (Courtesy Frank Christy Collection.)

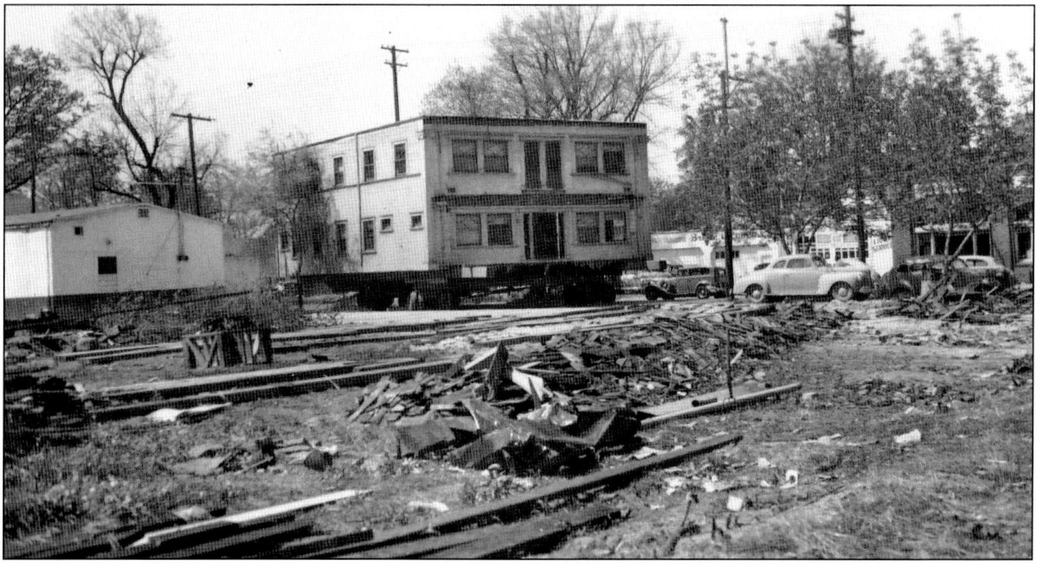

Redevelopment of Capitol Mall began in the late 1940s. This image, taken April 19, 1950, shows the last house being moved from Ninth and O Streets (as seen from Tenth and O Streets) as part of the Capitol Mall extension program. This project was undertaken because of the growth of state government after World War II. These sites eventually became Roosevelt Park and the Secretary of State Building. (Courtesy Eugene Hepting Collection.)

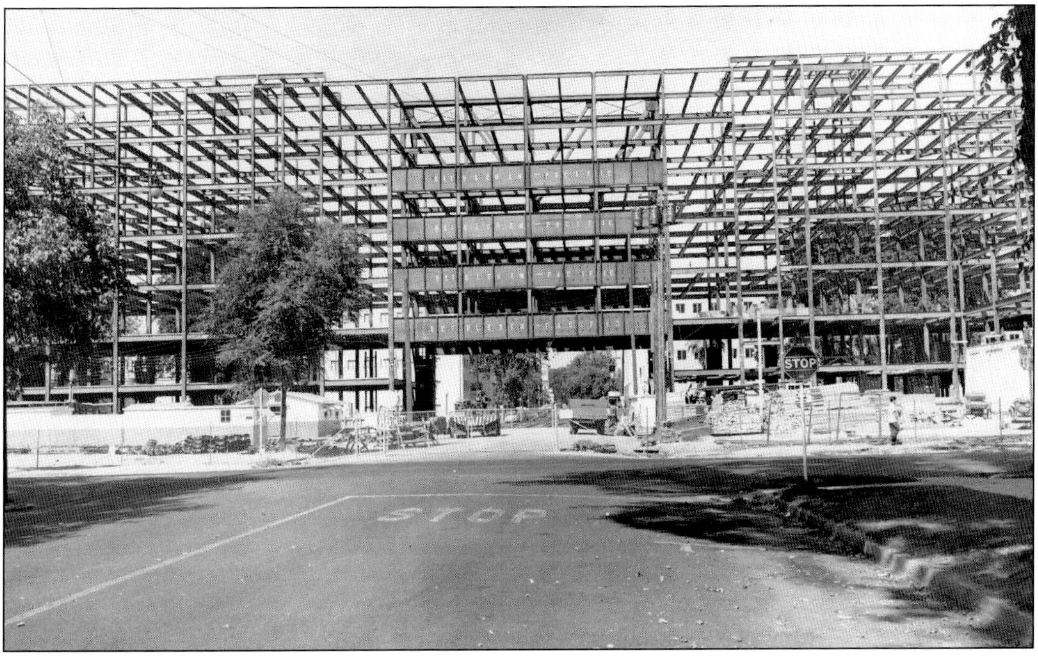

The Employment Development Department Building is under construction on September 26, 1954. The original plans for the structure had it blocking Eighth Street. The city objected to this, as Eighth Street was a main thoroughfare, and in a rare moment of acquiescence the state modified the plan to allow traffic to pass under the building. (Courtesy Ralph Shaw Collection.)

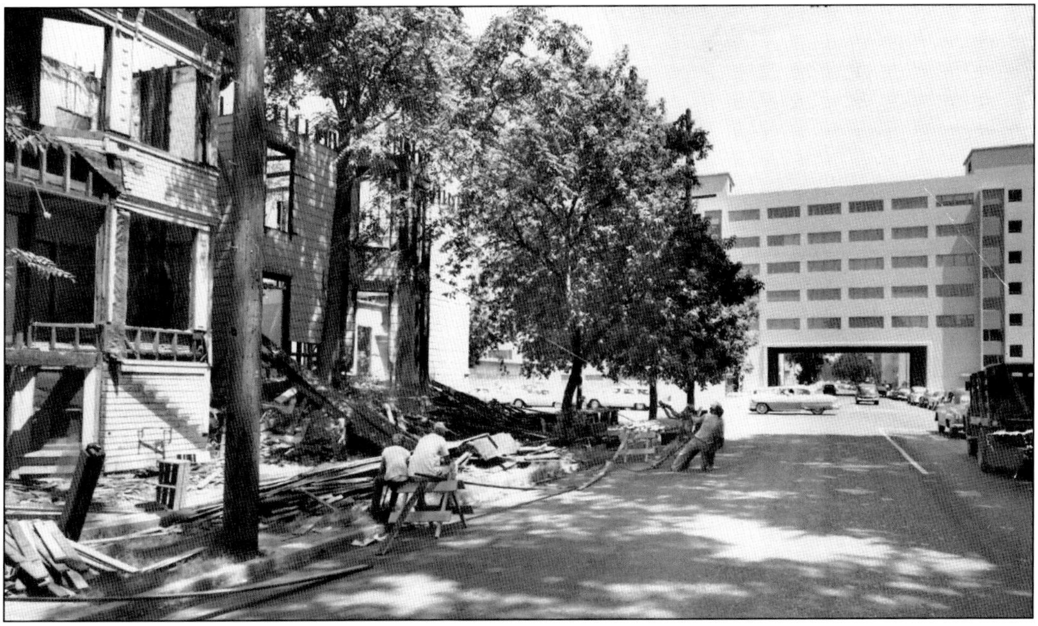

This June 28, 1956, photograph shows redevelopment at its most basic. The workmen are attempting to pull down a house on Eighth Street, near the recently completed Employment Development Department Building, using rope and muscle power. History does not indicate if this particular technique was successful, but the building did come down at some point. In its place stands a state office building. (Courtesy Frank Christy Collection.)

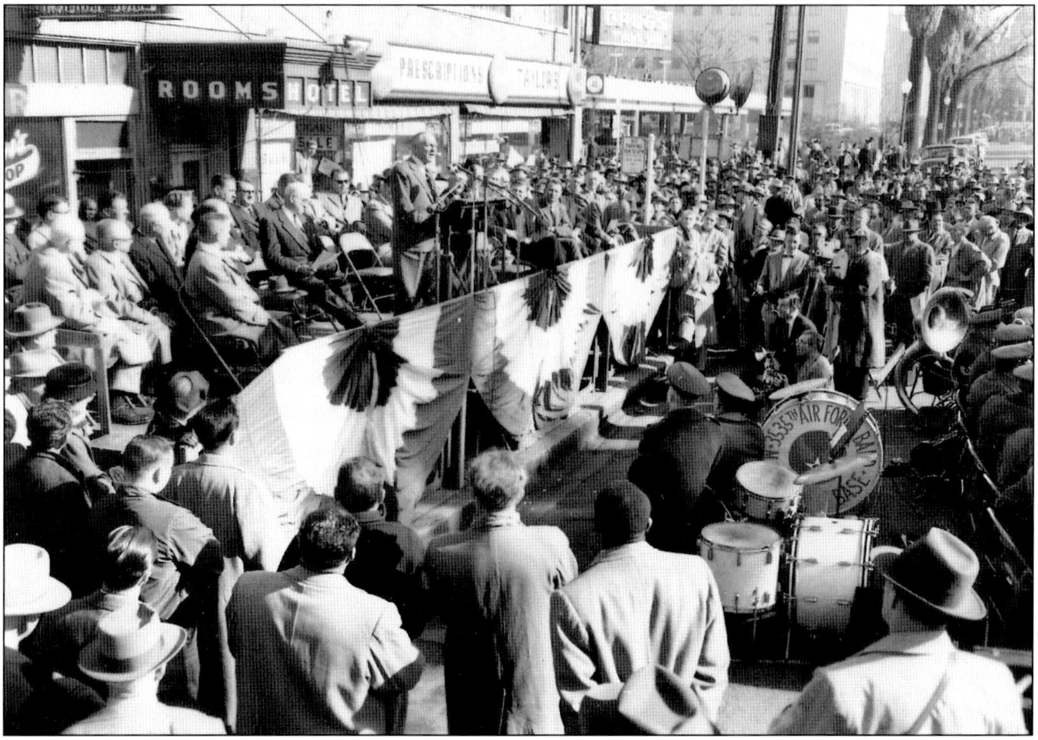

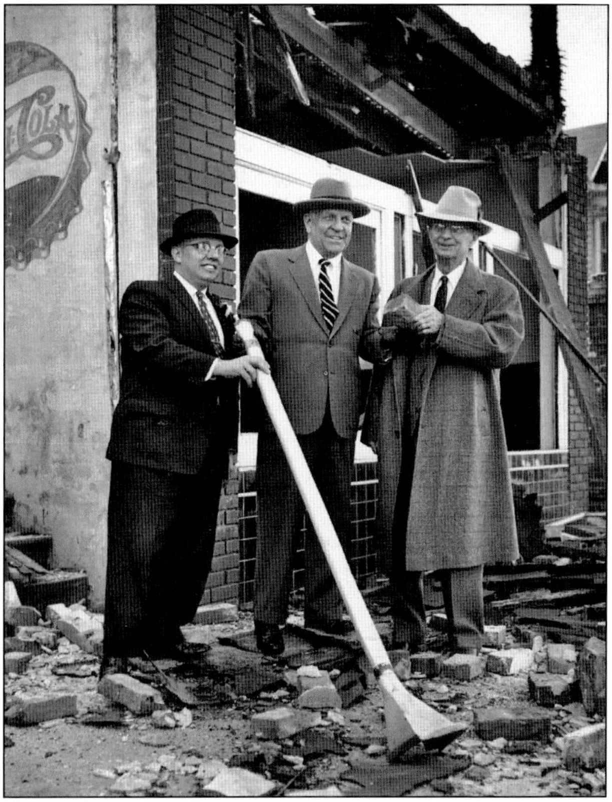

This ceremony, with Gov. Goodwin Knight speaking, took place on January 29, 1957, at 526 Capital Avenue and marked the first building officially demolished for the Capitol Mall Project. The event was quite well attended, including Mayor Clarence Azevedo and former mayor H. H. Hendren, who was instrumental in the early stages of the redevelopment project. (Courtesy Ted Leonard Collection.)

Pictured here are Mayor Clarence Azevedo, Gov. Goodwin Knight, and Fred Grumm, chairman of the Sacramento Redevelopment Agency, shortly after they wielded the first blows from the wrecking ball that officially started the redevelopment project. Originally, 526 Capital Avenue was built about 65 years before as a wedding present by Peter Bohl for his daughter Evelyn. (Courtesy Gunther Grumm Collection.)

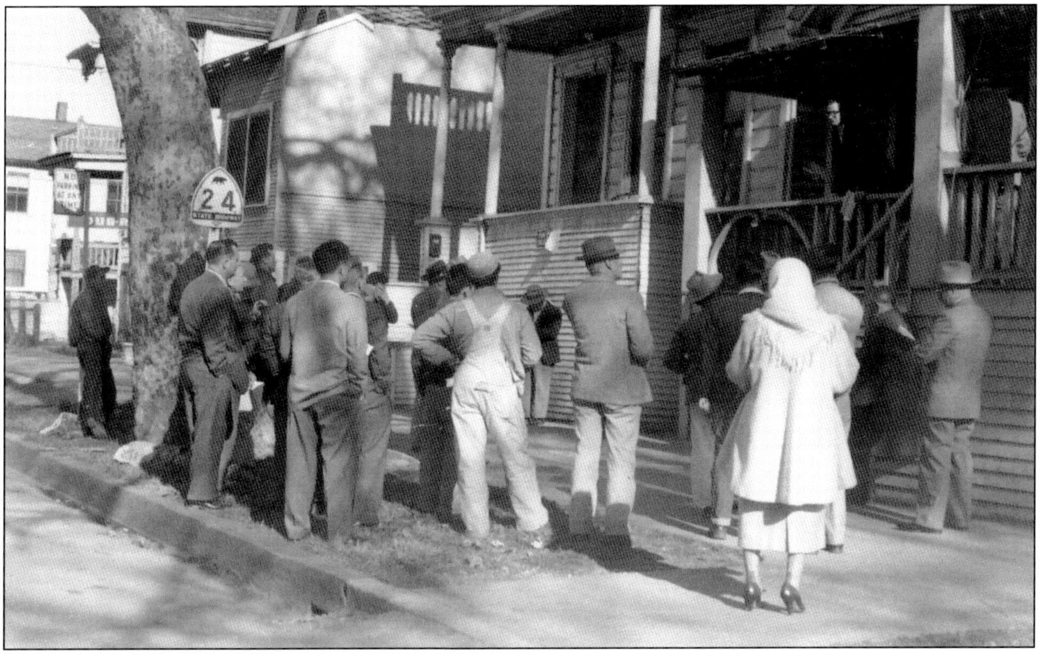

Part of the process of redevelopment included auctioning buildings for demolition on the site. This image is of the first auction, held on January 30, 1957, on Capital Avenue near Fourth Street. One of the reasons for the various redevelopment projects was the growth of state government and its need for office space. (Courtesy Gunther Grumm Collection.)

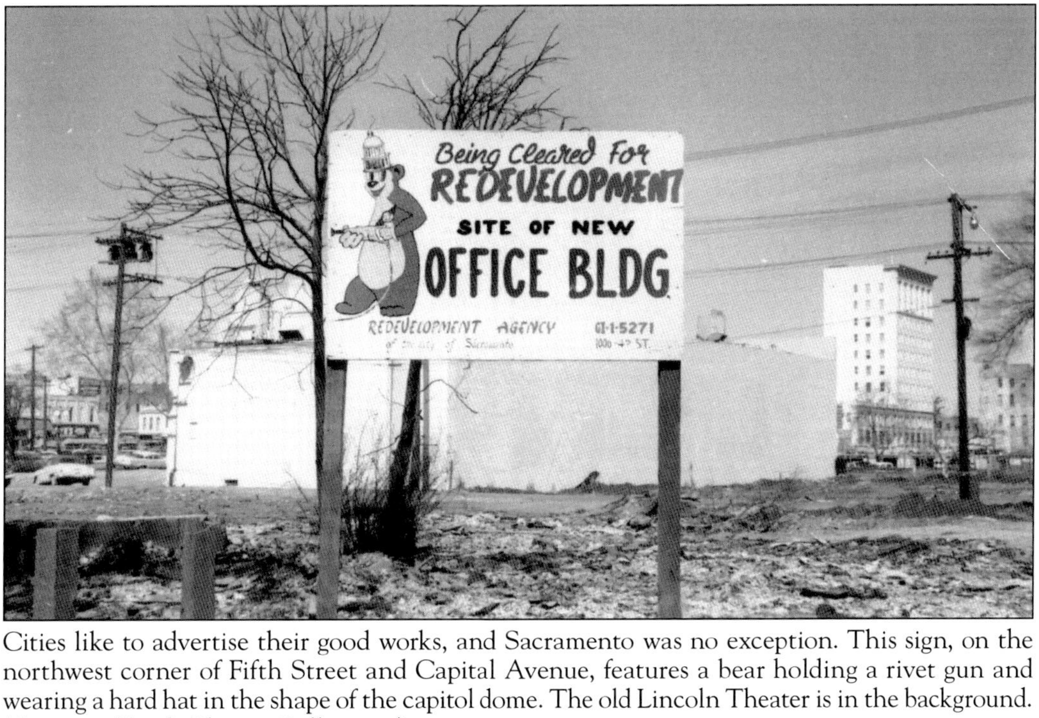

Cities like to advertise their good works, and Sacramento was no exception. This sign, on the northwest corner of Fifth Street and Capital Avenue, features a bear holding a rivet gun and wearing a hard hat in the shape of the capitol dome. The old Lincoln Theater is in the background. (Courtesy Frank Christy Collection.)

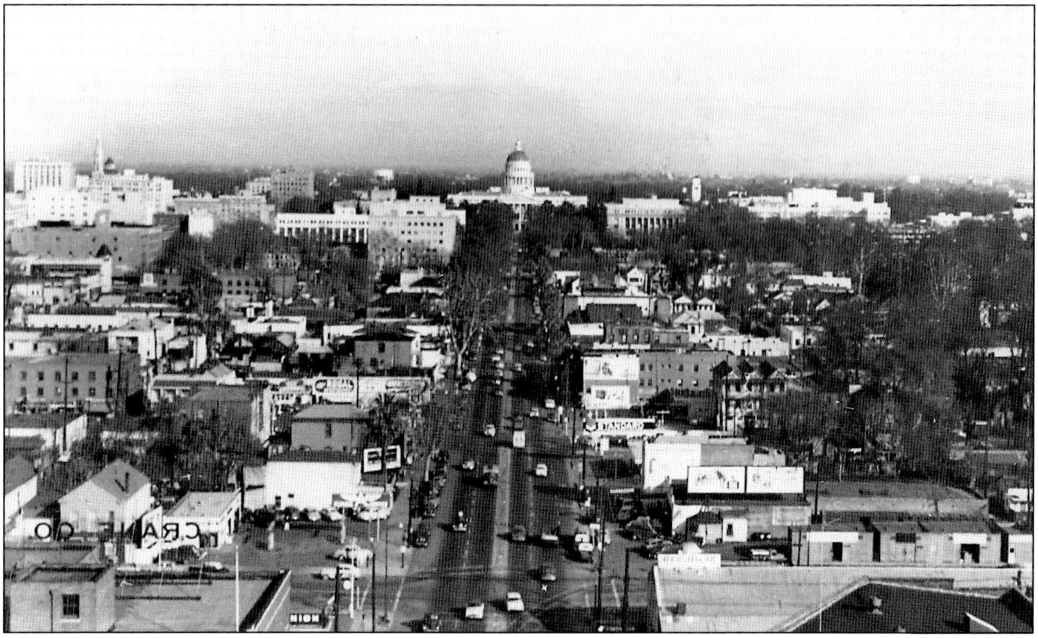

This is a photograph of Capital Avenue (formerly M Street) looking east in early 1957. The area was a mix of single-family homes, boarding houses, and small businesses that served the immediate neighborhoods. The image appears to have been taken from atop Tower Bridge and shows the area just prior to redevelopment. (Courtesy Frank Christy Collection.)

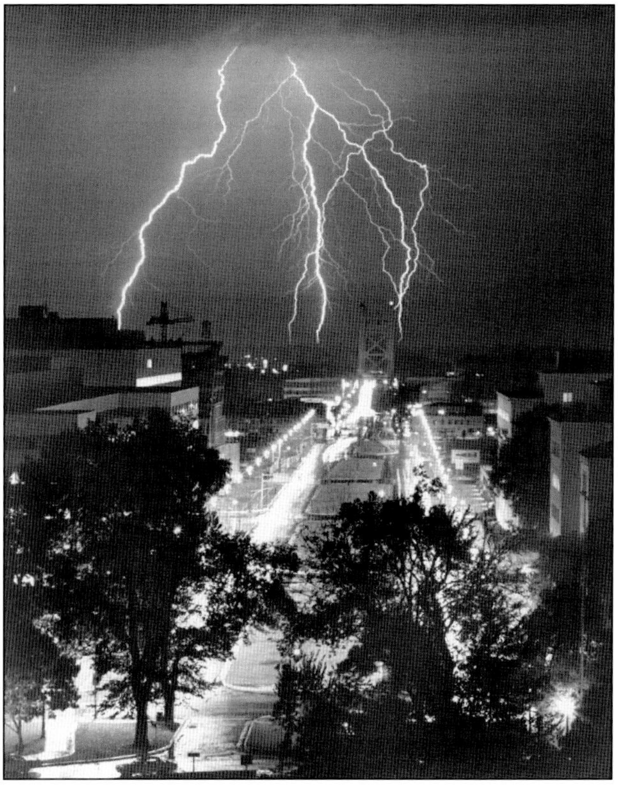

This is the completed Capitol Mall on September 25, 1962, looking west from the state capitol. It shows the wide, well-lit boulevard with the islands of grass in the center. It was built to give a favorable first impression of Sacramento as people arrived over the Tower Bridge. The scene is dramatically highlighted by bolts of lighting in this time-lapse image. (Courtesy Frank Christy Collection.)

Another reason redevelopment was undertaken is the deteriorating condition of most of the houses and businesses of the West End area, which this image clearly shows. City leaders were determined to change this situation and improve visitor's initial reaction to Sacramento. This is an alley not far from Front Street. The water tower in the background was located on Front Street near S Street. (Courtesy Ted Leonard Collection.)

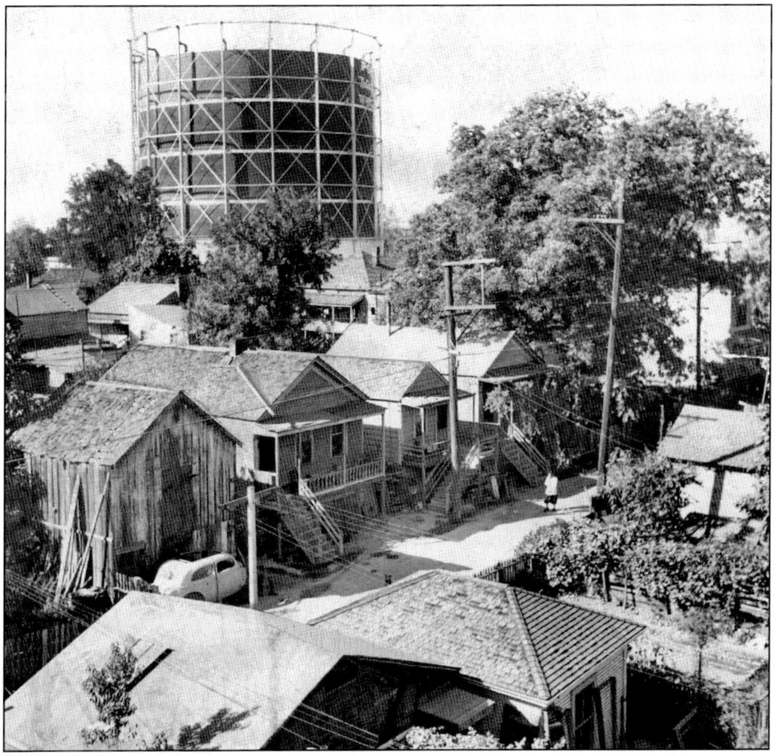

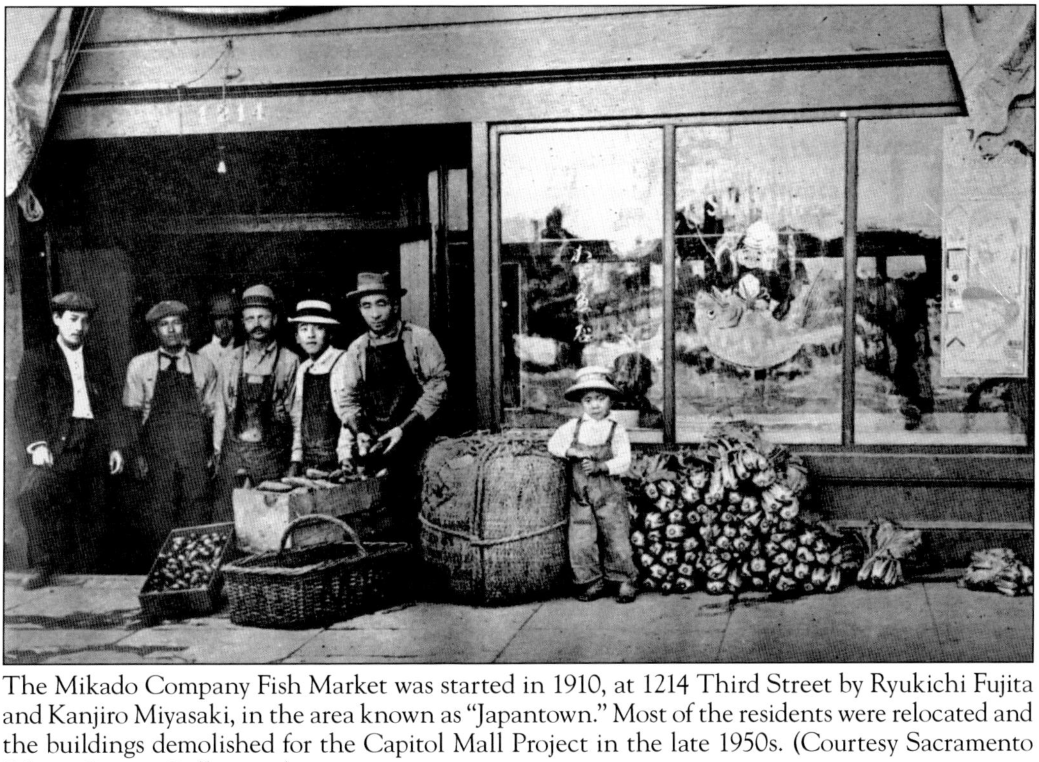

The Mikado Company Fish Market was started in 1910, at 1214 Third Street by Ryukichi Fujita and Kanjiro Miyasaki, in the area known as "Japantown." Most of the residents were relocated and the buildings demolished for the Capitol Mall Project in the late 1950s. (Courtesy Sacramento Ethnic Survey Collection.)

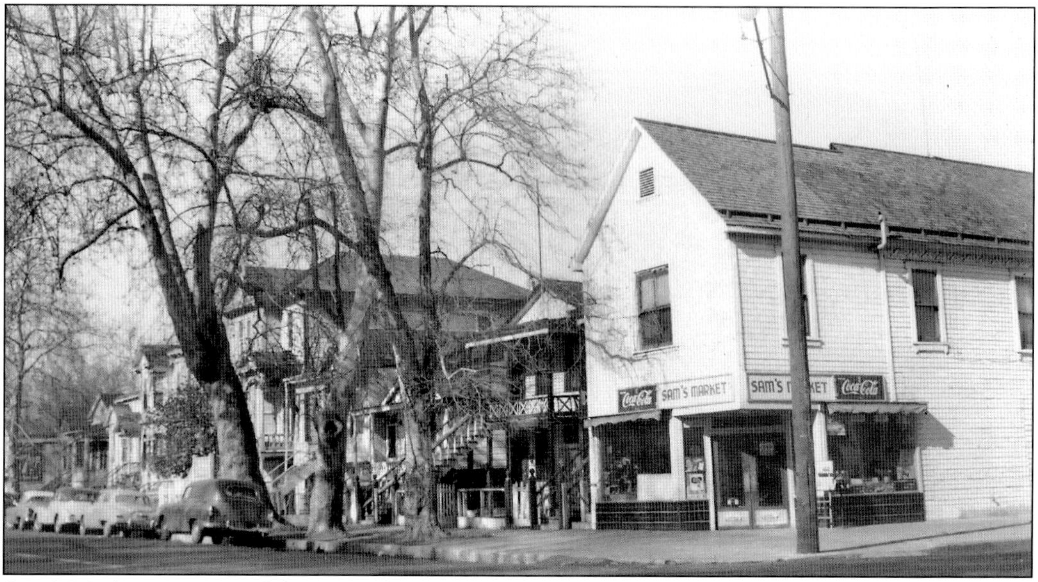

Sam's Market was one of the many businesses relocated for the Capitol Mall project. Located at the corner of Fifth and N Streets, it was an important part of the Chinese community for many years. This image was taken January 21, 1957, shortly before the business was relocated and the building demolished. (Courtesy Eugene Hepting Collection.)

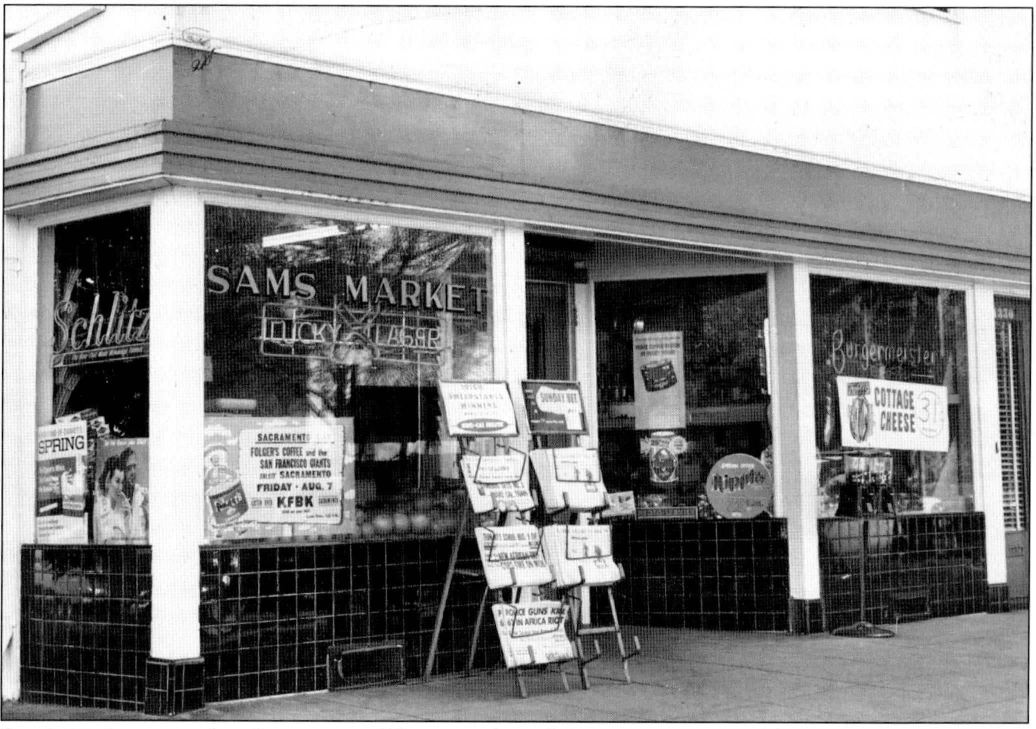

Sam's Market moved to the corner of Fourteenth and O Streets as part of the Capitol Mall project. The market today is still owned and operated by the same family and is a popular destination for lunch by many state employees. It is an example of relocation that worked because of the very reason for the move—state offices and employees. (Courtesy *Sacramento Bee* Collection.)

This aerial photograph of Sacramento's West End on February 23, 1969, shows Lincoln Junior High School in the upper right corner. This entire section, including the school, was razed or moved as part of the long-term redevelopment and eventually replaced with state office buildings, such as the Board of Equalization, Lincoln Plaza, and the Gregory Bateson Building. (Courtesy *Sacramento Bee* Collection.)

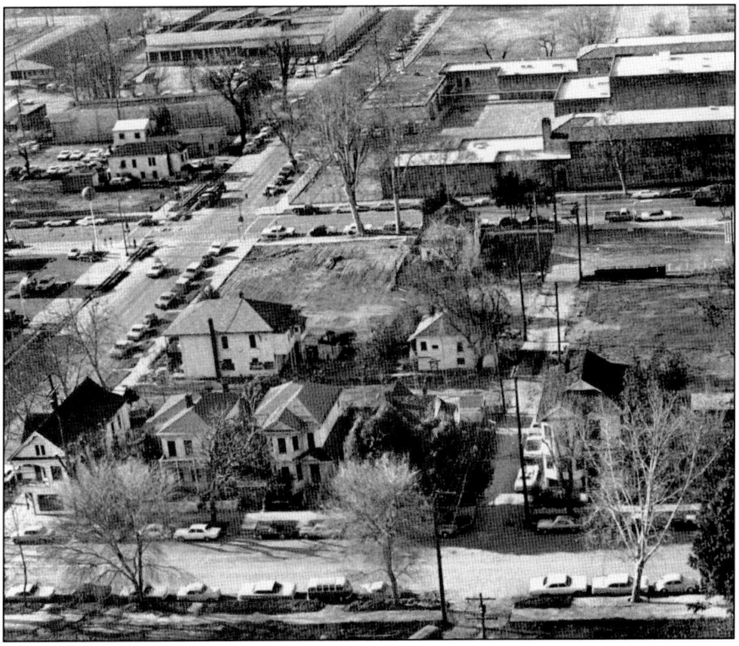

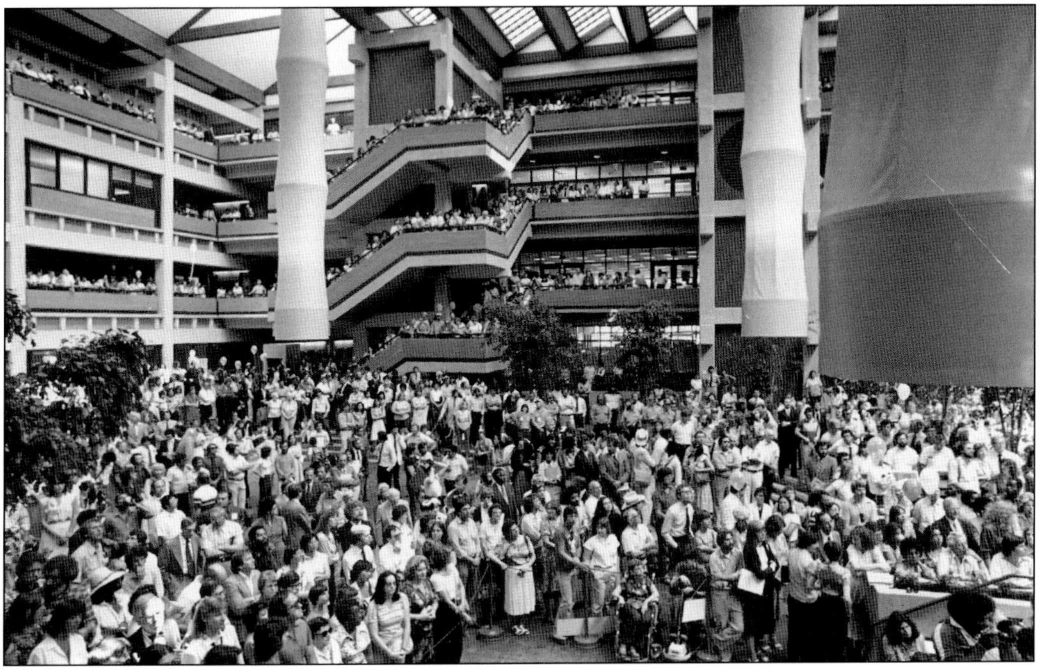

On May 1, 1981, Gov. Jerry Brown dedicated Lincoln Plaza on the former site of the Lincoln School. Unlike most other state buildings, its design included a large atrium with the offices surrounding it, as shown in this image. (Courtesy *Sacramento Bee* Collection.)

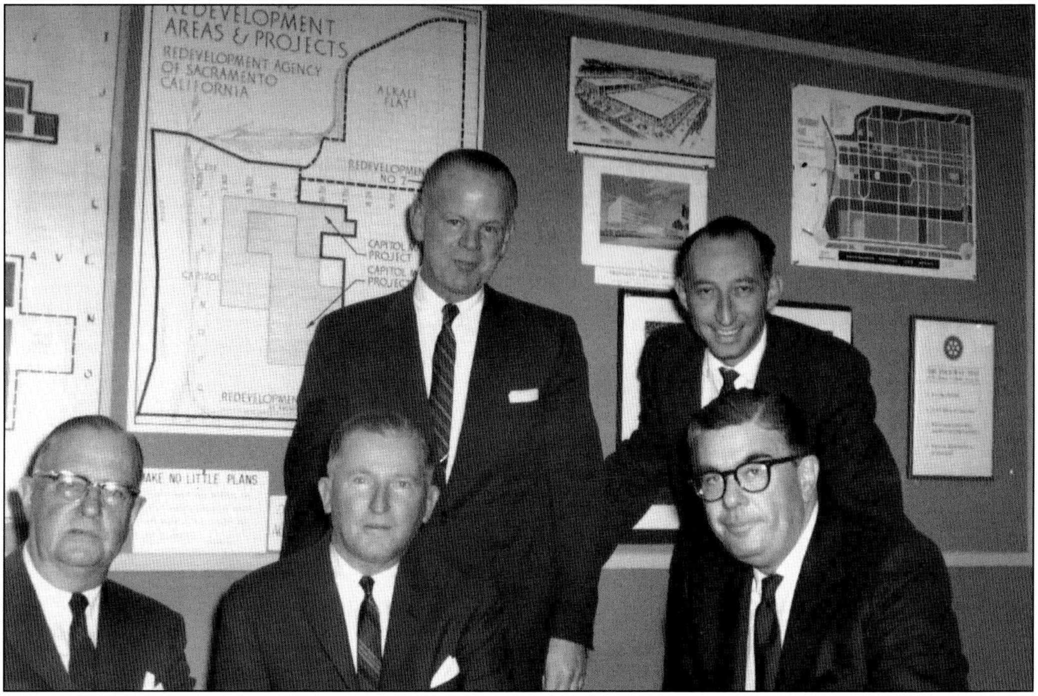

On January 30, 1961, Macy's submitted their proposal for a store in Sacramento. Pictured at the Sacramento Redevelopment Agency are, from left to right, ? Read, Ernest Malloy (president of Macy's), Garrett McEnerney II (counsel), John L. Egan (vice president, branch development), and Jerome Lipp (executive director, Sacramento Redevelopment Agency). (Courtesy Ted Leonard Collection.)

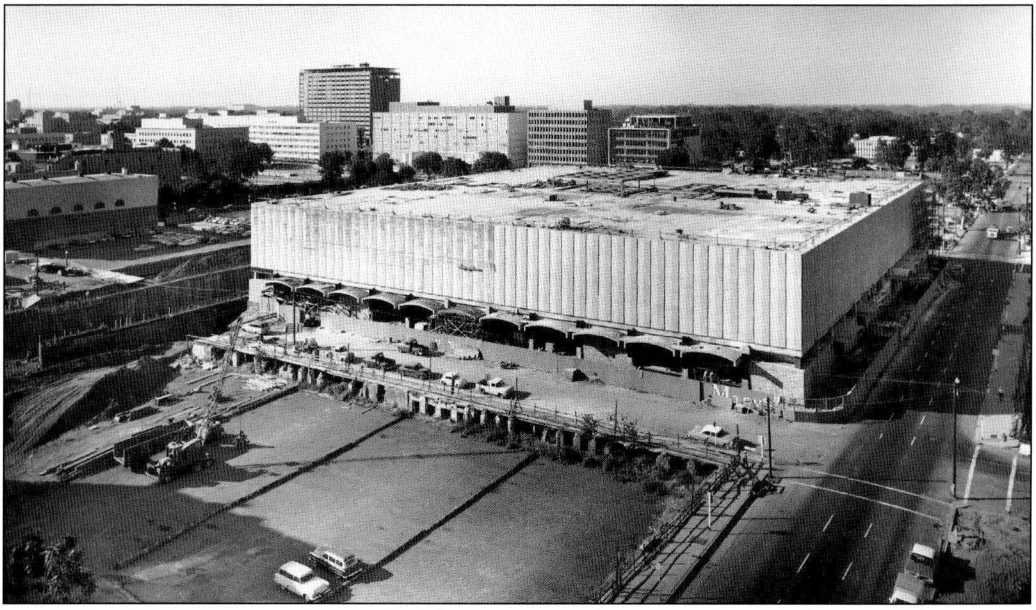

In March 1961, the city council rescinded the Maximum Floor Area Ratio for the Macy's department store site as a condition of their original proposal. The open area in front of Macy's, formerly the Morris Hotel, clearly shows the original street level in this 1963 construction photograph. The Fifth Street underpass is under construction at left. (Courtesy James E. Henley Collection.)

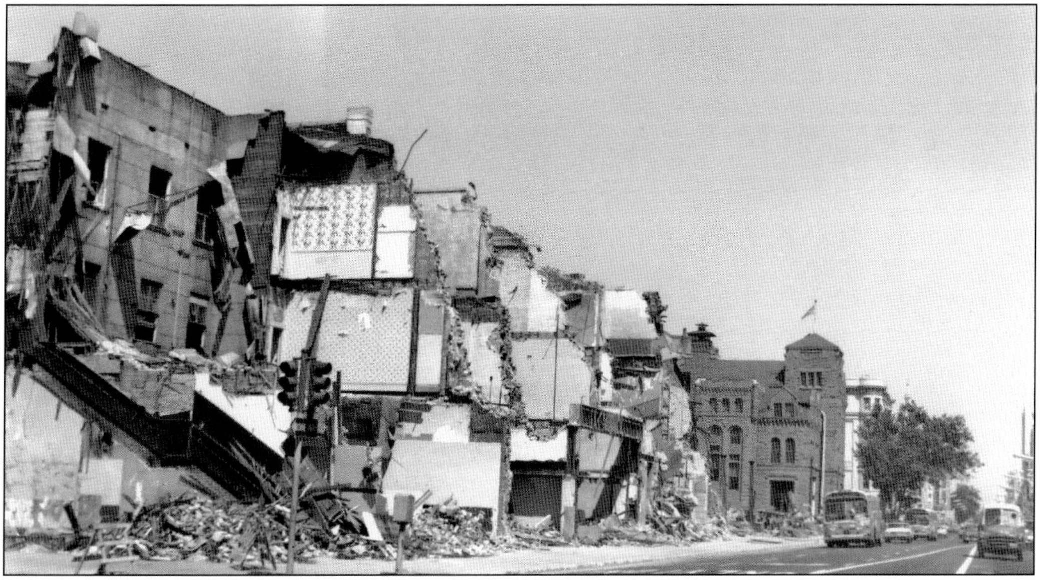

Demonstrating how quickly a city can change, this dramatic photograph of the demolition on K Street was taken June 27, 1963. The photograph, looking east from Sixth Street, includes the old "pink" post office in the background. Some of the businesses affected on this block were the Golden Eagle and Bell Hotels, the Fox Capitol Theater, Fun Center Amusements, and United Cigar and Liquor. The post office was demolished in 1967. (Courtesy Eugene Hepting Collection.)

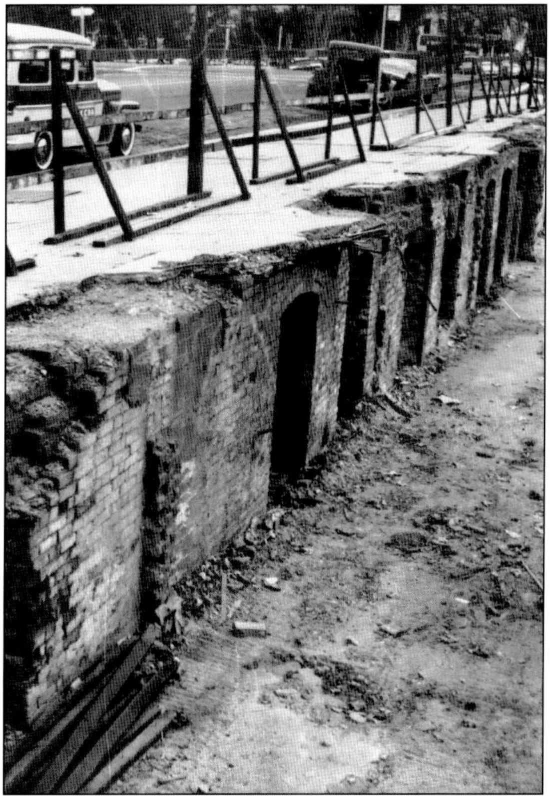

During the various redevelopment projects, many examples of the 19th-century efforts to raise the streets in the business district were uncovered. That project, begun in earnest after the flood of 1862, raised the streets to their current level using brick piers as support, as this image from April 29, 1959, of the alley between Third, Fourth, J, and K Streets clearly denotes. (Courtesy Ted Leonard Collection.)

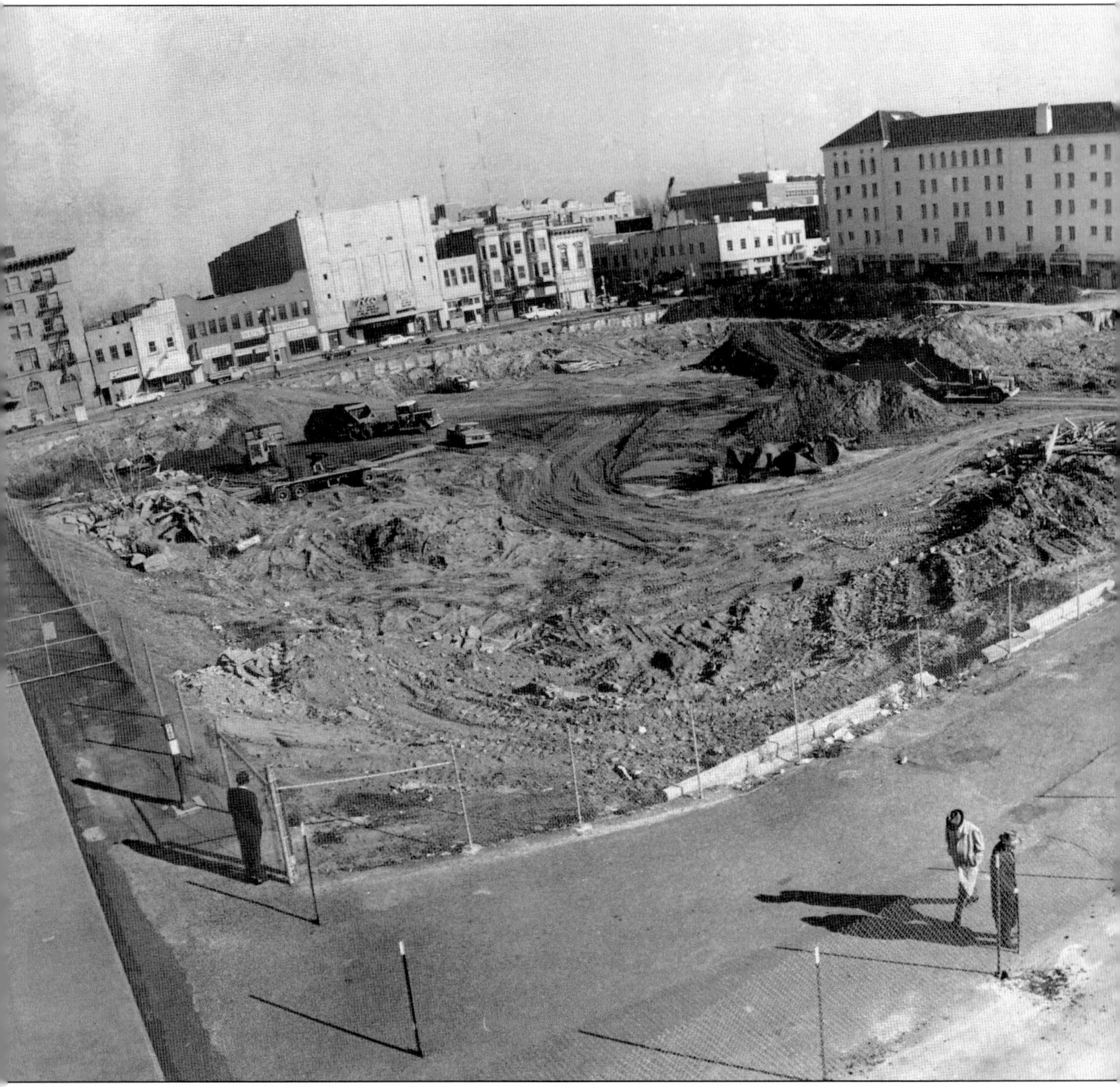

Taken on December 4, 1968, this wide-angle photograph shows the area bounded by Fifth, Sixth, J, and L Streets being prepared for construction of the underground parking garage of the Downtown Plaza. Above the parking garage, the new Weinstock's and an I Magnin were built, among several other stores. This version of Downtown Plaza did not fare particularly well, and

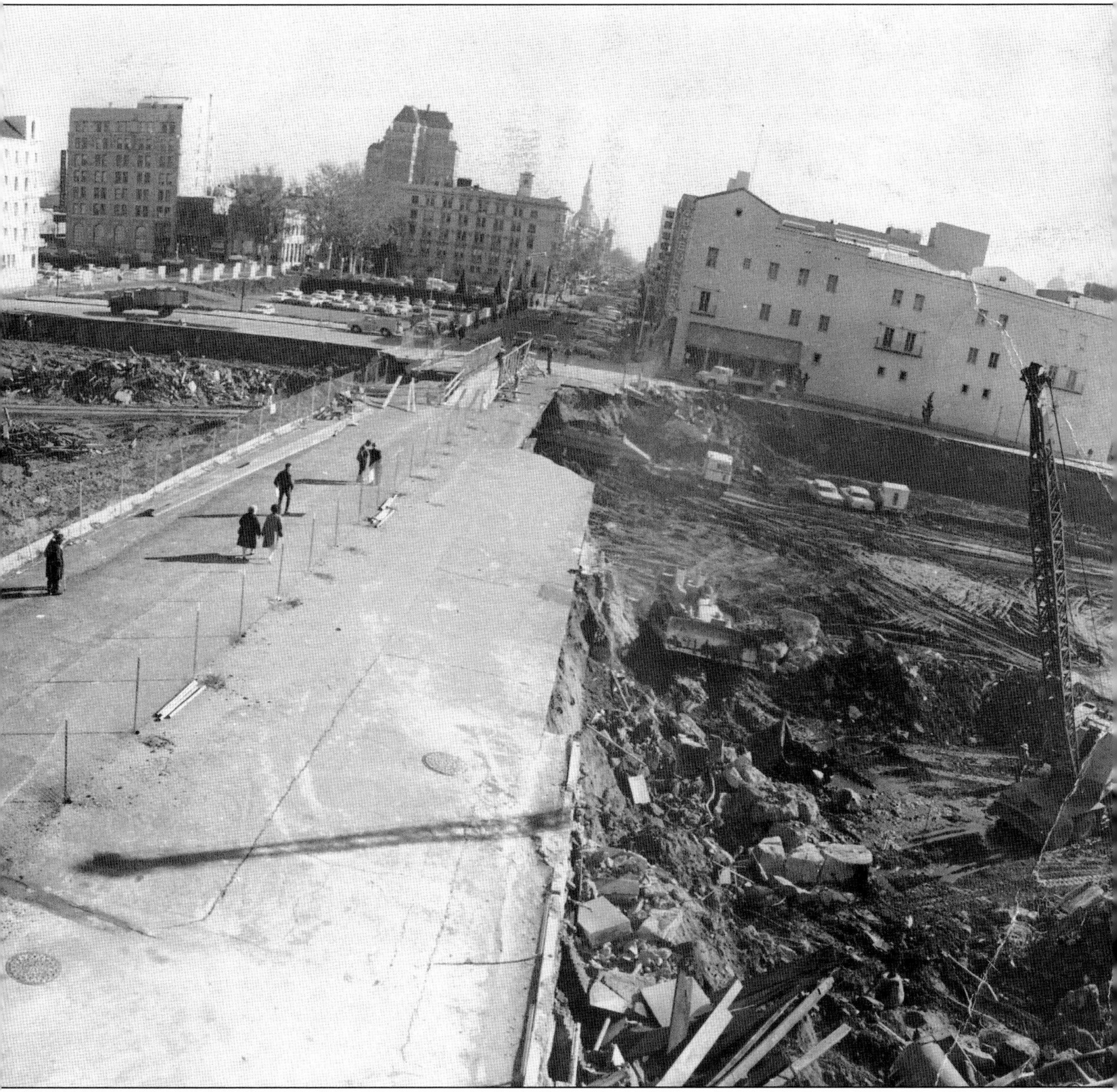

in the 1990s it was completely redone into a larger, open-air mall with two levels. Weinstock's was sold to Macy's, and I Magnin closed. The pedestrians are on K Street, which was closed to traffic up to Twelfth Street shortly after this photograph was taken. (Courtesy *Sacramento Bee* Collection.)

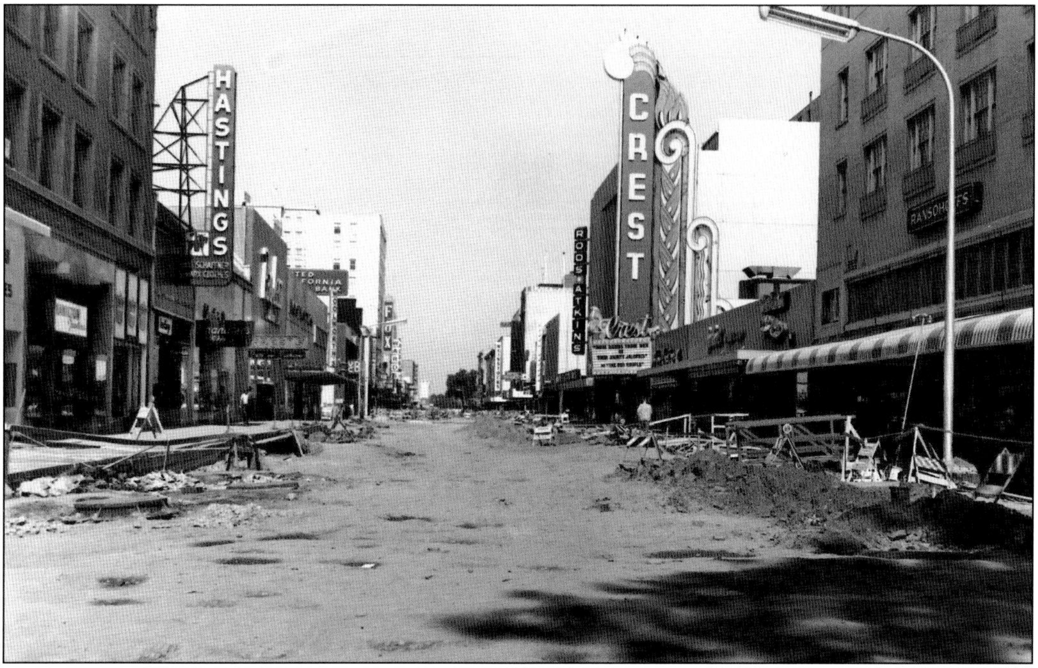

This photograph, looking west from Eleventh Street, shows K Street being transformed into the K Street Mall on August 10, 1969. The street was permanently closed to traffic up to Twelfth Street. Visible in the photograph are Ransohoffs, the Crest Theater, the Fox Theater, and Weinstock's. (Courtesy Frank Christy Collection.)

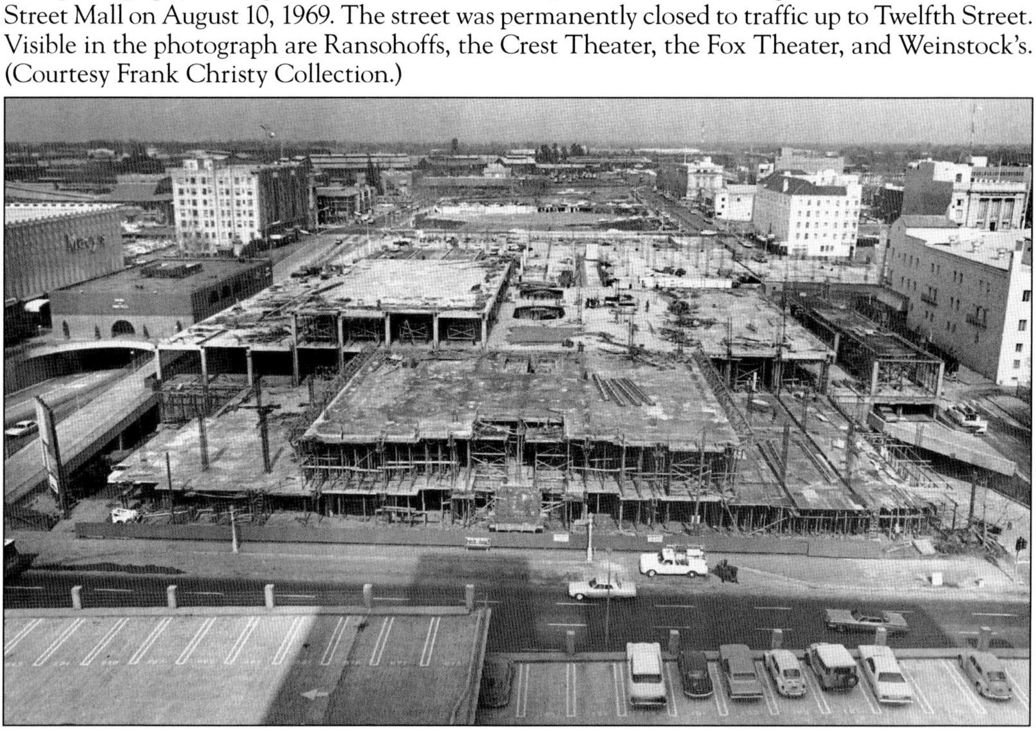

K Street has always been the heart of the business district. The mall project, pictured here under construction in 1970, was intended to highlight it. This photograph is looking north with L Street in the foreground. Macy's and the Fifth Street underpass are to the left, with the Traveler's Hotel just beyond and Breuner's at right. (Courtesy James E. Henley Collection.)

With automobile traffic having been removed, K Street became a pedestrian mall with sculptures, water features, and plants. The view is to the east from about Sixth Street, taken on December 27, 1972. This particular configuration was later removed to accommodate the light-rail system, which began service in 1986 and runs between Seventh and Twelfth Streets on K Street. (Courtesy *Sacramento Bee* Collection.)

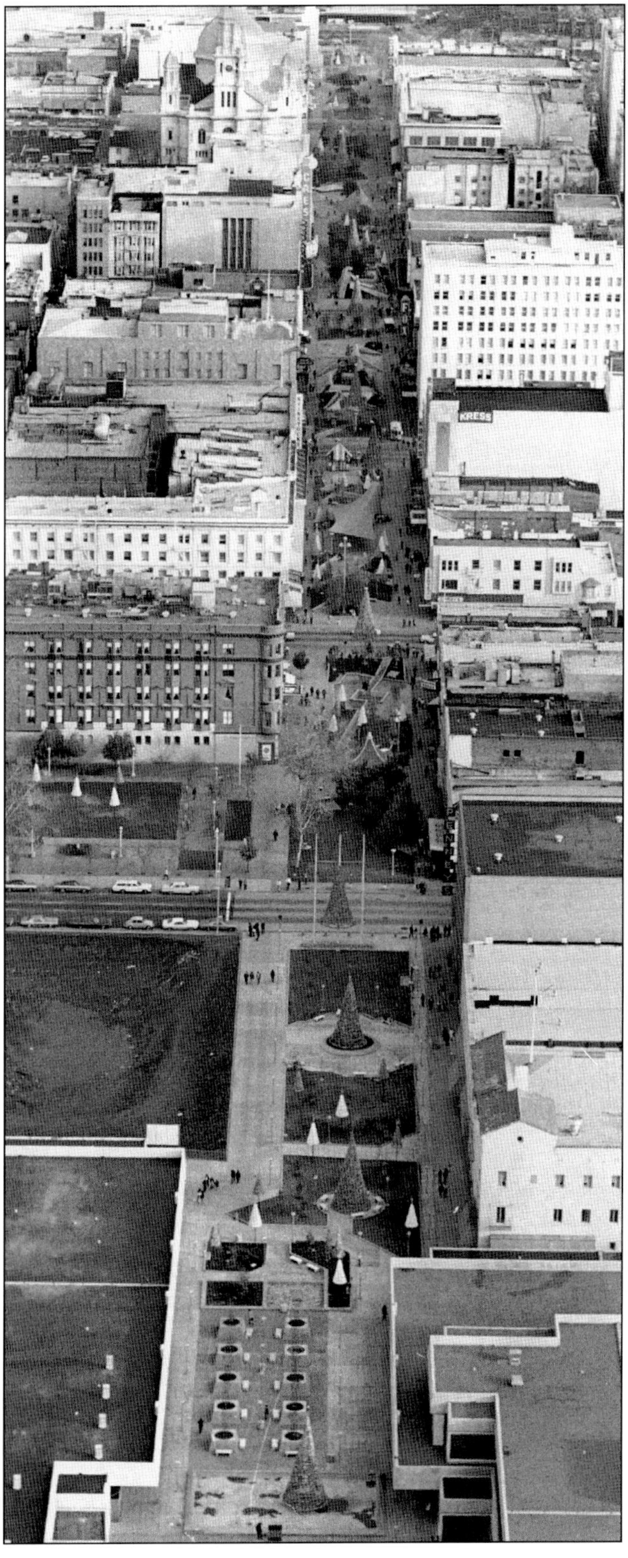